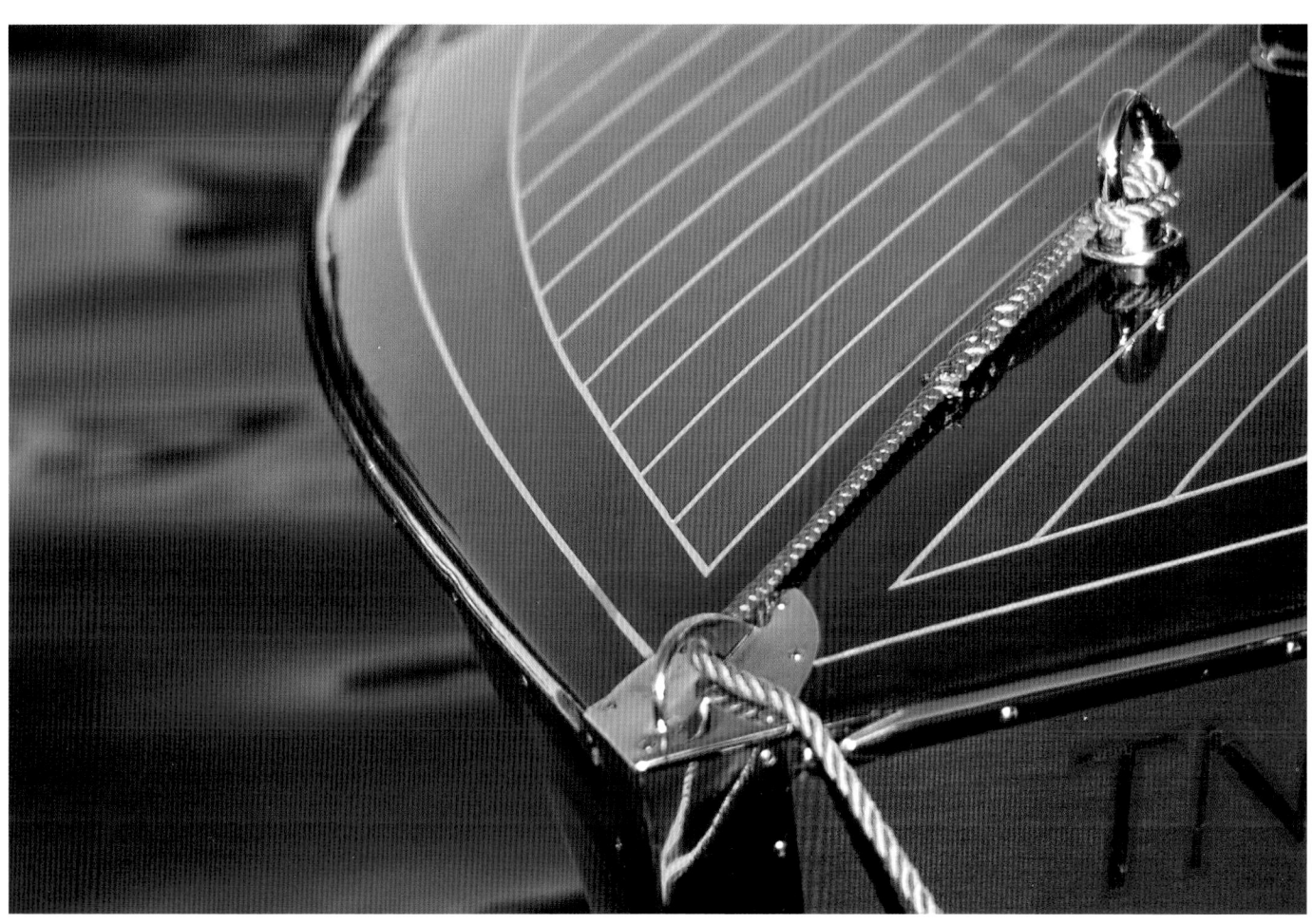

CHRIS-CRAFT
BOATS

ANTHONY MOLLICA JR. AND JACK SAVAGE

MBI Publishing Company

First published in 2001 by MBI Publishing Company,
Galtier Plaza, Suite 200, 380 Jackson Street,
St. Paul, MN 55101-3885 USA

MBI Publishing Company books are also available at
discounts in bulk quantity for industrial or sales-
promotional use. For details write to Special Sales
Manager at Motorbooks International Wholesalers
& Distributors, Galtier Plaza, Suite 200,
380 Jackson Street, St. Paul, MN
55101-3885 USA

Library of Congress Cataloging-in-Publication
Data available

ISBN 0-7603-0920-5

On the front cover: *top right:* The 1955 model year
saw big changes in the Chris-Craft line-up, and
among the new entries was the Capri Runabout,
offered in 19- and 21-foot lengths. The Capris
replaced the Rivieras, and featured a wrap-around
windshield, a stem with pronounced rake, and bull-
nose bow sans cutwater. *Classic Boating magazine*
Center: This 1941 38-foot cruiser featured a sedan
setup with the single-level coveredf deckhouse and
cockpit. **Lower right:** Chris Smith & Son's earliest
standardized 26-foot Runabout, such as the restored
Godfather VI, had no windshield. It was powered by
a war-surplus Curtiss OX-5 engine marinized
by the Smiths.

On the frontis: The bow of the 1942 17-foot Deluxe
Runabout *Second Time Around* features the distinctive
prewar dark-stained mohogany covering boards and
kingplank.

On the title page: Chris-Craft's first successful
standardized Cruiser was the 1929 38-foot
Commuting Cruiser, commonly called the
Commuter. Its all-varnished mahogany hull
resembled the appearance of a large runabout.
Classic Boating magazine

On the back cover, top: The 1938 19-foot
Sportsman, featured a rear-facing aft seat and a
middle "cockpit" with single seats on either side of
the motor box, was a hybrid sold as a "Utility
runabout." *Robert Bruce Duncan*
Bottom: Chris-Craft's "Freedom Fleet" in 1955
included the radical new Cobra, which took the place
of the 19-foot Racing Runabout in the line-up.
Unlike the split cockpit racer, however, the Cobra
was a very fast single-cockpit sports boat.
Classic Boating magazine

Edited by Paul Johnson
Designed by Dan Perry

Printed in China

Contents

Acknowledgments

Interest in fine wooden boats began long before they were affectionately referred to as antiques or classics. Even when there were strong signs that wooden boat construction was losing ground to a growing preference for the carefree appeal of fiberglass construction, many of us refused to heed the warning signs. When the final mahogany Chris-Craft was delivered to its owner in 1972, the reality of our loss finally began to be understood. Even then, many of us did not act decisively to preserve every available detail of the wooden boat era.

Fortunately, the Smith family members and their employees were consummate record keepers, and Chris-Craft enthusiasts are fortunate to have those archived at the Mariners' Museum in Newport News, Virginia—we are indebted to the museum and its staff for their enthusiastic assistance with this project. No less important are those writers and researchers who have come before us, publishing their work in books, magazines, and antique boat club newsletters, thereby laying the groundwork and thus aiding our own research.

Corporate records only tell part of the story, and the contributions of individual boat owners and marine enthusiasts play a vital role in the creation of a book such as this. Firsthand stories,

rare photographs, and personal experiences bring important aspects of our work to life and add immeasurably to the quality of the history of this boat-building story. We gratefully acknowledge their important contributions to our understanding of Chris-Craft's role in recreational boating, aspects of construction, merchandising, and product performance.

Our sincere thanks to the following contributors:

Don Babcock, Philip Ballantyne, Jeffrey Beard, Sean Berry, Jack Bingham, Chris Byrnes, Jerry Conrad, Linda DaBica, Bill Danforth, Dorris Deason, Roy Dryer, John Dubickas, Ken Eckfield, Doug Elmore, Terry Feist, Lisa Flick, Fred Genaw, Joe Gribbins, Scott Gross, Todd Heinrich, Peter Henkel, Rebecca Hopfinger, Bill Irwin, Jack Irwin, George Johnson, John Kellogg, Diane Laenen, Don MacKerer, Bill Magee, Craig Magnusson, Robert Merin, Jim Murdock, Gerry Pederson, John Pemberton, Paul Pletcher, Sam Rivoli, Jeffrey Rodengen, Karine N. Rodengen, Bill Siegenthaler, Chris Smith, Jeffrey Stebbins, Phoebe Tritton, Jim Wangard, Norm Wangard, Hank Why, Wilson Wright.

Thanks are due, also, to the owners and restorers of the many boats featured in this book. It is their willingness to spend money and time in pursuit of preservation that make modern appreciation of antiques possible.

—*Anthony S. Mollica, Jr. and Jack Savage*

Foreword
by Chris Smith

hen my family, owners of Chris-Craft for nearly 40 years, sold the company in 1960, it broke my heart. But, looking back, I suppose it came at a good time. The third generation was close to retirement and the company president, Harry Coll, was from outside the family. The boat industry was changing, and the era of the classic wooden boats, for which Chris-Craft was famous, was coming to an end. Ultimately, I've come to believe that it was a good move—at least I had a lot of fun with the money!

My grandpa, Christopher Columbus Smith, died in 1939, when I was 12 years old. I remember him as always having a cigar in his mouth, dressed in farmer's overalls and slipper-style shoes. In the early days, he and his brother—my dad called him Uncle Hank—were professional fishermen and hunters. That's what they did for a living. And in the winter months, they would trap and go fox hunting in the St. Claire flats near Algonac.

As their reputation as outdoorsmen grew, people would hire them as guides when they came up to go pleasure hunting. Grandpa and his brother would use

the duck boats they built. "Gee, this is a pretty nice boat," the hunters would say. "How about building me one?" And that's how the business just got going. Early on, Grandpa would hire local farmers to build boats in the winter, put one coat of varnish on them, then store them to be sold later.

In the early 1920s, when Grandpa, my dad Bernard and my uncles Jay W., Owen, and Hamilton started the company that would become Chris-Craft, Grandpa already had this 26-footer. But he didn't have plans or anything. First thing Mac MacKerer did was make a drawing. Mac wanted drawings of everything.

The biggest event in my life as a young boy was learning how to swim, because once I could swim, my mother would let me go to work with my father. On rainy days, I would play inside the factory. But my favorite spot at the Algonac plant was wherever we tested the boats.

My dad loved to test the boats—he preferred to be in the factory rather than in the office. And a lot of evenings we'd go out and test the boats and motors and, of course, his own personal boats were always test beds—he was always monkeying with something different. In fact, back in the days when my family owned the company, we all had cruisers that were all test beds, and we were always experimenting with the new this or the new that to see how it worked. No doubt that was one reason for the company's success.

I remember well one summer day they had just built a varnished Racing Runabout—this was in the 1930s—it was a brand-new prototype boat. My father , along with Uncle Jay and Owen told me to "go get that 16-footer—we want to see it." I ran over to the covered boat well. I managed to get the engine started and drove the boat over to the dock where they were. But as I came into the dock, the engine stalled and I ran that brand-new boat smack into the dock. We all heard wood crunch, but nobody said a word. Finally, my Uncle Owen spoke up. "Son, you're going to fool around here until we pay you to stay away!"

I wasn't fond of college, so I did two years of apprenticeship at Chris-Craft. The first year I did a little of everything. The second year, I worked with Mac MacKerer. He taught me a lot about design and production. But there were other lessons to learn as well.

I recall being back at the Algonac plant once, and I stopped in Harsen's office while there. I wanted to make a suggestion of one kind or another about a boat. He is a man of very few words, really. He looked at me, then said, "I don't care what you like, or even what I like. We're going to build what we can sell." Boy, I learned something there.

For that reason, the Cobra was not one of my favorites because it was not a money-maker. It was so expensive to build, and we sold few of them. I suppose my favorite boat was the 22-foot Utility, because my father had one. In that way I'm probably a lot like many classic Chris-Craft owners, whose favorites are determined by nostalgic memories from childhood.

I take great pride in seeing the modern appreciation of the boats my family's company built. I hope you enjoy the boats featured in this book as much as I have throughout my lifetime.

Chris Smith, namesake of his grandfather, Christopher Columbus Smith, and the youngest of six children of Bernard Smith, worked for Chris-Craft for most of his life. He was one of the few members of the family to continue to work for the company following the sale by the Smith family to NAFI in 1960, and he continued through various owners and management until his retirement in 1986. Still a resident of Holland, Michigan, Chris helped Grand Craft build some of the Chris-Craft replicas.

Introduction

Chris-Craft has a long and distinguished history. It was truly a giant among recreational boat-builders in the twentieth century, providing years of memorable fun and relaxation for generations of boaters and their families. Chris-Craft still exists today, and was recently acquired by Stellican Ltd., a London based investment firm, after its owner, OMC, filed bankruptcy.

When did Chris-Craft start? It's not hard to find modern references that date the company to the 1870s, when Christopher Columbus Smith, the patriarch of the Smith family and namesake of Chris-Craft, was still a teen-ager, helping his older brother, Hank, build small boats for hunting and fishing. Chris Smith later brought his sons into the family business, and as chronicled in Chapter 1, they became internationally famous as builders of the world's fastest boats in the early part of the 1900s.

From our perspective, however, the company that came to be known as Chris-Craft began in 1922, when father Chris and sons Jay, Bernard, and Owen sold the original family boatyard to Gar Wood and started a new venture. That final rendition of Chris Smith & Sons Boat Company signaled a new direction, as they focused on building stock boats using automotive-style assembly line techniques, at prices that made them a dream come true for a broader spectrum of boaters than ever before. They weren't the only boatbuilders with that idea, but they were the most successful, and the Smith family would go on to survive the Depression, shine during World War II, and dominate the pleasureboat industry during the baby boom. By the 1960s, traditional wooden boats were rapidly being replaced by fiberglass, and Chris-Craft was not immune. The last wooden Chris-Craft was built in 1972.

This book focuses on the 50 years, 1922–1972, that Chris-Craft, nee Chris Smith & Sons, built stock wooden boats. They are today's antiques and classics, growing simultaneously more appreciated and rarer as time passes.

In fact, in the years since Chris-Craft's last wooden boat, interest in antique and wooden boats of all marques has grown exponentially. In the case of Chris-Craft, longtime Chris-Craft design and production head Bill MacKerer, and others, helped jump-start the Chris-Craft Antique Boat Club in 1973. Under the guidance of executive director Wilson Wright, the club has flourished, today boasting some 3,000 members and a respected quarterly newsletter, *The Brass Bell.*

Since the late 1980s, Chris-Craft enthusiasts have enjoyed Jeffrey and Karine Rodengen's book, *The Legend of Chris-Craft*, an immense work that chronicles the business history of the company in detail. Looking to expand on that and other published works, we have chosen to focus our efforts more on the boats themselves than the company history.

Following the introductory first chapter, we've attempted to tell the stories first of the Runabouts, then Utilities, Cruisers, the plywood Kit Boats and Cavaliers, and the Sea Skiffs. The final chapter chronicles the development of Chris-Craft's marine engines during the wooden boat period.

As many readers know, the first Chris-Craft was a 26-foot "Runabout," or decked boat with distinct cockpits. The "Utility" was a product of the Depression, and is a widely accepted term for boats that that are generally 15 to 29 feet in length, with an open, rather than decked-over, interior and a small box-like enclosure over the engine. Cruisers are larger craft that typically include berths and a galley. Chris-Craft built many models of all three, using with few exceptions "Chris-Craft Grade" Philippine mahogany to construct planked V-bottom hulls.

Kit Boats and Cavaliers differ in that they were built using marine plywood for the bottom, sides, and decks, and were offered as Chris-Craft's value line in the 1950s and 1960s. Sea Skiffs were round-bilge lapstrake hulls, Chris-Craft's version of the classic sea skiff, built in Utility and Cruiser styles starting in the mid-1950s.

Like the automotive industry, Chris-Craft introduced the following year's models in the second half of the calendar year, and frequently offered discounts for orders placed in the fall. Consequently, a number of units of a model that was new for 1955, for example, would have been built in 1954. But in order to be consistent with sales catalogs, we have endeavored to match models with their official model years as we relate the chronologies of Chris-Craft's various boats.

We hope you enjoy this cruise through Chris-Craft history, and find it as enlightening to read and explore as we did to research and write.

—Anthony S. Mollica, Jr. and Jack Savage

CHAPTER 1

FROM DUCK BOATS TO MOTOR YACHTS
The Chris-Craft Story

When Harsen Smith, chairman of the board of Chris-Craft, appeared on the cover of *Time* magazine for a story on "The New Boom in Boating" in May 1959, it in many ways represented a climax for the Smith family. From humble beginnings, Harsen's family—grandfather Christopher Columbus Smith, father Jay W., and uncles Bernard and Owen—had created what was by then a boating empire, the world's largest builder of motorboats. Chris-Craft employed thousands of others across four divisions, building and selling mahogany, plywood, and steel boats small and large from more than a half-dozen plants and offices across the country. Despite fierce competition, they were the undisputed kings of recreational boatbuilding.

Today antique and classic Chris-Crafts continue to spark remarkable interest. The Chris-Craft exhibit at The Mariners' Museum is called "The Affordable Dream." Along with artifacts and photos, the exhibit features *Miss Belle Isle* (foreground); a Model 65 15-1/2-foot Utility, *Era Past* (left); and a 19-foot 1935 Double Cockpit Forward Runabout. *Courtesy The Mariners' Museum*

The famous *Miss Detroit*, winner of the 1915 Gold Cup Trophy and the boat that helped form the Smith–Gar Wood partnership, is shown running at full speed in this rare Warren Sheppard painting.

Baby Speed Demon II, built by Chris Smith for Stuart Blackton, won the 1914 Gold Cup and set a speed record in becoming the first Gold Cup racer to exceed 50 miles per hour.

True to form, the *Time* PR coup was likely one more clever ploy among the many deft moves made by multiple generations of Smiths over the nearly 40 years of Chris-Craft. Less than a year later, in January 1960, the Smith family astounded the boating world by announcing that they had sold the company to National Automotive Fibers, Inc., better known as NAFI. Although the story at the time was that the Smiths were cashing out as a result of a chance meeting, rarely did anything significant happen at Chris-Craft without careful planning and detailed research. After moving the company headquarters from Algonac, Michigan, to Pompano Beach, Florida, in 1957 and installing Harry Coll, the first non-family member, as president, it was time to advertise. What better place than the front page of America's premier newsweekly?

Before Chris-Craft

This remarkable family business can conceivably trace its beginnings to 1876, when two brothers, Henry "Hank" Smith and his 15-year-old brother, Chris, started building duck boats and fishing skiffs for local hunters, out-of-town "sports," and later for use as rentals at their boat livery. At the time they started building boats, Chris said, "It just seemed like a good way to earn a living."

Their father, James Smith, had been born near Syracuse, New York, in 1823. When he was still a young man he settled in the Algonac region of Michigan, some 40 miles north of Detroit on the St. Clair River. The river connects Lake Huron with Lake Erie in a region with a long history of shipbuilding. The elder Smith ran a blacksmith shop and was a skilled gunsmith, but preferred hunting and making guns to operating his shop, a preference enjoyed by both sons—Henry, born in 1851, followed by Chris in 1861. The family grew up near the marshlands of the St. Clair River. The surrounding flats area had abundant wildlife and fish, and it was perfect for simple lightweight craft used by outdoorsmen, who came often enough to make Algonac a seasonal tourist destination.

Hank and Chris became skilled hunters and savvy woodsmen, ultimately able to make their living by providing supplies and acting as guides for other sportsmen. Chris spent a few summers working as a deck hand on the Great Lakes steamers before deciding that he could do better building boats with his brother in Algonac. When Chris wasn't building small boats, he was carving decoys, fishing, hunting, or telling stories. These were his great pleasures, and he was particularly good at them.

In 1884, when he was 23, Chris married Anna Rattray from nearby Harsens Island. Anna and Chris had four sons and two daughters, and when the children were old enough to handle tools, Chris had them in the family boatshop helping build rowing, sailing, and small motor-propelled boats. In 1899, Chris became the Algonac postmaster, and for the next 12 years the official U.S. Post Office of Algonac was located in the front section of his boathouse. A town leader, he would also serve as president of the Algonac Chamber of Commerce and on the School Board.

Racing Fame

By 1904 the widespread interest in faster boats prompted the founding of the American Powerboat Association. As early as 1906, Chris Smith's boat shop was building 26-foot boats that would reach speeds of 18 miles per hour.

As interest in boat racing gathered momentum, the improved efficiency and reliable performance of automotive engines advanced rapidly and provided an increasingly reliable source of power for marine applications.

The advancing power of marine engines, in turn, focused more attention on hull design as another way to achieving greater speed. Smith was quick to experiment with the potential advantages of one or more steps in the bottoms of his boats, which allowed the forward portion of the hull to stay off the surface of the water at speed, reducing drag.

In 1910, Chris met John J. "Baldy" Ryan, a successful Cincinnati movie theater owner who spent his summers on Harsens Island, and who had money and enjoyed spending it. He loved to gamble and had become increasingly fascinated with the new fast boat phenomenon, which soon would lead him to the Smith brothers boat shop.

Ryan wanted a new boat that would be able to go faster than the boat of another local sportsman, Neil McMillan, whose Smith-built *Dart* was capable of doing 26 miles per hour. Smith assured Ryan that he could build him a boat that would make 30 miles per hour, and they struck a deal.

Ryan was so taken by his new boat that racing became his new pastime. When Ryan learned that Hank Smith had decided to leave the boat livery to open a grocery store, he offered to become Chris' business partner, providing capital for what would be called the Smith-Ryan Boat Company in 1911. With Ryan's backing, Smith began to develop a series of single-step hydroplanes, most of which took on the name *Baby Reliance.*

The Smith-Ryan *Reliance*-style race boats were exhibited at a number of boat shows, and the builders guaranteed speeds in various price ranges up to 50 miles per hour for $20,000. Ryan was a tireless promoter with enormous energy, and the new *Reliance* designs captured the interest of the emerging racing enthusiasts. One of the people who decided to purchase two *Reliances* was a friend of Ryan's, J. Stuart Blackton, formerly of England and then living on New York's Long Island. Blackton's successful ventures with Vitagraph Pictures had resulted in substantial, overnight wealth. He became devoted to spending his newly acquired fortune in whatever way pleased him most.

Fulfilling the boatbuilding needs of both Blackton and Ryan kept Chris Smith and his sons working long days and developing time saving techniques. The Smith-built boats were winning races and providing important recognition for them everywhere they raced. Smith's modest boat shop was thrust into new prominence with each race won. Blackton's *Baby Speed Demon II*, designed with a shallow step bottom, won the 1914 Gold Cup Regatta with an average speed of over 50 miles per hour, setting a Gold Cup speed record.

Bernard Smith steadies the funnel during the refueling of *Baby Reliance II*, a Smith-Ryan hydroplane driven by J. Stuart Blackton in the 1912 Harmsworth Trophy Race. *Edwin Levick*

But before the Smiths were able to capitalize on this important racing victory, Ryan and Blackton's extravagant lifestyles—as well as World War I—had dwindled their personal fortunes. They would never race again, and the balance of their remaining debts to the Smith Boat Company would go unpaid.

Chris then hooked up with a group of Detroit businessmen determined to topple the East Coast dominance of unlimited speedboat racing. They formed the *Miss Detroit* Powerboat Association and contracted the Smiths to build a new racing hydroplane to challenge for the 1915 Gold Cup. Smith turned to employees Jack and Martin Beebe, who had been the principal designers and builders of *Baby Speed Demon II,* and they set out to make sure the new *Miss Detroit* was even faster. It was a major project for the Smiths and the stakes were high—eastern racing groups did not take seriously the possibility of a midwestern racer taking the trophy home. However, that's exactly what happened as the 25-1/2-foot Smith-built single-step hydroplane *Miss Detroit,* powered by a 250-horsepower Sterling engine, was crowned the new Gold Cup Champion in 1915.

This victory should have been all that the Smith family needed to become an important builder of contemporary race boats. Then the victorious *Miss Detroit* syndicate—which included wealthy Detroit sportsmen such as Hugh Chalmers, head of the Chalmers Motor Company; publisher William

Miss Detroit III with riding mechanician, Jay Smith, waving and Gar Wood standing at the wheel as they return after testing her Grant-Liberty V-12 engine performance in preparation for a major race. *Morris Rosenfeld*

Scripps; Horace Dodge of Dodge Brothers Automotive, and C. Harold Wills of Wills Saint Clair Automotive—announced that it, too, had run its treasury dry. Once again, the Smiths were left with bills unpaid by wealthy racing types.

The Gar Wood Connection

Then along came industrious young businessman Gar Wood. Wood was a skilled engineer, a highly successful entrepreneur, and an aspiring boat racer. He had recently moved his factory from St. Paul, Minnesota, to Detroit to be closer to the major automotive and truck manufacturers for whom he was supplying hydraulic lifts. Wood was invited by a

friend to attend a business luncheon in downtown Detroit where the partners of the *Miss Detroit* syndicate were planning to sell their race boat to the highest bidder to raise enough money to pay off their debt to their financially strapped boatbuilder in Algonac. As it turned out, Wood was the only bidder, and shortly after his bid was accepted, he traveled to Algonac to inspect his purchase.

Chris Smith and Gar Wood were independent, creative achievers who shared a passion for fast boats. Individually, they approached challenges and solved problems with widely differing styles. It seemed remarkable that these two talented men would establish a genuine respect for each other so quickly. Their common goal was to be the best in the world of speedboat racing. The Smiths knew fast boats and powerful engines; Wood had the money and the will to win.

Wood ended up with more than the *Miss Detroit*, ultimately purchasing the assets of the C. C. Smith & Sons Boat & Engine Company. He relieved the Smiths of nagging financial concerns while allowing them to continue to operate. Furthermore, he wanted them to build a new, faster version of *Miss Detroit* in time for him to race for the 1917 Gold Cup Championship. He also offered paid positions at his hoist factory for Chris' sons if boat building slowed for any reason over the next year or two—which was possible, as orders for Chris Smith & Sons pleasure boats could dry up as the United States became involved in World War I. With a firm handshake in Chris Smith's living room, the men formed a partnership.

Smith's outstanding woodworker, Napoleon "Nap" Lisee, designed and completed *Miss Detroit II* precisely on schedule for the 1917 Gold Cup Regatta trials. *Miss Detroit II,* now using the same Sterling engine from the original *Miss Detroit,* set a Gold Cup record of 56 miles per hour with Wood and Jay Smith at the controls. The new partnership was off to a strong start. Wood felt he could do better and told Lisee to prepare designs for *Miss Detroit III.* This time he powered the new craft with a converted Curtiss Model 12 aircraft engine, which propelled Wood and Jay Smith to Gold Cup victory again in 1918. It was the first time aircraft power had been successfully used in boat racing. In 1919 they won the Gold Cup in the same boat with a Packard-built Liberty aircraft engine.

The Wood-Smith team proved to be the most accomplished combination of designer, builder, "mechanician," and driver in the history of racing. These men would share experience, skills, wisdom, theories openly to learn from each other and to reach the absolute pinnacle of success in unlimited racing and boat-building. Gar Wood and his brothers, along with Chris Smith and his sons, Jay W. and Bernard, made Gold Cup history. They proceeded to build four new *Miss Detroits* and the first two *Miss Americas.* They traveled to England to win the prestigious British Harmsworth Trophy for America and return home as international heroes. Aided by Wood's flair for promotion and publicity, the Smiths would become boatbuilders of international prestige.

Jay and Bernard Smith, in particular, were gaining valuable experience during the racing partnership with Wood. They traveled the world, rubbed elbows with the rich, and no doubt garnered valuable insight about building and running a business. They also added to their practical knowledge of what made powered boats run well. All of this would all serve them well when they decided to strike out on their own.

After their fifth consecutive Gold Cup victory and new world-record speed of more than 80 miles per hour in *Miss America II* in 1921, the Gold Cup Rules Committee was under pressure from the eastern yacht clubs to alter the eligibility rules. They wanted to disallow the use of unlimited hulls with steps and the aircraft engines of the Wood-Smith team. Over the winter the Gold Cup rules were modified, restricting virtually all of the new technology that Gar Wood and the Smiths developed. The rationale was that these unlimited hydroplanes were out of the reach of most racing enthusiasts, and the committee favored replacing them with what it described as "gentlemen's runabouts." While the rules change ultimately diminished the prestige of the Gold Cup, it succeeded in boosting the development of the stock Runabout and stirred interest among families to try boating as a new summer activity.

The First Chris-Crafts

In 1921, Chris was 61 years old and likely not eager to break the security he enjoyed with Wood as his partner. But for 37-year-old Jay W. and 33-year-old Bernard, who were essentially contemporaries of Wood, the time had come to put their considerable talents and energy toward their own future and build a manufacturing concern much like Wood. Their relationship with Wood had been valuable and prosperous, but the time was right for the Smiths to move on.

Gar Wood and Jay Smith were successful teammates for the Gold Cup Championship Regatta in 1921, racing the first *Miss America.*

The original Chris Smith & Sons Boat Company buildings in Algonac that the Smiths sold to Gar Wood in 1922 to help finance and build the new factory that would become the home of Chris-Craft.

They were in a position to acquire a supply of war surplus airplane engines that could be marinized for use in stock runabouts—in fact, they were already offering a Standardized Runabout through Central Marine Service Corporation in Detroit. Chris, Jay W., Bernard, and Owen Smith, armed with $8,000 in capital, sold their remaining interest in the old family boatyard to Wood. The Smiths put a down payment on 20 acres of waterfront at Point du Chene in Algonac, where they would start fresh, and formed the new Chris Smith & Sons Boat Company in February 1922.

Unlike the previous incarnations of Smith boat-building companies, however, they would not seek to be patrons of the rich, building custom boats on order. Following the lead of Henry Ford and others in nearby Detroit, they set out to build stock boats for Everyman, driving prices down by streamlining the building process. As it turned out, their timing was superb. After initial postwar

weakness, the technology-driven economy in the 1920s would flourish. More important, perhaps, the spirit of the Jazz Age was ideal—America embraced the image of fast cars, fast boats, and fast times.

By April 1922, the 30 men on the Smith payroll had the first boats ready for delivery. They averaged one powerboat and one rowboat per week during this first season. By September they completed and delivered 22 26-foot powerboats and 22 rowboats, which was a reasonable start.

However, the Smiths received immeasurable help from Gar Wood, who had contracted them to build 33-foot *Baby Gar* hulls, which they then delivered to Wood's facilities. Wood's staff installed the marinized Liberty aircraft engines, water tested them, and prepared the finished boat for delivery. The Smiths also continued to provide all modifications and repair work on Gar Wood's *Miss Americas* and *Miss Detroits*. This was steady work from a financially sound source, and no doubt aided the Smith's cash flow significantly.

It was a favorable plan and worked well for the first two years. As the Smiths' business grew, building *Baby Gars* for their old partner at a bargain price generated little profit, and the arrangement began to interfere with their regular production volume. Production of new Smith boats increased to

Jay Smith on the left with Gar Wood at the steering wheel of an early Smith-built 33-foot *Baby Gar* runabout, powered by the Liberty aircraft engine made famous during World War I. *Morris Rosenfeld*

Master boatbuilders George Joachim and "Nap" Lisee, at their giant lofting table. Both men were lured away from the Smiths by Gar Wood, with whom they built eight more *Miss America* race boats, allowing William "Mac" MacKerer to head up design and production at Chris-Craft for more than 40 years.

33 motorboats in 1923 and 48 units in 1924. It was during this period that their new marque, *Chris-Craft,* appeared frequently in their promotions and advertisements for their 26-foot Standardized Runabout. The name was suggested by Jay's youngest brother, Hamilton, and first appeared in 1922 on Col. Jesse Vincent's Smith-built Gold Cup–winning boat, *Packard Chriscraft.* The name caught on and before long was commonly used to identify *all* the Smith-built boats. In 1925 their sales vaulted to 111 units, frequently compromising their ability to produce *Baby Gar* hulls on schedule for their old partner.

Wood decided it was time to build the *Baby Gar* runabouts in his own Algonac boat shop, severing the formal working arrangements with the Smiths for the first time in a decade. The Smiths were too busy building boats to be overly concerned. However, friction between the two was created when key employees from the new C.C. Smith Boat & Engine Company were persuaded to leave in order to work at Wood's operation building race boats and *Baby Gars.* Most notable among those returning to work for Gar Wood was the talented team of Napoleon Lisee and George Joachim. Lisee would design and build all of Wood's *Miss America* race

boats and Joachim would eventually be the stylist for their production craft. This departure of their best craftsman was a blow to the Smiths and intensified their rift.

The World's Largest Builder of Mahogany Runabouts

Fortunately for Jay W. and his brothers, young William MacKerer was willing to come back to Algonac. With a background in naval architecture and experience working for both George Crouch and John Hacker, MacKerer first met Chris Smith at the New York Boat Show in 1916, came to work in Algonac initially in the spring of 1922, then left, supposedly after butting heads with the elder Lisee. When Lisee joined the Gar Wood payroll, MacKerer returned. Except for a layoff during the Depression, he would stay with Chris-Craft his entire life.

MacKerer was a dogged recorder of facts and procedures who maintained detailed notebooks of boat specifications—the Smiths' as well as the competition—a habit that would lead to the detailed volumes of engineering that cataloged all Chris-Craft operations in later years. He was charged with improving speed of production in the factory, and the evidence suggests he was able to do just that. In 1926 production

Jack Clifford, the talented sales manager from the Wills Saint Claire Automobile Company, joined Chris-Craft in 1927 to organize and expand its national dealership program.

and sales increased by a relatively modest 20 percent to 134 units. In 1927, with the introduction of the new 22-foot Cadet model, they built boats year-round for the first time and increased production by an astounding 225 percent, to 447 units, topping $1 million in gross revenue. Chris Smith & Sons had become more than player in a market that included dozens of Runabout makers. It was without question the industry leader.

Jay W. was named president of the company in 1927. Bernard was named vice president and treasurer, and their father, Chris, became chairman of the board. It would be a year of tremendous growth and change for a five-year-old company. They had developed and brought to market their own engine, a 200-horsepower V-8 called the A-70. While they would begin using a new marine engine from Chrysler as well, by manufacturing their own engines they were able to drive down prices of finished boats still further. With production on the increase, they moved to expand their sales effort, hiring John E. "Jack" Clifford as sales director, opening the first franchised dealerships, and offering a consumer payment plan. By the end of 1927, there were 26 buildings covering nearly 3 of the 20 acres on Point du Chene.

With the adoption of a true marine engine, the Smiths also could exhibit at the National Motor Boat Show in New York. They would learn to use the show to project production volume, size up the competition, and extract advance orders from a growing dealership network. When the Boat Show concluded, the Smiths would have enough information to plan their production schedule with remarkable accuracy, and dealers understood that ordering ahead was the only way to guarantee having new Chris-Craft boats to sell during the peak season.

The growth would continue—to 830 units and more than $2 million in 1928, then 946 units of 18 different models (including a Commuting Cruiser) and more than $3.2 million in 1929. Boat sales continued to hold firm in early 1930 in spite of the stock market crash. The Smiths' success had attracted attention worldwide, including that of some New York investors. *Motor Boating* magazine featured this flattering story about Chris-Craft's success in the July 1930 issue that announced the formation of a new Chris-Craft corporation with plans to take the company public:

The Chris Smith's desire to build fast family motor boats for general service caused the company

The cover of the 1929 catalog— it featured 18 models from 22 to 38 feet. In less than eight years, Chris Smith & Sons Boat Company had grown to be a $3.2 million concern, spawning plans to go public. The stock market crash of October 1929 would eventually change those plans drastically. *Courtesy The Mariners' Museum*

Chris-Craft

to abandon their racing activities and enter the field of standardized boat production. For eight years Chris-Craft business has been confined to this type of boat. Residents of Algonac have seen the old boat works sprout new buildings at frequent intervals until the present plant rivals the mammoth manufacturing plants of its near-by metropolis, Detroit. The peaceful channels of St. Clair Flats are daily torn by dozens of speeding Chris-Craft being tested before shipment. Drowsing along in its rural setting, Algonac has wakened to find itself the site of one of the greatest industries in the world.

In 1922 the capital of the Smith & Sons Boat Company was $8,000—plus three generations of boat-trained Smiths. The growth of the company, out of earnings, without refinancing, into a business of many millions is an event of importance not only to placid Algonac but to financial pessimists who said boats were luxuries and that people simply would not buy enough of them to build any such manufacturing business.

Sales, according to Jay Smith, president and general manager, have continued to surpass his most optimistic estimates as well as baffle those timid souls who thought that motor boats could never be manufactured and sold in volume. Nobody knows whether, like the great growth in motion pictures, people want luxuries in good times or bad, but the truth of the matter is that motor boat sales are mounting, depression or no depression. The upward trend of Chris-Craft sales, unbroken since 1922, has recently taken a still more pronounced upward turn. Thus far in 1930, records show gains every month as compared to corresponding months last year.

So, what was once nothing more than a cherished ambition to Chris Smith is now to be made a reality through the formation of Chris-Craft Corporation, a greatly enlarged company to manufacture and market Chris-Craft motor boats.

Working control and management of the newly formed company remains in the hands of the present Smith family. Chris Smith, founder of the original company and now Chairman of the Board of Directors, will continue as Chairman of the Board of the new organization. Jay W. Smith, Chris' eldest son, and active head of the company for the past several years, will continue as president and general manager. Directors, in addition to these two individuals, will include Bernard Smith and Owen Smith of Algonac, and a newly elected director,

RUNABOUTS

Robert Heller of New York City, representing the bankers, Childs, Jeffries & Company, Incorporated.

Upon completion of the expansion program application, the firm will move to list the stock on the New York Curb Exchange, thereby opening up to the public an investment opportunity in a comparatively new and rapidly growing industrial field. Only one class of stock, no par value common, will be issued. This is the first financing, other than out of earnings, that has ever been done by the company. This expansion comes as a result of successive years of rapid growth.

In noticeable contrast to the general hesitancy in current business activity, Chris-Craft plants are and have been running at capacity to meet the demand from record sales. Highway congestion has made the modern power boat desirable. Shipments are at the present time running substantially ahead of last year, a banner year in the history of the company.

Bad Times for Boats

After generating more than $300,000 profit in 1929, the Smiths knew the Depression had arrived when they posted a $100,000 loss in the last quarter of 1930. The stock

Chris-Craft simultaneously promoted the idea that its boats were affordable for Everyman yet fit for a king—and emphasized the royal nature of Chris-Crafting by creating this coat of arms. At the crest is an outline of Miss America I; the bendy (diagonal bars) represent superiority among rivals. The ancient galley in the upper right is an emblem of honor for acts of heroism on the sea, and the flying geese in the lower left signify strength and speed.

in the post–World War II period—to take on more responsibility as vice president. They continued to plan for better times, even taking advantage of depressed prices to break ground on a new building. Like other builders, they introduced stripped-down Utility boats in order to sell—or at least attempt to sell—at the lowest retail price possible. The practical, open-hulled boats found a following not only among the thrifty, but also among sportsmen and those with families, and would ultimately outlive the Runabout style.

In the fall of 1935, Jay Smith announced that Chris-Craft sales of new boats finally exceeded their previous high of 1929, MacKerer returned, and Wayne Pickell was hired as sales manager. It had taken six years to reach the sales dollar volume level previously achieved before the Depression. Many established boat-builders were not so fortunate. The long struggle not only made the Smiths an even more resilient operation but wiped out much of the competition. Sea Lyon, Dart, and Dee Wite all succumbed, as did Dodge in 1936, leaving Chris-Craft to battle it out with Gar Wood, Hacker, and Century. Chris-Craft's dealer network stretched worldwide and was the strongest in the industry, and its new confidence was evident with its introduction of 66 new models for 1936.

Good Times Return

In late 1936 Chris-Craft resumed year-round production and introduced 97 models for 1937. Then a labor strike in 1937 decreased the anticipated production volume, left the door open for competitors such as Gar Wood, and resulted in its workers becoming unionized. It also changed, forever, the relationship between Chris-Craft's management and labor, and distanced the Smiths further from the men who were their neighbors as well as the labor force. It would not be the last labor action—there were more strikes just two years later and again in late 1941—and Chris-Craft would begin looking to establish production plants elsewhere to mitigate the labor issues in Algonac. More than 20 years later, the decision to move Chris-Craft headquarters to Florida may have been made easier by the rift that opened during the 1937 strike.

Once back in production, Chris-Craft's management resolved to carefully watch its rivals and the market for success with a new design or feature. Most competing builders specialized in a particular type of craft or a particular size range of models, whereas by the late 1930s Chris-Craft offered a wide range of craft—Runabouts, Utilities, and Cruisers—from 15-1/2 to 55 feet. In the years ahead when a boatbuilder found sales success with a specific niche, Chris-Craft was ready to move in and offer its own version. In 1949, for example,

Christopher Columbus Smith, the patriarch of the Smith family and cofounder of Chris-Craft with sons Jay, Bernard, and Owen, passed away in September 1939. In 1988 the National Marine Manufacturers Association enshrined Chris Smith into its Hall of Fame for generating substantial and lasting contributions toward the advancement of the marine industry.

market was moribund, and the two senior partners from the House of Morgan who had put down a reported $250,000 deposit as an option to buy one-third of Chris-Craft pulled out of the deal. However, the ever prudent, always cautious family from Algonac had stipulated that if the investors changed their minds, they would forfeit the entire deposit. For the next 30 years, Jay Smith never hesitated to openly admit that the pre-Depression miracle fund "saved us." The deal-never-done also left another legacy: Chris Smith & Sons Boat Company became the Chris-Craft Corporation— still owned by the Smiths.

The Depression was internationally devastating. All boatbuilders struggled to survive, but it yielded some advantages. Chris-Craft would lay off most of the workforce, including MacKerer and Clifford, which allowed Jay W.'s son Harsen—who would go on to lead the company

Chris-Craft introduced a 21-foot Express Cruiser that was identical to the bread-and-butter model of the Cruis-Along fleet, and offered it at $145 less. Chris-Craft's 1954 18-foot Sea Skiff was a dead ringer for the popular Lyman Islander and Century Viking 19. Chris-Craft's experience in volume production made it a formidable force to any boatbuilder that had developed a successful product. With their huge dealer network, Chris-Craft could swiftly bring a rival to its knees with well-financed national promotions.

Sales climbed sharply between 1937 and 1941, and Chris-Craft's designs and superb styling led the industry. The small and midsize family cruisers were beginning to capture the fancy of new boating enthusiasts in the rapidly emerging marinas and yacht clubs. On September 9, 1939, patriarch Christopher Columbus Smith died at age 78. While his passing was noted with sincere sadness in Algonac as well as throughout the industry, it did not affect operations. Jay W. and his brothers had been in full control for more than a decade.

The same month that Chris Smith died, the company that was his legacy announced plans for a new manufacturing facility on 22 acres across the state from Algonac in Holland, Michigan, where workers trained as furniture makers needed jobs. By late that year the plant was operational, managed by Harry Coll, an old college friend of Harsen's. Years later, Coll would be the first non-family member to be named president of Chris-Craft.

In January 1941, Chris-Craft arranged with Cadillac, Michigan, to acquire an additional 125,000 square feet of production space in an available structure. In less than five weeks after the deal was made, production of 18- and 22-foot Utility boats was under way. This aggressive expansion program was, in part, motivated by the need to meet the rapidly growing demand for its boats. It was also fueled by its awareness of the growing world conflict. The next generation of Smiths knew that if war was to come to America, their production capabilities could become an important factor in the nation's defense efforts. In either case, it made sense to expand and be ready for increased civilian production or the opportunity for military contracts. With full confidence, Chris-Craft announced its largest fleet, 110 models, for the 1941 season.

The War Years

When their archrivals at Gar Wood were awarded a sizable government contract to build target boats for the U.S. Army in the late 1930s, Chris-Craft also took interest in the potential need for military craft. It fell to Harsen Smith to look into securing defense contracts. In early 1940, Chris-Craft decided to participate in a special government design

competition for the development of a new 30-foot landing craft. In September its prototype was ready to be shipped to Virginia Beach, Virginia, for a series of tests arranged by the Department of the Navy. Although it lost the contract to Higgins, Chris-Craft's prototype performed extremely well, and it gained valuable experience in the techniques of working successfully with the government. In February 1941, Chris-Craft signed its first military contract, to supply marine engines for boats from another builder. This contract was followed by an order for 27 standard 22-foot Utilities for the U.S. Army Air Corps, to serve as rescue boats for downed

The 1930s were difficult times, but a decade after the remarkable year of 1929, Chris-Craft was again doing well—well enough to produce this color cover for the 1939 catalog. Barrelbacks were all the rage, and Chris-Craft had become an established builder of stock Cruisers. *Courtesy The Mariners' Museum*

With the coming of World War II, Chris-Craft entered into government contracts to build plywood landing craft and other models for the armed forces. By all accounts the Smiths and their employees did themselves and their country proud, applying their industry-leading production techniques to build some 10,000 landing craft. *Courtesy The Mariners' Museum*

army target boats, 42-foot command boats, and 60-foot quartermaster boats. Chris-Craft was able to meet and often exceed all the volume the army and navy required. Maintaining the rigorous wartime production schedules served as advanced training in construction technology that would lend itself to even greater peacetime production efficiency. Managers learned to incorporate styling changes quickly, and increase their profit margins while staying competitive. Through the defense contract to build the Higgins-spec landing craft, they learned about building plywood boats and were introduced to Thiokol sealant—helpful when it came time to launch the Plywood Boat Division and Sea Skiff Division in the 1950s.

The war and government contract work may have interrupted its post-Depression recovery, but it was not a setback regarding growth, technical development, and national recognition for its service to the country. All through the war years, Chris-Craft continued its commitment to colorful, full-page ads showing their military craft in action or providing a glimpse of attractive postwar designs for its customers to anticipate. Its unwavering dedication to attractive advertising made *Chris-Craft* a term so common that even non-boaters began using it to identify all pleasure craft.

Postwar plans were more than dreams on paper. Always mindful of an eventual return to recreational boating, in 1943 Chris-Craft acquired land in Grand Rapids, Michigan, and Jamestown, New York, for future expansion. The Grand Rapids site later would be used to house the Outboard Motor Division before it was shut down in 1953, while the Jamestown parcel was sold in 1949.

Chris-Craft's experience and production methods proved to be outstanding among military contractors. By early 1945, Chris-Craft had delivered 10,000 landing craft to the government and had received the Army-Navy Award for Excellence at each plant on more than one occasion. Of course, it was rewarded financially as well—though profits were limited by law during the war, Chris-Craft revenues topped $20 million annually as a result of the government contracts. Coming out of the war, the company would be well positioned financially to do battle in the marketplace.

As soon as the Allied victory was ensured, thoughts of peacetime boat production were on management's mind. As early as January 1945, plans were being developed for the anticipated postwar fleet of exciting new designs. Chris-Craft often received letters from men in the service anticipating an end to the war and expressing their desire for their own powerboat. For many GIs, the thought of returning home and owning a boat of their own became both an inspiration and an obsession that helped motivate them in the darkest days of combat. It became increasingly clear that large numbers of

aircraft. In May 1941, three slightly modified Chris-Craft stock cruisers promptly filled another government purchase order. Then shortly after the Japanese attack on Pearl Harbor in December, Chris-Craft was awarded its first major government contract.

Just as its 1942 catalog was being printed in early October 1941, the labor union staged an ill-timed strike. Less than a year before, the union had signed a carefully negotiated two-year contract. Management was caught by surprise and was becoming increasingly distrustful of the union's methods. By mid-November, Chris-Craft obtained a restraining order directing the union membership to cease its threats of violence, intimidation, and interference with the orderly conduct of business. Three weeks later, on December 7, 1941, the nation was at war. Chris-Craft's modest inventory of 1942 boat models was sold promptly and marked the end of its pleasure boat production for the next four years.

When America went to war, Chris-Craft was prepared to convert its factories to full production for the military. Its success in building boats on production lines proved to be valuable in fulfilling ambitious defense needs, including the 36-foot landing craft, 36-foot navy picket boats, 27-foot

returning troops, as well as civilians, were dreaming of their personal boat as a vision of the reward they deserved for their role in this terrible war.

The Postwar Transition

Demonstrating typical Chris-Craft preparation, the first postwar recreational boat was shipped in July 1945, just weeks before the bombs that ended the conflict in the Pacific. Chris-Craft's transition to peacetime production was smooth and successful. Unlike many of its rivals, it decided to make only moderate styling changes for its initial return to pleasurecraft. Early production concentrated on the most popular prewar models.

Early production concentrated on the most popular prewar models while incorporating clever style changes, such as the turtleback white bow cap on new Cruisers, that helped distinguish the post-war models from their pre-war predecessors.

While its rivals were busy redesigning and retooling to make totally new boats, Chris-Craft was rolling out new models to eager buyers. This quick start and the strength of its purchasing power put Chris-Craft in a better position to acquire mahogany and to build engines, both of which would become annoyingly scarce in the early postwar years. These frustrating shortages, alone, were enough to reduce the

number of aspiring postwar boatbuilders and improve Chris-Craft's position.

As always, Chris-Craft adapted. Unable to acquire a large enough supply of quality Philippine mahogany, it used Spanish cedar and painted the hulls because the wood did not take stain and varnish well. As during the Depression, only the most popular models were offered. Still, from 1946 to 1949, Chris-Craft solidified anew its position as leader of the powerboat industry, opening one new plant along the Mississippi in Caruthersville, Missouri, and another in Chattanooga, Tennessee. It watched as long-time rival and neighbor Gar Wood Boats, no longer under control by Gar Wood himself, closed its doors in 1947. By contrast, Chris-Craft would make $1.5 million on $14.5 million in revenue in fiscal year 1950.

Baby Boom Boating

In the 1950s, Harsen Smith would lead Chris-Craft through a decade of uninterrupted growth. Without a Depression or World War to sidetrack it, the Smith family business would expand exponentially.

The lineups of Runabouts, Utilities, and Cruisers would continue to be refined. Chris-Craft stylists would look more than ever to the automotive industry to provide inspiration for design cues, no doubt prompted by marketing departments that were looking to piggyback on America's increasing fascination with the car. Chris-Craft realized its potential strength by offering a complete range of boat types. Customers who enjoyed their first boating experience more often than not expressed their pleasure by moving up to a faster or a larger boat. For many boaters the nearly annual trade-up to a new or finer model became a natural progression, facilitated by the strong market for used boats.

With outboard motors becoming ever more popular, Jay W., Harry Coll, and others led the development of Chris-Craft's own outboards. Needing entry-level boats to hang the motors, Chris-Craft launched the Kit Boat Division in 1950, making it possible for even kids to buy and build their own Chris-Craft. Enticing ads in *Outdoor Life*, *Sports, Afield* and *Field and Stream* and a dozen other periodicals promised to fulfill dreams. And each time a Kit Boat sold, the owner became a potential lifetime customer.

Chris-Craft made mistakes, too, of course. Its Outboard Motor Division was scrapped after Carl Kiekhaefer and the manufacturers of Mercury outboards stirred up enough legal issues regarding patent infringement on the lower end unit of the 10-horsepower Commander outboard. The Grand Rapids outboard motor facility was shut down as a result of the legal issues, and it was an expensive and no doubt embarrassing move at the time. In the early 1950s, it spent considerable time developing an aircraft rescue boat

The 1950s were a decade of uninterrupted expansion for the marine industry, and Harsen Smith helped Chris-Craft capitalize on that growth. Harsen, Jay W.'s son, was groomed for the job from early on in his life. He appeared on the cover of *Time* magazine in May 1959–by the following January, the Smith family sold Chris-Craft to National Automotive Fibers, Inc., for $40 million. ©*Time Inc.* *Reprinted by permission.*

By 1969 the wooden boat era was effectively over, prompting the company to run a contest to find the oldest living Chris-Craft. The winner at the time was *Miss Belle Isle*, a 1923 26-foot Standardized Runabout, shown here in front of the Chris-Craft headquarters in Pompano Beach, Florida. The boat was purchased from the owner by Chris-Craft, and ultimately donated to the Chris-Craft Collection at The Mariners' Museum in Newport News, Virginia. *Courtesy The Mariners' Museum*

based on U.S government specs for the Korean conflict. After much frustration with the federal bureaucracy, Chris-Craft abandoned the project. In 1957, Chris-Craft purchased a small builder of 15-foot fiberglass runabouts called Lake 'n Sea, but the fiberglass technology it used was flawed, the boats came to be known as the "Leak 'n Sink," and Chris-Craft quickly sold the company.

But compared with the successes, the failures during the Smith years were of little consequence. In 1954, Chris-Craft took on the makers of round-bilge lapstrake skiffs with the launching of its own Sea Skiff Division, opening a new plant for the purpose in Salisbury, Maryland. Over the course of the next 16 years, Chris-Craft would establish itself as a major builder of lapstrakes, contributing still more to the bottom line. In 1955 the Kit Boat Division became the Plywood Boat Division, offering value-priced prebuilt Kit Boats,

and then subsequently was renamed the Cavalier Division in 1957. The plywood Cavaliers, offered with the option of a fiberglass-over bottom, were a value line that brought thousands to the Chris-Craft fold and held off the incursion of all-fiberglass competition for a decade. Chris-Craft also purchased the Roamer Boat Corporation, maker of steel-hulled Cruisers, when it came up for sale in 1955, and built a new facility in Holland to expand the production of steel-hulled (later aluminum) boats.

Legend for Sale

But there was no more astounding news in Algonac than the announcement in 1957 that the Smiths would be moving the company headquarters to Pompano Beach, Florida. Not only had the Smith family been building boats in Algonac since the 1870s, they had been employing locals regularly for 50 years. Chris-Craft had brought international prestige to the small town, and moving the headquarters away was for many a slap in their collective face. But realistically, Chris-Craft was an international, multimillion dollar concern with manufacturing facilities spread across the country. Critical field testing and development was hampered by Michigan's winter weather. Attracting top industry talent to a small, northern town had to be difficult. By the late 1950s, Chris-Craft's second generation—Jay W., Bernard, Owen—were of retirement age, and any number of members of the family spent time in Florida already, where corporate taxes were more favorable.

Not that they needed it, but the move and construction of the new Administrative Headquarters and Manufacturing and Engineering Center were financed in part by subdividing and reselling portions of the land they purchased in Pompano Beach. By November 1957 the Chris-Craft Division had made the move.

The following year, Chris-Craft named Harry Coll president, the first non-family member, and only the third person after Chris and Jay W., to hold the position. Harsen continued as chairman of the board. Coll's appointment signaled, perhaps, the second generation's determination to move on, test the market and if the price was right, perhaps even cash out. By February 1960, that's exactly what the 55 Smith-family stockholders did, selling to NAFI for $40 million. While Harsen, then 53, would leave and manage the Smith-family trust, his old college friend Harry Coll would stay on. One of the only Smiths to remain with Chris-Craft after the sale was Bernard's son Chris, then a relatively young man who would work for a variety of owners over the next 30 years.

Modernizing Chris-Craft

In retrospect, the Smiths picked an ideal time to sell their company. The fiberglass revolution was under way in the marine industry, and Chris-Craft seemed uncharacteristically behind the curve. It would take a massive effort—and considerable capital—to prepare the company to compete in the plastic arena. Consequently, the decade of the 1960s was a time of considerable change for Chris-Craft.

In 1962, NAFI announced the purchase of Thompson Boat Company of Cortland, New York, maker of fiberglass Runabouts with the Volvo-based inboard-outboard hybrid transdrive. They would use Thompson by Chris-Craft to launch the Corsair fleet of outboard and transdrive Runabouts and small Cruisers.

Perhaps more shocking to Chris-Craft customers, in 1964 NAFI introduced a 35-foot sloop-rigged fiberglass sailboat called the Motor Sailer, instigated by Cornelius Shields of Shields and Company, a major stockholder of NAFI. It

would go on to offer additional sailboat models, including a 30-foot Capri and 30-foot Shields One-Design stock racer, as well as a lineup using American Indian names. Sailboats would be part of the Chris-Craft fleet through 1976.

More influential, perhaps, was the 1964 introduction of the 38-foot all-fiberglass Commander Cruiser line, the largest all-fiberglass boat to be built at that point. It was developed in the Holland plant, was powered by twin V-8 engines, and sold for less than $30,000. It was competitively priced and outfitted, promised less maintenance, and soon was joined by sister models in other lengths.

Although fiberglass would enter the Chris-Craft bloodstream relatively quickly following the ownership change, the ensuing decade was still dominated by wood. Enclosed-cockpit wooden Runabouts would run aground after 1961, when the last Capri came off the line. But Utility-style Sport Boats would enjoy healthy sales for most of the 1960s, initially with Ski Boats, Holidays, Continentals, and subsequently with the new Super Sports. On the Cruiser side of the business, the traditionally planked Constellation fleet, with lengths from 28 to 65 feet, continued to have a strong following and were offered into the early 1970s. Plywood Cavaliers and lapstrake Sea Skiffs also stayed afloat through most of the decade.

But by 1965 when Bill MacKerer officially retired after more than 40 years with Chris-Craft, the future of the commercially viable, mass-produced wooden powerboat was apparent. Americans were embracing new politics, new music, and new technology. In the boating world, fiberglass was the standard, and wood was old-fashioned.

Herbert Siegel had engineered a takeover in 1967 and was named chairman of the board in early 1968. By many accounts, Chris-Craft was from then on a different kind of company—corporate headquarters were moved to New York, and the Boat Division became a less significant part of Chris-Craft Industries.

The wooden boat era could be said to have ended in 1969. The Cavalier Division was shelved, and the last Utilities were offered in 1968. The Constellation line was whittled down to three lengths while a 60-foot all-fiberglass Commander Motor Yacht topped the Cruiser fleet. The fiberglass Commander line even included a 19-foot high-performance double-cockpit forward Sport Boat—a fiberglass Runabout. Harry Coll retired late in the year. The day of the wooden powerboat was done.

Chris-Craft would go on—a brand name so strong it could withstand the energy crisis of the 1970s, poor management, multiple owners, and bankruptcy proceedings— and it still exists proudly today. Today's Chris-Craft stylists have even returned to the designs of the classic era for inspiration for modern boats.

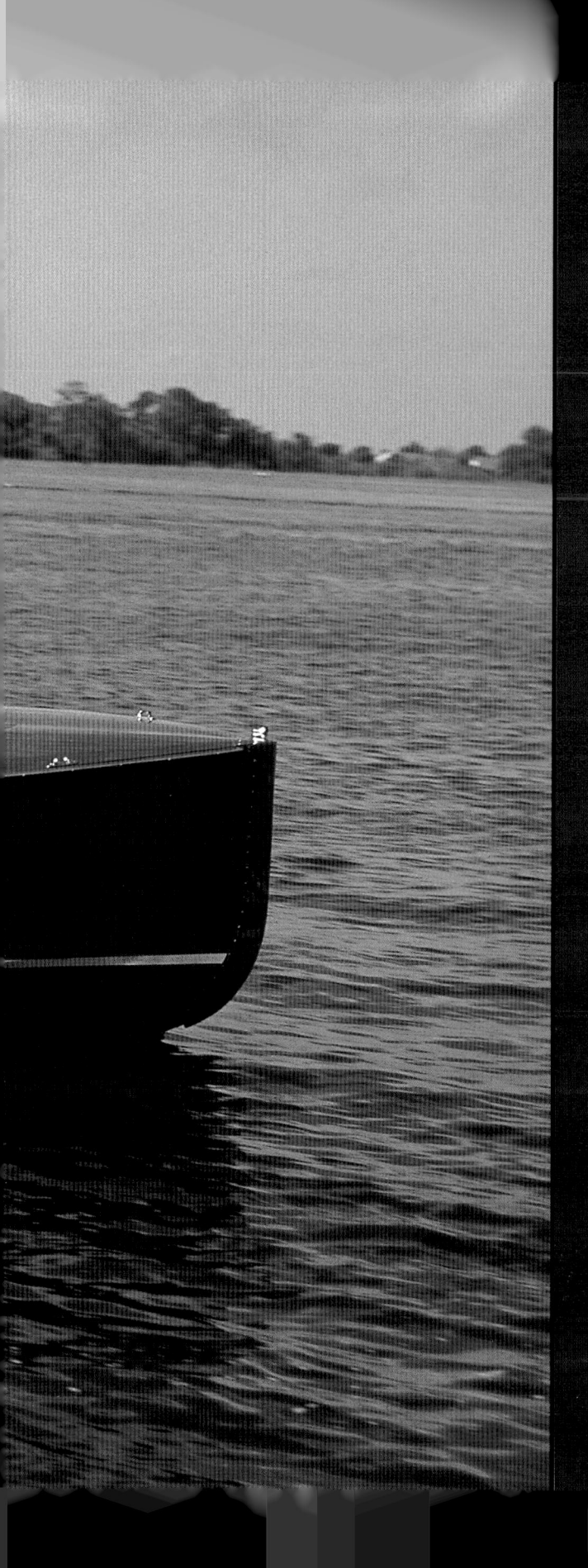

CHAPTER 2

RUNABOUTS
Speedboats for Everyman

long with others in the boatbuilding trade in the early 1920s, Chris Smith and his sons sensed that the post–World War I period was ripe for explosive growth in recreational power-boating. Known worldwide for their expertise in coaxing more speed than anyone else out of racing hydroplanes, the Smiths set out to capture a piece of the runabout market.

While the Smiths would—through the sheer volume of their output in the 1920s—do much to define what was known as a standardized runabout, they did not invent the V-bottom displacement hull it was based on. The hard-chine V-bottom evolved from the

Chris Smith & Sons' earliest standardized 26-foot Runabout, such as the restored *Godfather VI*, had no windshield and was powered by a war-surplus Curtiss OX-5 engine marinized by the Smiths. *Classic Boating Magazine*

When this mid-1930s triple came off the line, Chris-Craft Runabout design was in transition. Smooth decks and covering boards led to modest tumblehome aft, presaging the ultrastreamlined barrelbacks of the late 1930s, yet the flat windshield was a throwback to the early Standardized Runabout.

deadrise bottom design of pre-1900. Most early runabouts—a term coined for early automobiles—were round-bottom launches, often with fantail sterns, that handled the early, low-power engines of their day with aplomb. But as engine technology advanced, boat designers looked for hull shapes that could make use of added horsepower. One of the first to refine and popularize the V-bottom was naval architect William Hand Jr., who made his plans available in the early 1900s.

According to a 1940 *Motor Boating* article, the first V-bottom runabout with a forward cockpit (although controls were still aft) was a 25-footer, built by Hand around 1914, called *Ginger*. George Crouch, another influential

Miss Belle Isle, a 1923 26-foot Standardized Runabout, was made famous some 45 years later through a 1969 contest to identify the Oldest Living Chris-Craft. She was restored and donated to The Mariners' Museum in Newport News, Virginia, home of the Chris-Craft archives, where she remains on display today. *Courtesy of The Mariners' Museum*

naval architect, was building V-bottom runabouts capable of more than 30 miles per hour as early as 1913. Well-known designer John Hacker is credited with the first forward-cockpit, forward-control runabout design from the Albany Boat Corporation in 1916.

Following America's involvement in World War I, Ed Gregory installed 125-horsepower Hall-Scott engines in four 26-foot Hacker-built hulls, and called them Belle Isle Bearcats, after the Stutz Bearcat of automotive fame. It would not be the last time boatbuilders piggybacked on the marketing of the auto industry. The Bearcat—the hit of the 1920 New York Boat Show and considered the first standardized runabout with forward controls—featured two wicker chairs aft and was advertised as available for a pricey $6,500.

Throughout this period, Chris Smith and his sons Jay and Bernard, along with designer Napoleon Lisee, focused on the racing world. Their partnership with industrialist Gar Wood, begun in 1916 when he purchased secondhand the Smith-built *Miss Detroit*, led to domination of the class. The Wood/Smith team won five straight Gold Cups, establishing new speed records in the famous *Miss America* hydroplanes.

By the early 1920s, however, it was clear that the Smiths were looking to expand beyond the racing game. Central Marine Service Corporation of Detroit advertised a 26-foot Smith-built aft-cockpit runabout powered by the Hall-Scott engine for $3,950 in 1921—considerably less than the Bearcat—though, as author and marine historian Joseph Gribbins has pointed out, featuring the then old-fashioned long-deck-forward configuration.

By early 1922 the Smiths had sold their former boat shop to Gar Wood, used the capital to start the Chris Smith & Sons Boat Company, and set out to build and sell their

Facing stiff competition for the growing pleasureboat market, the Smiths introduced the 22-foot Cadet in 1927, the first of the Runabouts to be given a separate model name. Note the step-through seat back.

When Chris Smith and Sons introduced its second model after the 26-foot Standardized Runabout, the 22-foot Cadet, it boldly announced plans for production of no fewer than 500 units.

own standardized runabouts. They acquired a quantity of World War I surplus V-8 Curtiss OX-5 airplane engines that were cheap, plentiful, and able to be adapted for marine use by the Smiths themselves. Although purpose-built marine engines were available at the time, the resulting 90-horsepower Smith-Curtiss OX-5 engines, featuring an electric starter and transmission with reverse gear, would power the Smiths' standardized 26-foot runabout for the first few years of production.

Standardized Runabout

The production Standardized Runabout had a 6-1/2 foot beam, 24-inch draft, and could hit 30–32 miles per hour powered by the Smith-Curtiss. With the engine installed amidships, it was essentially a split cockpit configuration with controls forward. Early examples had no windshield, leather upholstery, linoleum floors, and two wicker chairs supplementing a bench seat in the aft cockpit. The carvel hull used double planking on the bottom, and single-planked board-and-batten sides. When introduced in 1922, it was advertised for $3,500 then $3,200.

Who designed the Smiths' first Standardized Runabout? Throughout Chris-Craft's history, no one person was typically credited with an entire design. Hacker's Belle Isle

Bearcat clearly provided some inspiration. Certainly Chris Smith and his sons had decades of practical experience at their disposal. Nap Lisee, the likely design genius behind the legacy of great race boats, was still on the payroll and probably had a significant hand in the new 26-footer. A. W. MacKerer, who first met Chris Smith at the 1916 New York Boat Show, was hired in 1922, but was still a young man in his 20s. According to his son Don MacKerer, Bill or "Mac" was not given the freedom to tackle design tasks until Lisee left to rejoin Gar Wood later on. MacKerer had, however, worked previously for both George Crouch and John Hacker.

The first "Chriscraft" was the *Packard Chriscraft*, a 26-foot runabout commissioned and piloted by Colonel Jesse Vincent of Packard Motorcar Co., in the Gold Cup race in 1922. Vincent won that race; Gar Wood, in another Smith-built boat, finished seventh. This result would in part spawn the oft-repeated belief that the Smiths and Wood became bitter rivals. In fact, the Smiths would continue to build the hulls of Wood's 33-foot Baby Gars through 1925, providing steady income for the fledgling Chris-Craft business.

Thanks to their racing background, the Smiths were well known around the world, especially among wealthy sportsmen who could afford big, fast runabouts. Chris Smith and his brother Hank served as guides for "sports" hunters and

The 22-foot Cadet lasted for three years; it was introduced in 1927 and offered into 1929. *The Laker*, docked on an early morning on Lake George, is a Cadet.

fisherman from Detroit, for decades—some of whom had started the Smiths in boatbuilding by asking them to build duck boats. These inroads provided excellent prospects for potential customers for their new Standardized Runabout.

And by the standards of the day, the plan worked. The Smiths shipped 24 of their new 26-footers in 1922, then another 33 units in 1923. The wicker chairs in an open aft cockpit would give way to a triple cockpit configuration. They increased the beam to 6 feet 8 inches on the 1924 models and sold 48 units.

The booming economy of the 1920s fueled the market. They would add windshields and sell 111 boats in 1925—an increase due to more efficient building techniques, but also in part to the end of their contract with Gar Wood to provide the 33-foot Baby Gar hulls.

In February 1926 the Smiths would take the next big step in the marketing of their Runabouts with the establishment of the first Chris-Craft dealer, E.J. Mertaugh of Hessel, Michigan. A New York office was opened a year later. In 1927 they hired John E. "Jack" Clifford, former sales manager for the Wills Saint Claire automobile in nearby Marysville, as general sales manager for the company. They

would begin offering credit terms to buyers. The Smiths were positioning themselves to be able to sell many more boats than the 134 units that went out the Algonac doors in 1926. All they had to do was build them.

The 22-Foot Cadet 1927–1929

By 1927, the year Jay Smith would be named president of the company, it was clear that the concept of the gentleman's runabout was a hit. "At last the day of the stock boat has arrived," announced *Motor Boating* in 1926. Not only were sales of the 26-foot Chris-Craft growing, but dozens of competing boatbuilders were staking out market share as well. John Hacker had introduced the Bearcat-based Dolphin models, available in various lengths and competitively priced, in 1923. Dodge, Gar Wood, and others were all trying to distinguish their products in an increasingly crowded market. A 1925 article in *Motor Boating* magazine touting the virtues of standardized runabouts and cruisers featured offerings from Gar Wood, Dodge, Belle Isle, Everett Hunter Boat Company, Fay & Bowen—Chris Smith & Sons was as yet just one more boatbuilder looking to cash in on a trend.

They also sought to continue to drive down the price of their boats. The 26-foot standardized Runabout began selling for $3,500 in 1922 and by 1926 was advertised for $2,900 equipped with the Smith Curtiss motor, a reduction made possible through "greatly increased production with the added economies of quantity buying and a constantly reduced sales expense." It would appear that the Smiths' legendary thrift, in combination with MacKerer's extraordinary attention to detail and drive to make production cost-effective, allowed the company to offer more boat for less money. It was also true that the marinized OX-5 engines were getting long in the tooth, and Chris-Craft also had begun offering the 26-footers with either of two Kermaths, a 150-horsepower at $3,500 or 100-horsepower at $3,200.

But Chris-Craft was not the only company to find ways to sell boats for less. Ventnor's 25-foot runabout with a 50-horsepower Van Blerck, for example, was listed for a low $2,250 in 1926. In addition, the Indian Lake Boat Company of Lima, Ohio, had introduced its 26-foot Dart runabout in 1924, and would then introduce a 22-foot Dart Junior in 1927. In 1927, Gar Wood introduced the 26-foot Baby Gar Jr., a smaller version of the industry-leading 33-foot Baby Gar, and sold an impressive 103 units. In fact, the Smith family, overseeing a five-year old family business that had through 1926 pushed a total of 350 boats out the door, would have hardly been considered a favorite to ultimately outlast the well-financed boatbuilding efforts of Gar Wood or Horace E. Dodge.

Dodge jumped into the recreational boatbuilding business in 1924, advertising the Dodge Watercar, the "Motor Car of the Sea" in the April issue of *Motor Boating* for a mere $2,250. In December of 1924, Dodge hired aforementioned naval architect George Crouch. Dodge's first Watercar model was 22-1/2 feet, powered by a marinized Dodge auto engine. In 1926 he introduced a 26-footer powered by a Dodge Curtiss—the same converted 90-horsepower aero engine found in the Chris-Craft. By 1927, Dodge was marketing his Watercars in three lengths, 22-1/2, 26, and 30 feet, all built in a 75,000-square-foot building in Detroit outfitted specifically for standardized boatbuilding, following the lessons learned in the Dodge automotive business.

In that context, the Smiths understood that while the market was strong, the competition was fierce, and sales growth depended on expanding their offerings and by extending the number of people who could afford a Chris-Craft. In order to stay ahead of the competition and take full advantage of its sales ability, Chris-Craft needed additional standardized product. Thus was born the company's second stock runabout, the Chris-Craft Cadet.

This 1929 28-footer, *Kath II*, shows not only the upswept forward deck styling, but the exquisite detail of a late-1920s Chris-Craft. Note the considerable forward flare.

The Cadet was introduced at the National Motorboat Show in New York in January 1927, and was initially available with a 70-horsepower Kermath that gave it 25 miles per hour for $2,250. In 1928 the triple-cockpit 22-footer could be ordered with either an 82-horsepower Chrysler that produced 30 miles per hour or the 100-horsepower Chrysler Imperial engine, the latter pushing it to a listed top speed of 35 miles per hour. In 1929, its final year, it was also powered by the 106-horsepower Chrysler Imperial. The Cadet was discontinued in favor of the new upswept deck-style Runabouts after three years, 1927 through 1929.

The Cadet is significant in that the Smiths and their employees used it to make substantial improvements in their mass production techniques. When the new model was announced, the Smiths claimed they planned for the then-unheard-of 500 units a year. And, in fact, their overall output went from 134 boats in 1926 to 447 boats in 1927 and a staggering 830 units in 1928. A reporter visiting the Algonac plant in the late 1920s marveled at the fact that varnishing was the only aspect of building the Cadet that was completed by hand. All other facets of construction involved the use of power tools, with crews of men assigned to one given

Along with the adoption of the upswept deck, restyling in 1929 included a nickel silver instrument panel, as shown on *Why Not*, a 1929 28-foot Runabout. It was fitted with two cigar lighters, a No. 35 spotlight, and a dash-mounted pull-handle that engaged the fire extinguisher. The Star Pathfinder compass was a dealer-installed extra.

task. By May of 1927, according to Jeffrey Rodengen in the *Legend of Chris-Craft*, production of the Cadet had reached three boats a day.

While many companies would build quality runabouts over the years, Chris-Craft evolved into the world's largest by building them faster and more cost-effectively.

The 1928 26-Foot Sport Hydroplane

At the 1928 Boat Show, the Smiths would astound the crowds and the competition by offering 11 different models. Granted, some of those were simply the same hull with a different engine, but in an industry in which many regional builders were doing well to put out 11 boats total, Chris Smith and Sons were blowing away the competition and establishing themselves as the "World's Largest Builder of All-Mahogany Boats." In addition to the 26-foot "40-mile Chris-Craft" and the 22-foot Cadet, Runabouts would become available in 24-foot and 28-foot lengths. Sedan versions of the 26-footer were offered, and it would also be the year of the first Chris-Craft Commuters, the beginning of the company's cruiser lineup.

Production numbers show that diversity of their lineup was the key to their growth. Records from 1928 indicate

that they built 331 Cadets and 296 24-footers, but only 134 26-foot Runabouts—the same number as in 1926, when they had just the one stock Runabout. In addition, they built 33 26-foot sedans, 6 28-footers, 10 30-footers, 2 of the new 38-foot Commuting Cruisers, and 2 "experimental" hulls.

Experimental? At the 1928 New York Boat Show, the company displayed a new model that apparently was never put into production, a 26-foot "Sport Hydroplane" with a stepped bottom (as compared to the displacement hulls on the other Runabouts). The 26-footer carried a 200-horsepower Chris-Craft engine that would push it to a claimed 55 miles per hour. It was advertised for $7,200, which put it considerably above the heart of the Chris-Craft lineup. The two experimental hulls may have been Sport Hydroplanes, and they may have been created in order to show off the new Chris-Craft engine.

It was also in 1928 that the company began building its own engines to supplement the Chrysler and Kermath marine powerplants that were available in a Chris-Craft Runabout. With development overseen by Gar Wood's former racing mechanic, none other than company president Jay Smith, it introduced the A-70, an 828-ci 90-degree V-8 that made 200-horsepower. Power output increased to 225 horsepower

By 1930, when Chris-Craft built this upswept-deck Model 103 24-footer, shown cutting through the brisk autumn waters of Lake Winnipesaukee, the company offered Runabout models in six lengths, from 20 to 30 feet. *Hepcat* was originally powered by a Chrysler 125-horsepower Model LM engine.

In 1930, Chris-Craft added the 20-foot Model 100 to the lineup and—as with the Cadet—predicted it would build 500 units. The diminutive upswept-deck triple returned for 1931 as the Model 200, like *Lagniappe*. The Depression took its toll, and it would be the last year of the upswept style.

in 1929. Soon after, they introduced a second engine, the 225-horsepower A-120. Being able to control cost and quality in its powerplants only made the company more competitive and helped expand its Runabout lineup even further.

Upswept Deck Runabouts 1929–1931

With sales of the standard 26-foot Chris-Craft triple flat in spite of substantial overall growth, it was time for some restyling. After all, 26-footers were—with some modifications—more or less the same boats that came off the drawing board in 1922 and may have started looking a little stale. Other makers were starting to make styling changes, so the Chris-Craft would change as well.

The result was the upswept deck style, a design thought to be Bill MacKerer's first real design work for the company. The forward deck rose gradually as it approached to windshield, and louvered vents replaced chrome portholes along the raised engine compartment, which was also upswept at the rear to mimic the forward deck. Dash instruments were incorporated into a single chrome and nickel-plated instrument panel inset into a curved mahogany dashboard, making for a far more elegant presentation in the forward cockpit. Gone was the walnut steering wheel, replaced by a more modern-looking black automotive-style wheel.

In its first year, the upswept deck styling was featured on 24-, 26-, 28-, and 30-foot Runabouts, all triple cockpits. The 24-footer featured slightly less beam (6 feet 4 inches), used the 106-horsepower Chrysler Imperial engine to reach 33 miles per hour, and sold for $2,750. The 26-foot hull was offered as 7 of the 18 models offered in 1929, including 3 runabouts and 4 sedans. The 26-foot Runabout prices ranged from $2,975 with the Chrysler six-cylinder to $4,300 powered by the Chris-Craft engine, which gave it a claimed 45 miles per hour.

Nineteen twenty-nine also marked the introduction of Custom Runabouts, in 28- and 30-foot lengths. The 28-footer was offered as a Runabout with either the 225-horsepower Chris-Craft for $4,975 or a 200-horsepower Kermath for $300 less, as well as in sedan configurations.

For the 1930 model year, developed in mid-1929, the Smiths added a 20-foot Runabout. Also sporting the upswept forward deck, the triple cockpit Model 100 was powered by a 75-horsepower Chrysler and sold for just $1,895. As with the Cadet, which was discontinued after 1929, the company said it planned to build 500 units of the 20-footer.

The Cadet was replaced by the 22-foot Model 101/102, which also featured the upswept style. Continued were the 24-footer, 26-footer, and the 28- and 30-foot Custom Runabouts.

Although the magnitude of the economic problems facing the country wouldn't become glaringly apparent to the Smiths until well into 1930, the 1931 lineup did feature a still-smaller Runabout, the 17-foot Model 199. It was propelled to 25 miles per hour with a little 41-horsepower engine and could carry six passengers in its two cockpits. It sold for $1,295.

The 1931 catalog was the first to divide the 37-model lineup between runabouts and cruisers. The 17-, 20-, 22-, 24- and 26-footers were offered as Standard Runabouts, while the 26-, 28-, and 30-foot hulls could be ordered as more luxurious Custom Runabouts. Also offered that year were 26- and 28-foot Convertible Sedans—Runabouts with folding tops over the aft cockpit.

The company that incorporated as Chris-Craft in 1930 was at the top of its game in 1929. All models were called Chris-Crafts, because the name had become an established and respected brand. In less than eight years, it had grown from a small family business reliant on a few wealthy clients to the largest builder of recreational powerboats. But the greater challenge would be finding a way to survive the coming Depression.

Level Riding Runabouts 1932–1934

While no one knew how long the depressed economic times would last, it was clear by the time the 1932 models

Long-time Chris-Craft dealer Irwin Marine maintained a stable of 26- and 28-foot 1929 and 1930 upswept triples that were run as party boats and thrill rides. There were as many as seven *Miss Winnipesaukees* operating on Lake Winnipesaukee. This restored 26-footer still graces the waters of the big New Hampshire lake. *Robert Bruce Duncan*

For 1932, Chris-Craft modified its Runabout hulls and advertised its new "Level Riding Principle." The 26-footer became a 25-foot Custom and featured less draft and freeboard, giving the driver better vision over the forward deck. Stylistically, the Runabouts took on a flush deck appearance with additional tumblehome aft, as shown on *Recovery*, a 1934 25-foot Custom Runabout.

came out that major changes—if not desperate measures—would be required. From the heady days of offering more than three dozen models, Chris-Craft cut back to less than half that many, some of which were not stock boats at all but rather available on special order.

Advertisements for the 1932 fleet extolled the virtues of Chris-Craft's new "level riding principle." In theory, the hulls were modified to promote coming on plane quickly and giving a smoother ride, allowing the driver and passengers in the forward cockpit to see directly ahead.

And in fact, the hull specifications were modified. The venerable 26-footer, for example, became a 25-foot Custom (Models 306–308). The beam was identical, at 6 feet 8 inches, but with less draft and 5-1/2 inches less freeboard (distance between the waterline and the deck) forward. Stylistically, the Runabouts imitated the flush deck approach that had been adopted on Gar Wood and Dodge models previously. There was more flare forward and tumblehome (reverse flare, if you will) aft, and cockpits featured trim with rounded corners, softening and streamlining the overall look in acknowledgment of the design movement that would define the 1930s. These were not yet barrelbacks, however, and the conversion to a fully streamlined look wasn't yet complete. Some of these boats still used the flat, rectangular folding windshields of the 1920s. Later versions featured V-windshields—fixed or folding—that would grace many of the Runabouts into the 1940s.

The 18-foot models 301 and 302, which replaced the 17-footer of the previous model year, continued to have two cockpits, one forward and one aft of either a 55-horsepower or 85-horsepower engine. They sold for $1,095 (Standard) and $1,395 (Deluxe). The 21-foot triple cockpit models 303–305 replaced the 20-footers, and included the Custom 21-foot model with a 125-horsepower Chrysler six, promising 36 miles per hour for $2,395. Model 309 was a 27-foot triple, replete with the new styling cues that sold for $4,975 with a 250-horsepower Chris-Craft eight-cylinder engine.

15-1/2-Foot Model 300

In addition to styling changes and hull modifications, Chris-Craft introduced a new boat in the 1932 Runabout lineup. Model 300 was a slim 15-1/2-foot Runabout with a beam of 5 feet 4 inches and 17 inches of draft. A 55-horsepower Chrysler four-cylinder pushed the split-cockpit hull to a claimed 32 miles per hour—all for the economy-minded price of $795. This diminutive Runabout would be called the 300 Deluxe a year later, and would be joined by the Model 400 Special, which was the same boat fitted with a four-cylinder Gray Marine engine and priced even lower, at $595. Still, these wouldn't be the least expensive Chris-Crafts—the

By 1932 the Depression had reached Algonac and boat sales plummeted. All but a few employees were laid off from the factory. It's likely that one or more members of the Smith family originally built this 25-foot Custom triple.

In 1935 the 21-foot triple cockpit Custom Runabout was pushed to 22 feet with more beam, and when equipped with the 150-horsepower Chrysler eight-cylinder engine could reach the magic 40 miles per hour. Note the curved cockpit trim on *Miss Flagship*.

1934 model year included the Model 65, based on the same hull but in the new Utility configuration complete with 32-horsepower engine and tiller steering, for all of $495. The Runabout version stayed in the lineup in 1934 with a price increase to $845 and $945, depending on the engine choice.

While runabouts were sold during these dark days of the Depression, this was the era of the birth of the basic utility-style boats. Created to push retail prices down, the Utilities would prove to be more practical and gain popularity—ultimately pushing the runabout aside. After all, a sports car is fun, but a four-door sedan is what you need when it's time for the family vacation.

Double Cockpit Forward Runabouts

In 1934, Chris-Craft added a Double Cockpit Forward version of the 18-foot Deluxe Runabout. Rather than two cockpits split by an engine mounted amidships, the engine was placed in the stern, allowing "Direct Drive" of the propeller—the advantage being avoiding the power lost when a transmission is used. A press release published in *Motor Boating* credited this development to Jay Smith: "He has designed it from stem to stern—even to the motor and the unique way of installing the motor, which has eliminated the always troublesome gear box construction." Given that

the dire economic conditions had forced the company to lay off virtually everyone, including inhouse designer MacKerer, during the period leading up to the Double Cockpit Forward, it's certainly plausible that Jay designed and engineered the boat.

The promotional article went on to describe the boats: "They are finished in natural mahogany with chrome trim and V-type sloping windshield. Both cockpits are of the large, roomy, airplane type with high lazybacks, deep cushions, and box springs. Unusually large leg room has been provided, and the lazyback dividing forward and aft cockpits is of rounded sloping design, which harmonizes with the general streamline appearance of the craft." Chris-Craft held a contest for a slogan for the new configuration. "Ride gaily through the spray, the chummy Chris-Craft way" was the winner—promoting the friendlier aspect of two cockpits no longer divided by a decked engine compartment.

The concept was good enough to expand in 1935 to the new 16-foot and 19-foot Runabouts in 1935. The 16- and 18-footers were also available in split-cockpit configuration.

Special Race Boat 1934–1940

When the Smiths started the company in 1922, they left world-class racing behind. Outside of the Packard Chriscrafts in the early 1920s, the experimental Sport Hydroplane in 1928, and the various custom orders that came in from time-to-time, they had stuck to their mission and built stock runabouts for the general public.

Double Cockpit Forward Runabouts were offered in 16-, 18-, and 19-foot lengths in 1936. they ranged in price from $945 for the smallest to $1550 for the 19-footer equiped with a 93-horsepower engine that made a claimed 36 miles per hour. *Karine N. Rodengen*

Jay Smith was credited with the design of the new Double Cockpit Forward Runabouts introduced in 1934, such as this 16-footer. Featuring the V-windshield and "airplane type" cockpits, they used a stern-mounted engine with direct drive. *Courtesy The Mariners' Museum*

Boaters being who they are, however, stock runabout racing was a popular activity, and the men of Chris-Craft knew full well that speed sold boats. A Cadet ad in 1927 touted the impressive list of "Smith Built Champions" from Baby Speed Demon to the *Miss Detroits* and *Miss Americas,* while extolling the virtues of the new 35-mile per hour 22-footer that had won both heats in its class in the Boston Regatta.

According to a Jim Wangard article in *Classic Boating,* Chris-Craft shipped two 26-foot triples in 1934 equipped with a racing version of the A-120 engine (the A-120A), fitted with dual carbs and high compression heads that generated 350-horsepower. The boats, named *Madashumi* and *Jay-Dee II,* raced in Florida regattas. *Jay-Dee II* sported a white bottom, red sides, and helped its owner, Jack Dunn, promote his Chris-Craft dealership. Both boats still exist today. Although seven of these early 26-foot Special Race Boats were reportedly built between February 1934 and July 1936, they were not made available to the general public—that would come later.

In Algonac, Chris-Craft was returning to profitability in 1936. Not only was the economy recovering, but the Depression had wiped out much of Chris-Craft's competition. Dodge closed in 1936, joining Dart, Dee-White, Ditchburn, and others in the boatbuilder boneyard. Chris-Craft, however, was ready for new growth, and the Runabout fleet was expanding once again. A new 19-foot Special Race Boat was

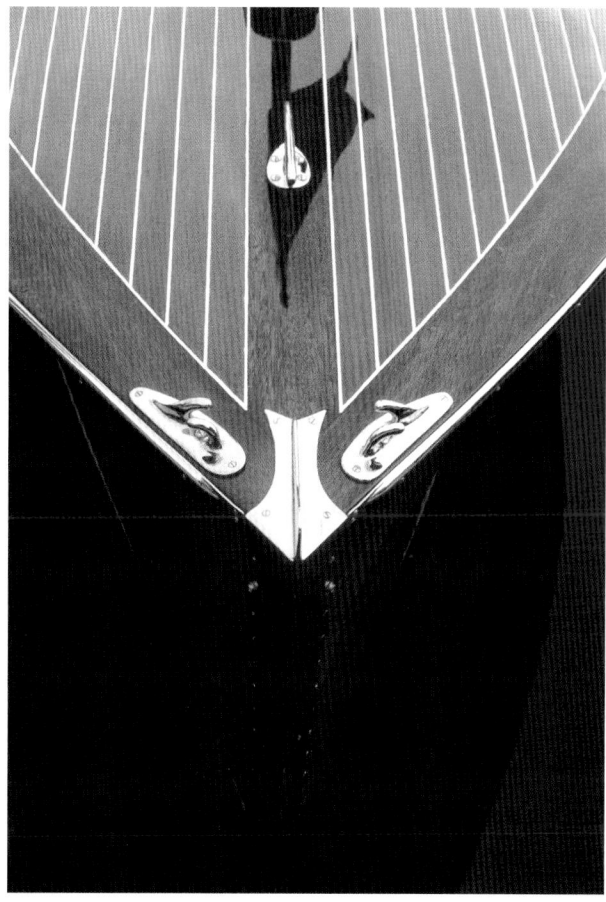

The pointed bow of the 1937 25-foot triple-cockpit Custom Runabout *My Girls.* Chris-Craft brightwork typically used a red mahogany stain contrasted by the dark walnut stain on the covering boards and kingplank.

The 16-foot Special Raceboat was one of the first Runabouts in the Chris-Craft lineup to feature the barrelback stern in 1936. *Blue Chip* is a 1937 version—the aft cockpit could be covered by a removable hatch.

Left: Postwar Runabouts like this 1952 riviera exchanged the contrasting dark-walnut stained kingplank and covering boards of the prewarboats for the bleached blond kingplank, cockpit trim, and engine hatch covers. *Classic Boating magazine*   **Above:** By 1939, Chris-Craft designers embraced the streamlining craze with the barrelbacks. *Solitude* ia a 22-foot Custom Runabout originally listed at $2,550 powered by a 135-horsepower MR engine.

Note the fully rounded cockpit trim and dual Bugatti-style windshields on *Sashay*, a 1939 22-foot Custom Runabout.

Even as the storm clouds of war approached, Chris-Craft continued to refine the design of the Runabouts. In 1941, the bows of Customs, such as the double cockpit forward 19-foot Custom (left) and the 23-foot triple (center), were rounded to give them a "torpedo" look to match the barreled sterns. The 17-foot Deluxe Runabout, right, kept her pointed bow. *Courtesy The Mariners' Museum*

In 1940, Runabouts like the 23-foot *Lady of the Lake* featured Bugatti-style windshields and banjo-style steering wheels. This particular example sports twin Chris-Craft 121-horsepower KB engines.

among the 14 Runabout models offered in 1936, initially featuring a 155-horsepower Lycoming powerplant (later boosted to 175-horsepower in race tune) that could push it up to 47 miles per hour, faster than the 27-foot Custom and its 250-horsepower engine. The production 19-footer was based on a stock hull, but was made lighter by using main and intermediate frames 1/8 inch thinner than stock as well as thinner bottom planking.

It could seat five—three in the forward cockpit and two in the small aft cockpit that had a removable hatch. Hulls were painted white, while kingplanks and covering boards sported bright contrasting colors—red, yellow, or blue—suggesting racing stripes and perhaps foreshadowing the two-tone styling of postwar Runabouts. There were some 49 of the 19-foot Racing Runabouts built from 1935 to 1938.

In 1935 the Motor Yacht Club de la Cote d'Azur (MYCCA) commissioned several 18-foot Runabouts, based on the 19-foot stock Racers, to be used as stock racers in France. Featuring painted hulls using the contrasting colors of the French flag, the MYCCA boat was a hit at the 1936 Paris Boat Show.

For the 1937 model year, Chris-Craft came out with a 16-foot version of the Special Race Boat, having dropped the other 16-foot Runabouts that year. Standard color scheme was a patriotic red, white, and blue. The hulls of the little split cockpit race boat featured substantial tumble-home aft, leaving a semicircle transom that was Chris-Craft's first "barrelback."

The 16-footers differed from their 19-foot sisters in that they used Direct Drive: the 95-horsepower K engine could push the boats to 39–41 miles per hour—6 miles per hour faster than the 17-foot Deluxe offered the same year—for $1,350. A year later, buyers could pack the 131-horsepower into the little racer and hit up to 43 miles per hour for $200 more. The 16-foot racer stayed in the lineup through 1940, when it was replaced for 1941 by the 16-foot barrelback Hydroplane, sold "for racing only."

In 1937, a Special Race Boat version of Chris-Craft's 27-foot Custom was added to the Racing Runabout production lineup. Like the earlier 26-foot *Jay-Dee II*, these were powered by Chris-Craft's A-120A 350-horsepower V-8. For $5,950, buyers could thrill their passengers with speeds up to 54 miles per hour. It would stay in the fleet through 1941.

Custom Runabouts 1935–1938

In 1935 the 21-foot Custom was pushed to 22 feet with more beam, and was offered not only with the two Chrysler six-cylinders but with the 150-horsepower Chrysler eight-cylinder engine as well. The bigger engine helped it reach the magic 40-mile-per-hour mark—another 40-mile Chris-Craft. There were fewer changes in the 25- and 27-foot Customs, which soldiered on with the 22-footer as the triple cockpit models of the Chris-Craft fleet.

Mid-1930s Customs were distinguished from most of the Double Cockpit Forwards and Deluxes not only by length and number of cockpits. Brown leather supplanted Red or Blue Russaloid upholstery, and the folding V-windshield was favored over the fixed Vee. As would be the case into the 1940s and 1950s, "Custom" meant top-of-the-line luxury in the Runabout fleet.

In 1937 the Double Cockpit Forward 19-footers would be sold as 19-foot Custom Runabouts. By 1939 the 19-foot Custom would entirely displace the 19-foot split-cockpit Racing Runabout.

Engine options expanded for the Customs in 1937, ranging from the 85-horsepower unit that pushed the 19- and 22-footers to 34 miles per hour and 31 miles per hour respectively, to the 275-horsepower V-8 Chris-Craft that propelled the 27-footer at 45 miles per hour for $4,950. The 27-foot hull was also sold as a Special Race Boat, equipped with the Chris-Craft A-120 tuned for competition and putting out 350-horsepower for a claimed 52–54 miles per hour.

The 19-, 22-, 25-, and 27-foot Customs stayed in the lineup in 1938 with various engine options, including twin

Sideplanks, walnut-stained covering boards and aft deck converged on a barrel-shaped transom on this 19-foot Custom Runabout. *Classic Boating magazine*

121-horsepower engines available on certain cruiser models. A twin-engine 22-foot Custom was rated at 43 miles per hour, 6 miles per hour faster than the next fastest of the same length. The twin-engine 25-foot Custom mustered 41 miles per hour, a hair slower but $1,000 less expensive than the same boat equipped with a single 212-horsepower engine. Ditto the 27-footer, which could be had for under $4,000 if ordered with the twin KB engines.

Barrelbacks 1939–1942

The streamlining craze—evident throughout industrial design—progressively influenced production boat design in the 1930s. John Hacker pushed the streamlining envelope earlier than, and as much as, any naval architect of the era. Bill MacKerer and his team of engineers at Chris-Craft were not ones to be left behind, even though the complex shapes featured in the ultimate barrelback models took more time to produce than the efficiency-minded managers in Algonac were likely to have preferred.

For Chris-Craft, the apex of the streamlined look came in the 1939–1942 Custom Runabouts, known informally as barrelbacks or barrelsterns, in which stern of the boat is wider

45

at the waterline than at the deck, forming a near perfect semicircular transom. The barrelback Customs were bracketed by two Racing Runabouts—as noted previously, the 16-foot Racing Runabout was the first to feature the pronounced tumblehome that brought sideplanks, covering boards, and aft deck together at the half-barrel-shaped transom, and the 1941–1942 16-foot Hydroplane would close out the barrelback period.

As represented by the 1939 19-foot Custom Runabout, the wide covering boards were sloped, rounding the transition from sideplank to deck from the stern to the stem. Early versions used a single-plank covering board, later split lengthwise with the seam sometimes caulked white. The traditional V-bottom led into modest forward flare. The Customs featured varnish over Chris-Craft's red mahogany stain sides and decks contrasted by the dark walnut-stained covering boards and kingplank. The stock 1939 and 1940 models were fitted with a two-piece Bugatti-style windshield, while later versions typically used the four-piece folding V-windshield. As was the tradition in the Custom line, cockpits were upholstered in leather and fitted with elegant three-spoke banjo-style steering wheels. From 1939 to 1942, 391 19-foot Custom Runabouts were built.

The 1942 17-foot Deluxe Runabout featured the elegant V-windshield and carried six in two forward cockpits. *Second Time Around* was equipped with a 95-horsepower K engine, giving her a claimed 35 miles per hour.

A war-abbreviated 1942 lineup included the last of the triple cockpit Runabouts, and the last of the barrelbacks. They featured folding V-windshields and rounded torpedo bows.

Although stylish, the rounded covering boards of the late prewar Custom Runabouts like the 1942 19-footer *Emerald Cut* were more complex to manufacture. The V-windshields could be folded.

In 1939 the 25-foot Custom was dropped from the catalog, and a year later the 22-footer was newly listed as a 23-foot model, the better to bridge the gap between the 19-foot and 27-foot Customs. The 23- and 27-footers continued in 1941, the year Chris-Craft modified the Customs with the rounded torpedo bow, a look Gar Wood adopted on its runabout line in 1939. In 1942 the 27-footer was dropped from the abbreviated 1942 lineup.

Decades later, the barrelbacks are some of the most highly prized antique Runabouts, with restored examples fetching tens of thousands dollars. The 1942 23-foot Custom Runabout would be the last triple cockpit model offered by Chris-Craft, the end of an era. The Custom would be reinvented with dramatic styling changes in the postwar period.

16-Foot Hydroplane

The 16-foot Racing Runabout—one of Chris-Craft's first barrelbacks when introduced in the 1936 catalog—was replaced in 1941 with a speedy new barrelback stunner, the 16-foot Hydroplane. As its name suggests, it featured a flat, stepped bottom that—like its Smith-built ancestors that had conquered the world of speedboat racing more than 20 years

before—let the forward hull break free from the water as it planed. Straight-line speed was its forte, and since it was far less stable than the displacement hulls of other production runabouts, it was sold "for racing only."

To power the Hydro, Chris-Craft used a hopped up version of the Model K six-cylinder engine, the KB, that put out 121 horsepower with triple downdraft carburetors that protruded through the engine hatch with a fin-like carb cover. For only $1,690, the Hydro gave speed mavens a 50-mile per hour ride—just a hair shy of the top speed of the nearly $7,000 race version of the 27-foot Custom. Of course, the single-cockpit Hydro could only seat two.

The 16-foot Hydroplane was included in the abbreviated 1942 lineup, but few were built in its two-year history.

Deluxe Runabout 1937–1942

Changes in 1937 included dropping all but the Special Race version of the 16-footer, and in its place came the 17-foot Deluxe Runabout, a modest model that would continue in one form or another through the late 1950s.

With a double cockpit forward configuration and fixed V-windshield, this handsome little boat was powered ini-

While most models in the immediate postwar period reprised prewar styling, the 20-foot Custom Runabout was the landmark exception. It featured a double cockpit forward configuration; tumblehome was modest with a convex transom and double-door engine hatch.

tially by the 55-horsepower and 85-horsepower engines, the latter giving her a top speed of 35 miles per hour and a retail price of $1,295. The 1938 1ine-up included the 17-footer equipped with the 121-horsepower KB engine, raising top speed to 39 miles per hour and the price to $1,490. By 1941 the 17-foot Deluxe had adopted the barrelback stern but kept its pointed bow, while the Customs took on the rounded Torpedo bows. It would stay in the lineup right up to the end of recreational boat production before the war, and then be revived without the barrelback stern after the war.

When the 1942 lineup was prepared in late 1941, it was pared down in anticipation of war. Among the offerings was another 17-footer, the Special Runabout, that featured fewer complex curves and was easier (and less expensive) to build. It sold for $350 less than a comparably powered 17-foot

Deluxe, and would be the basis for the postwar 17-foot Deluxe Runabout.

Another little boat—nominally a Runabout—that carried the deluxe moniker in the 1939 catalog was the 15-1/2-foot DeLuxe Runabout. Based on a Utility hull with different specifications than the Model 300 and her descendants earlier in the decade, the little Deluxe featured a forward cockpit created by an engine cover tucked under a center deck. The aft area around the engine box was open, Utility-style, with a bench seat. The 15-1/2-foot Deluxe would be offered in 1940 (as would a straight Utility version for $50 less), again in 1941, and in 1942 as the 16-foot Special Runabout. The same hull would be relaunched after the war as the 16-foot SR (Special Runabout) Rocket.

By the late 1930s and early 1940s, the line between runabouts and utilities was blurring considerably in Chris-Craft's

The bleached mahogany kingplank, cockpit trim, and engine hatch would establish a two-tone look that would last through the 1950s. *Legend* is a 1948 model.

The trend-setting 20-foot Custom was introduced for 1946 and offered into 1949, when this example was built. Note the rake of the flagpole. *Classic Boating magazine*

marketing. The 1939 catalog, for example, featured "Utility Runabouts," which were Utilities; "Sport Runabouts," which were the Sportsman and Custom Sportsman—also Utilities; and "Runabouts," which were Runabouts—except for the 15-1/2-foot Deluxe, which was really a Utility. And if that didn't confuse you, there were Utility Cruisers as well.

Reviving the Dream

Chris-Craft emerged from World War II stronger than ever, despite suspending recreational boat production for nearly four years. Although profits from government contracts to build landing craft were regulated, 1942–1945 were strong cash-flow years for the company, leaving it positioned to build on its dominance of the powerboat market in the late 1940s and 1950s.

While the postwar years would see Chris-Craft blow away the competition in total boats sold, the Runabout

would cease to be the flagship of the Chris-Craft line. As power-boating became more of a family-oriented activity, and as water sports became more popular, the full-cockpit Runabout style gradually fell out of favor. It was replaced by the more practical utility-style that had its origins in the sparse times of the 1930s. Runabouts like the Riviera, Racing Runabout, Capri, or the flashy Cobra may have conjured images of speed and style, but customers were more often voting with their wallets. The family-friendly Sportsman alone —the now-famous *U-22* of *On Golden Pond* fame—for example, sold over 20 percent more units than all Riviera models combined.

The postwar Runabouts can be divided into three general eras. From mid-1945 to 1948, prewar designs still dominated, and wood shortages led to painted hulls on some models. From 1949 to 1954, styling cues developed on concept boats spread to more of the lineup.

The 1955-to-1961 era was a distinctively automotive age, as designers looked more closely to Detroit than ever to grab the boating public's attention.

As with nearly all postwar consumer products, the first boats to come off the Chris-Craft production lines in mid-1945, and 1946 continued prewar styling. In spite of bold and creative concept boats drawn and advertised to keep the boys overseas dreaming of owning their new Chris-Craft once the enemy was defeated, it was a big enough challenge to convert from building plywood landing craft back to carvel-planked Runabouts without reengineering for all-new styles.

20-Foot Custom Runabout

But every lineup needs a model to lead the sales charge, and for the 1946 model year, there was one exception to the reliance on prewar styling. It was a bleached-blond standout, with styling that would redefine the look of Chris-Craft Runabouts for years to come. The 20-foot Custom Runabout was virtually all new, replacing the dark walnut stain for bleached mahogany kingplank, covering boards, cockpit trim, and double-door engine hatch cover. The blond mahogany contrasted sharply with the varnished decks and sideplanks for a radical new two-tone look. The double cockpits forward were luxuriously upholstered in red leather, and hardware included a folding V-shaped windshield with retractable hold-down brackets that was carried over from the last of the prewar Custom barrelbacks.

However, the barrelback styling of the prewar days gave way to more muscled curves from the creative mind of independent designer Don Mortrude, shapes that presaged automotive designs to come in the 1950s. The hull still featured some aft tumblehome, along with a convex "bubble" transom raked forward, contrasting smartly with the steeply aft-raked bow- and stern-poles, both bleached to match the kingplank

The post-war 16-foot Special Runabout was a Utility based on the pre-war Deluxe Runabout hull. It was sold as the SR Rocket and built from March 1946 through the end of 1948, with 1,040 units going out the door. The Rocket could be equipped with either the 60 horsepower B engine or the Chrysler Ace.
Karine N. Rodengen

and covering boards. The softly rounded bow was underscored by a rounded transition from sideplank to deck line, giving the boat a softer, poststreamlining look that many industrial designers favored into the 1950s.

When introduced in 1946, the 20-foot custom was offered with four engine options, starting with the 95-horsepower K, plus a 115-horsepower Chrysler that was soon dropped, the 130-horsepower M, or 145-horsepower ML. Prices ranged from $2,890 to $3,390, depending on the engine choice. When the 158-horsepower MBL became available in 1948, it was offered in the Custom ($4,260) as well as the Racing Runabout.

Marketing materials from 1946 indicate that a 23-foot version of the Custom Runabout was planned, but apparently never produced. It may have been a victim of the postwar shortages of quality Philippine mahogany, which also may have contributed to the company substantially reducing its model lineup in 1947—to the point of temporarily discontinuing the 25-foot Sportsman and the 20-foot Custom. The new factories were also coming on line, so changeovers in production lines may have also played a part.

But the 20-foot Custom was the top of the line, and while it wasn't produced in huge numbers—366 were built before the Riviera replaced it in 1949—it received the best wood and hardware of its time. The 20-foot Custom was a milestone runabout that gave birth to the bleached mahogany two-tone styling of a generation of Chris-Craft Runabouts and Utilities.

Special Runabout Rocket 1946–1948

This sprite little boat—based on the prewar 16-foot Deluxe Runabout—was called a Special Runabout (SR Rocket)—but it was in fact a utility, with the telltale engine box nestled up under a center deck that created a forward "cockpit." Such semantics were of no concern to postwar buyers, who liked it well enough to snap up 1,040 of them in just two years of production. The entry-level Rocket could be equipped with either the 60-horsepower B engine or the Chrysler Ace, and was offered with the traditional red mahogany stained and varnished, or with the hull painted Atomic Blue. The nifty "Rocket" logo was designed to extend the length of the painted sides as well. Though it was discontinued after 1948 (the 16-foot Riviera would be introduced in 1949, as would a 17-foot Special Runabout), the Rocket name would reappear in 1952.

17-Foot Deluxe Runabout 1946–1950

With company and Smith-family finances stabilized following the government contracts of the war years, Chris-Craft clearly felt bullish about the postwar powerboat market. With labor a perennial problem, it built new Runabout production plants in Chattanooga, Tennessee, and Caruthersville, Missouri, in 1947 to go along with established boatbuilding plants in Jamestown, New York, as well as Algonac, Holland, and Cadillac, Michigan. Knowing that Gar Wood Industries was closing down its Boat Division and eliminating a long-time competitor no doubt made the Smiths feel comfortable with their dominating position in the market. The market that Chris-Craft dominated would double in size—from 3.5 million to more than 7 million boats owned in the United States—in the 10 years between 1950–1960.

Among the models that would be built at Caruthersville was the 17-foot Deluxe Runabout. Unlike the utility-based SR Rocket, the 17-foot Deluxe was a true runabout of double cockpit forward configuration, a design reprised from before the war. Gone was the prewar 17-foot Deluxe, which was a barrelback. Instead, Chris-Craft used the less expensive prewar 17-foot Special Runabout hull to relaunch the postwar Deluxe, adding coil spring seats and upgraded hardware from the Custom. The bow was rounded to closer mimic the shape of the 20-foot Custom, and the hull was modified to handle more power. It was fitted the fixed-position V-windshield and traditional stained finish.

The little Deluxe could be purchased with one of several engine types, including the 121-horsepower KB engine that had been used in the prewar 16-foot hydroplane, and then the 131-horsepower KBL starting in 1948. The 17-foot Deluxe proved popular enough to see 1,880 built from 1946 into 1950 before it was replaced—along with the 20-foot Custom—by the Riviera line.

19-Foot Racing Runabout

From early on, the appeal of runabouts was speed, and the Smith family knew from experience that in good economic times they could build and sell a fast, stock runabout better than anyone in the business. Following in the marketing tradition of the "40-mile Chris-Craft" of the late 1920s and the design cues of the 1936 Racing Runabout, Chris-Craft reintroduced a prewar winner in 1947 (for the 1948 model year), the 19-foot Racing Runabout. The split cockpit model was most often sold with the 158-horsepower MBL engine that pushed the speedy craft to a claimed 44 miles per hour, all for around $1,000 less than the cost of the luxurious 20-foot Custom Runabout. There were also fewer than 100 Racers sold with the 130-horsepower MB, and a few with the 131-horsepower KBL.

The first 205 postwar Racing Runabouts featured painted red-and-white hulls. While prewar Racers also came painted, the early postwar models were likely painted due to

The 19-foot Racing Runabout came back into the lineup for 1948, with the first 205 featuring painted hulls—in part because of the shortage of "Chris-Craft grade" Philippine mahogany. The split cockpit model was most often sold with the 158-horsepower MBL engine that pushed the speedy craft to a claimed 44 miles per hour.

Once the Riviera joined the Chris-Craft lineup in 1950, the Racing Runabouts began sharing some hardware with it. *Fast Forward* is a 1950 model, number 279 out of a total of 503 built between 1947 and 1954.

the shortage of "Chris-Craft grade" Philippine mahogany following the war, forcing the company to substitute Spanish cedar and other wood types that did not take the traditional brightwork finish as well. The Racing Runabout model would turn out to be a stalwart of the runabout line through 1954, eventually featuring the varnished mahogany look with dark walnut-stained covering boards.

Once the Riviera joined the Chris-Craft lineup in 1950, the Racing Runabouts began sharing some hardware with it. When the postwar Racer was phased out in 1954, a total of 503 had been built. Today, the Racing Runabout stands as one of the most collectible models, fetching prime prices for well-restored examples.

Riviera 1949–1954

By 1949 it became apparent that the postwar styling of the 20-foot Custom Runabout was attractive to buyers—the relatively high price was less so. The Custom had been a stylist's exercise, designed to capture the imaginations of potential boat owners with less consideration given to ease of manufacturing. Given Chris-Craft's legendary drive to produce good boats for less money than the competition, it is no surprise that the company decided to make changes that would trim the production time and cost of its lead runabout.

The result was the Riviera, a boat that is considered by many the quintessential 1950s Chris-Craft Runabout. Featuring the same bleached mahogany styling cues as the 20-foot Custom, the Riviera was offered in 16-, 18-, and 20-foot lengths, with a variety of engine options.

Differences between the Riviera and its predecessor, the Custom, include elimination of the convex "bubble" transom; a single-door engine hatch fixed windshield; vinyl upholstery rather than leather; and less expensive hardware. The result was a boat that looked similar, but could be constructed more easily and sold for less.

The 16-footer could only handle the little 60-horsepower B engine, and consequently was found to be underpowered and didn't last. Some 174 were built between 1949 and 1951, when the shortest member of the Riviera family was discontinued.

The 20-footer was perhaps too easy to compare to the more luxurious older sister, the 20-foot Custom, and while the biggest Riviera remained in the runabout lineup through 1954, just 288 were built. It also had to compete head-to-head with the 19-foot Racing Runabout, which sold in comparable numbers.

The 18-foot Riviera, however, like Goldilocks' favorite porridge, was just right. Priced at $2,430, with the double cockpit forward (or "amidships cockpits" in Chris-Craft

The Riviera line was introduced in 1949, replacing the 20-foot Custom with similar looks at a lower price. *Honey* is a 1952 20-foot Riviera, one of only 288 20-footers built between 1949 and 1954.

marketing parlance) configuration providing a chummier ride with your friends than the split cockpit Racing Runabout, but still capable of hitting 38 miles per hour with the 131-horsepower KFL engine, the runabout crowd took to the medium-sized Riviera in more substantial numbers—some 1,210 were built before the Riviera line was replaced after 1954.

Rocket Runabout Redux, 1953–1954

The Rocket name was used on the little utility-based Special Runabout from 1946 to 1948, a relatively popular boat that was stowed away when the 16-foot Riviera and the 17-foot Special Runabout were introduced in 1949. However, when the smaller Riviera was scuttled after 1951, there was room in the lineup for a diminutive runabout, and Chris-Craft brought the Rocket back to the launching pad.

Although still based on a somewhat square-sterned utility hull, the second generation Rocket was more of a true runabout than its predecessor, being decked over rather than sporting the engine box of its older sister. It featured traditional varnished mahogany finish rather than the two-tone look. The 17-foot runabout would continue in the lineup through 1958, but it would cease to be called the Rocket after 1954. Some 243 Rockets were built in 1953–1954.

The Freedom Fleet

The 1955 Chris-Craft lineup, revamped thoroughly with stunning new models and designs, was by some measures the peak of Chris-Craft's long history. Not since the national boat show of 1929 had Chris-Craft enjoyed the combination of market dominance, strong economy, and—with the Korean conflict left behind—prospects for peaceful prosperity. It would have been difficult to guess at that point that the 1955 "Freedom Fleet," which *Motor Boating* magazine called the "biggest and most important model changeover in the history of the corporation," would also be the beginning of the final era for classic wooden runabouts.

While the fiberglass revolution had not yet taken hold, it was well under way among builders of dinghies, small sailboats, and outboard runabouts, and within 15 years, fiberglass construction would displace the traditional wooden hulls that had defined Chris-Craft. In spite of the exciting new styling represented by the 1955 Cobra and Capri Runabout models, the more practical utility styles had been overtaking runabouts in the small boat category for years, and Chris-Craft's stylish Holiday and Continental models would continue the trend. In addition, Chris-Craft launched its Sea Skiff Division of round-bilge lapstrake boats in 1954, with 18-, 22-, and 26-foot open hulls at attractive prices.

Rivieras were initially offered in three lengths, 16, 18, and 20 feet. The 16-footers were not known as great performers and were soon dropped, but the 18-footer was just right, selling 1,210 units over five years. *Sliver* is a 1952 18-footer. *Classic Boating magazine*

Also lurking to knock the traditional runabout off its perch as the speedy sports car of the waterways was Chris-Craft's own value-priced Cavalier line. The plywood-built Cavaliers—an outgrowth of the kit boats that were sold to compete with the entry-level outboard market—offered customers just as much fun in a less expensive package, and reached out to beginning boaters who embraced the increasing horsepower of outboard motors.

Cobra 1955

Undoubtedly the leadoff hitter of the new 1955 Freedom Fleet was the Cobra, meant to take the place of the venerable and far more traditional 19-foot Racing Runabout. Offered in 21-foot and 18-foot versions, the Cobra featured a distinctive single vertical dorsal fin in the style of the Ventnor Runabouts

of a decade before. More to the point, however, the Cobra was meant to draw into the boat dealerships the same clientele that was drooling over the new Chevrolet Corvette (which, when introduced in 1953 was one of the first cars with a body constructed entirely of fiberglass). More powerful than the imported sports cars that started the trend, the American version featured lots of engine in a two-seater format, and the Cobra was designed to follow suit.

The Cobra featured the blond kingplank that marked most of the postwar runabouts, and a raked stem with a bull-nose bow but it was bated on the hull of the 19-foot Racing Runabout it replaced. It shared hardware with its sister runabout in the 1955 lineup, the Capri. The fore deck of the 21-footer was a beamy 8 inches wider than its Racing Runabout predecessor, giving it a look some say mimics the three-point hydroplanes of its

Chris-Craft's "Freedom Fleet" in 1955 included the radical new Cobra, which took the place of the 19-foot Racing Runabout in the lineup. Unlike the split cockpit racer, however, the Cobra was a single cockpit sports boat designed to ride the enthusiasm generated by the new Chevrolet Corvette. *Classic Boating magazine*

time. As *Motor Boating* noted, "[Cobras] are distinguished by bows that lean ahead, sheer lines that taper close to the water at the transom, curved swept-back windshields, lavishly appointed cockpits, raised engine cowls, graceful tailfins and an abundance of speed."

Such a shape was not fast, easy, or inexpensive to build—forward sideplanking was particularly time-consuming to shape and fit. A remarkable styling exercise, the Cobra did not fit Chris-Craft's usual parameters for ease of construction.

While the golden fin and deck lid of the Cobra were complex shapes, also ill-suited to assembly-line–style wood construction, such shapes were ideal for fiberglass. Chris-Craft had been using fiberglass in some hidden parts of cruiser cabin interiors, but the Cobra represented the company's first notable use of the new material, albeit not on anything so critical as a hull. But while it was a baby step in the direction the boating industry would eventually go, the market for a single cockpit runabout was small. Sales of the Cobra were weak, and Chris-Craft would not use it as an immediate stepping-stone to more fiberglass. The wooden carvel hull still had a few more years to go.

Rare and considered a uniquely stylish classic today, the Cobra was an expensive but powerful boat in its day. Only 106 were built, including 51 18-footers and 55 21-footers, and it was offered for only one model year. The shorter

versions retailed from $3,710 to $3,950 depending on the engine, though none were sold with the smallest engines—most were shipped with the 131-horsepower KBL that pushed the 18-footer to 39 miles per hour. The 21-foot model top price was $6,560 when powered by the 285-horsepower V-8 Cadillac engine that gave it a claimed 50–55 miles per hour, and 18 went out the door so equipped. Some 21 proud new big-Cobra owners opted instead for the 200-horsepower Chrysler Hemi at $5,690, while the balance of the 21-footers sported the 158-horsepower MBL, the engine of the 19-foot Racing Runabout that the Cobra replaced.

Capri 1955–1957

Although the Cobra would be short-lived, the other new runabout in the 1955 Freedom Fleet would, with modifications, last six years—long enough to end up as the last of Chris-Craft wooden runabout line. Offered initially in 19- and 21-foot versions, the Capri replaced the then six-year-old Riviera.

The early Capris were clearly styled to be the next in the line of postwar runabouts that began with the Don Mortrude–inspired 20-foot Custom and continued on in the Rivieras. Like its ancestors, the 1955–1956 Capri featured bleached mahogany kingplank, cockpit trim, and engine

hatch. Gone was the chrome cutwater, however, the Capri's raked stem and bull-nose bow remaining unadorned. A wraparound windshield further modernized and streamlined the look. Stock upholstery was white in 1955, red in 1956, and dark green in 1957.

The 19-footer could be ordered with a choice of K-series engines, ranging from the 95-horsepower K (33 miles per hour) to the 131-horsepower KBL (38 miles per hour), with prices starting at $3,390 and going up to $3,630. Some 786 19-foot models were sold 1955–1958.

The 21-foot Capri featured not only the more powerful M-series engines, including the 158-horsepower MBL (41 miles per hour for $4,280) and the 200-horsepower Chrysler Hemi V-8 (44–49 miles per hour for $5,290). Capri prices were only $300–$400 less than similarly powered Cobras, but the double cockpit Capri could carry six adults comfortably. In 1956 buyers of the 21-foot Capri could order their boats equipped with the 285-horsepower Cadillac V-8, which then could reach a claimed 43 miles per hour. Before the 21-foot Riviera-based Capri of 1955–1956 was replaced in 1957, 170 units went out the door.

17-Foot Runabout 1956–1958

After a year off in 1955 (except in Utility trim as the 17-foot Sportsman), the little traditionally styled 17-footer returned to the 1956 lineup minus the V-windshield and without the Rocket moniker that defined it in 1953–1954. Instead, a one-piece wraparound plastic windshield made it

Chris-Craft workers finish off the wooden hull of the first 21-foot Cobra in October 1954, in this recently discovered archival photograph. According to company insiders, the Cobra was not an easy boat to build. *Courtesy The Mariners' Museum*

The 1955 model year saw big changes in the Chris-Craft lineup, and among the new entries was the Capri Runabout, offered in 19- and 21-foot lengths. The Capris replaced the Rivieras, and featured a wraparound windshield, a stem with pronounced rake, and bull-nose bow sans cutwater. *Classic Boating magazine*

look more like a cousin of the Capri. The hull was shared with the 17-foot Sportsman Utility model, and could be ordered with any one of the K-series engines up to the 131-horsepower KBL, which made the cost $3,050 pushed her to 36 miles per hour.

Classic II is a 19-foot Capri with the 95-horsepower K engine capable of 33 miles per hour for $3,890 in 1957.

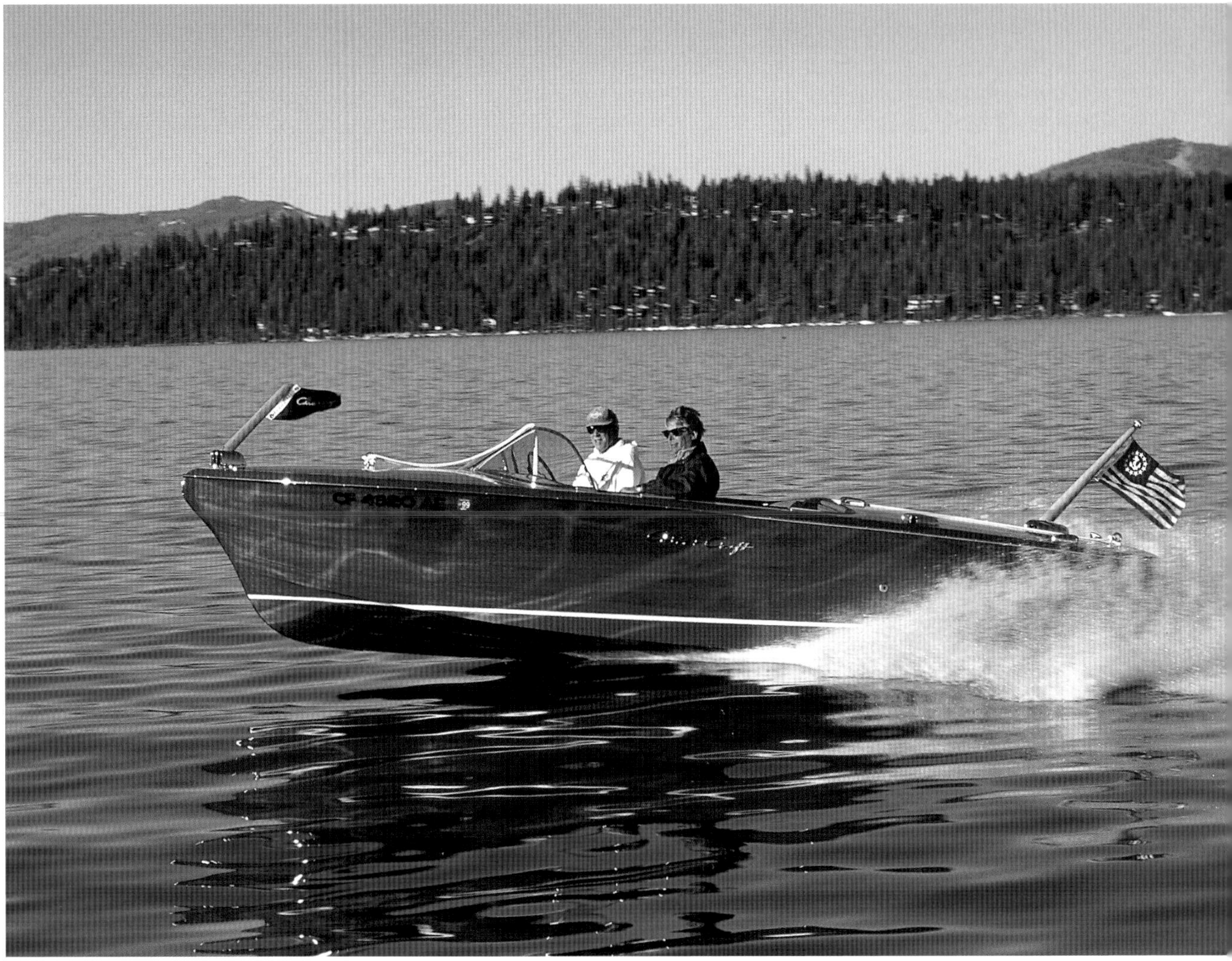

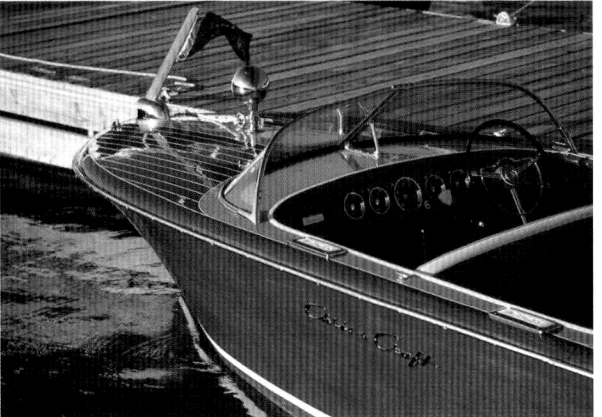

To make your 17-foot wonder—whether in runabout or utility configuration—into a Custom, the factory would "add chromium-plated stem band, panel cockpit with mahogany, finish bright, linoleum on floor," and charge you an extra $85. According to company records, Chris-Craft built 94 17-foot Runabouts for the 1956–1957 model years.

For 1958, when the Capri and Continental were sharing a hull and trying their best to look like something out of a Chevy plant, Chris-Craft reached back to the Riviera days and restyled the 17-footer with the familiar two-tone deck planking. It featured a gentle barrelback stern and shared a pointed bow (no bull nose for this pleasant little double cockpit job) with the 17-foot Sportsman. The price jumped to $3,280 when powered by the 131-horsepower KBL engine.

The look that blew away the industry on the Custom Runabout in 1946 was now a staid and traditional throwback when compared with the space-age style of the Silver Arrow. The style would last long enough for 236 units to go out the factory doors. By 1959 the 17-foot runabout would be replaced by a utility-style 17-foot Ski Boat with similar styling and slightly more beam.

Capri 1958–1961

After a brief respite in mid-1957, Chris-Craft reintroduced the 21-foot Capri for the 1958 model year. The Riviera-based hull was set aside in favor of a restyled Capri Runabout based instead on the new 21-foot Continental Utility hull. The Continental styling was a flashy take-off on the popular 1957 Chevy, complete with dual white painted automotive-style fins on the stern, a look the Capri would also emulate. The new Capri's aft deck sloped from the rear of the double cockpit to the transom, with an automotive-style interior matching the fins that housed the exhaust vents. The bull-nose was gone, and a distinctive air scoop on the forward deck ventilated the cockpit. Options included a convertible soft-top or sliding fiberglass hardtop reminiscent of offerings from Century. Only 44 units of the Continental-based 21-footer would be built from 1957 to 1959.

Silver Arrow

Listed in the 1958 sales literature as part of the "Capri Series" of Runabouts was Chris-Craft's latest step in the growing fiberglass arena. With the failure of the Lake n' Sea fiberglass outboard hulls behind them, Chris-Craft introduced the Silver Arrow, a 19-foot sport boat advertised as a "sports car for the waterways" that was a "honey for water skiing." Century and Correct Craft, among others, were making inroads among the burgeoning water sports set—the Silver Arrow was a measure of response.

The Silver Arrow was not a fiberglass boat per se, although according to research by Silver Arrow collector Al Casby, when development of the boat began in 1956, it was intended to be fiberglass throughout. But after their disappointing experience with the Lake 'n Sea outboards in 1957, as well as other problems experienced by rival builders, Harsen Smith was said to have pulled the plug on the Silver Arrow. As a compromise, however, the Smiths decided to build it using a conventional wood hull that was glassed over from the chine up, with wing-like tail fins lowing from the sides at the stern. The styling once again flowed from Don Mortrude's creative hand, and as Casby's research has shown, mimics almost exactly the "pagoda rear end" of the 1959 Buick. This half-and-half construction made for a boat that weighed more than 2,770 pounds, 400 pounds heavier than the 18-foot Continental or Capri

Strictly speaking, the Silver Arrow was a utility-style hull, with an open aft area and engine cover rather than enclosed cockpit. But the appearance of the Silver Arrow in

The Lake 'n Sea

In 1957 when Chris-Craft moved its headquarters from Algonac to pompano Beach, Florida, the move brought them into contact with a small company called Lake 'n Sea, builders of 15-foot outboard fiberglass runabouts. Small outboards were exactly the niche where fiberglass was making an impact at the time, and Chris-Craft bought Lake 'n Sea.

Alas, they couldn't make it work. Whether the company's technology was faulty or the wooden-boat men of Chris-Craft were beyond their areas of expertise, the boats apparently suffered enough problems from delamination to acquire the nickname "Leak 'n Sink." Chris-Craft sold the company not long after they bought it, and subsequently launched the fiberglass-covered (from the chine up) Silver Arrow, which they already had in development. It's as if they wanted to offer the public a fiberglass boat, but didn't really believe it would hold up, and so made sure there was a traditional wood bottom.

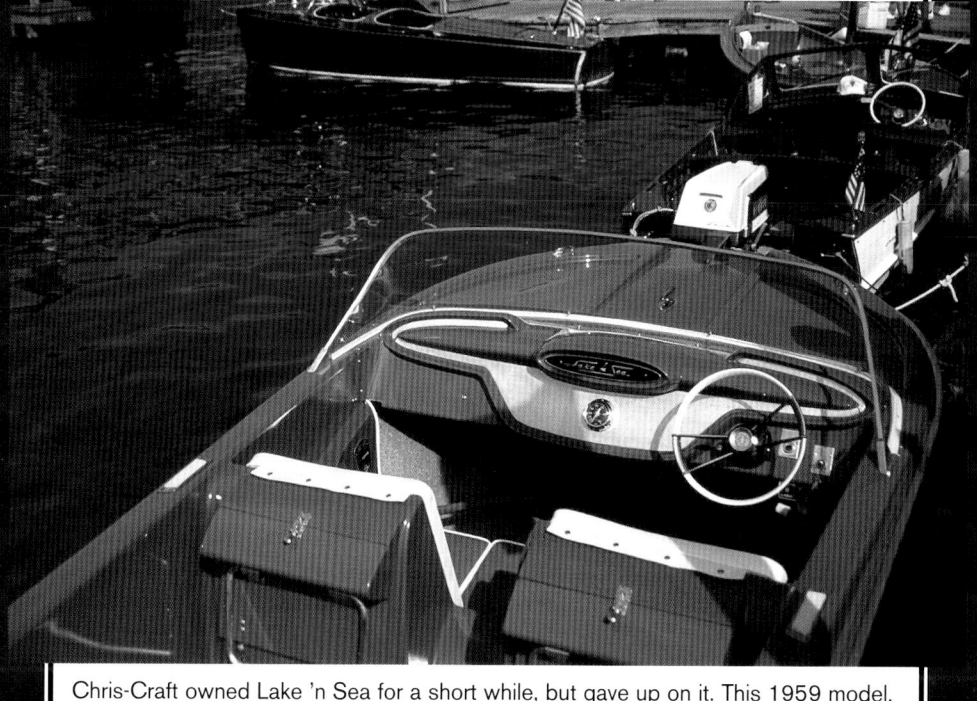

Chris-Craft owned Lake 'n Sea for a short while, but gave up on it. This 1959 model, which could have been produced after Chris-Craft sold the company, shows no signs of the delamination problems that gave the marque the "Leak 'n Sink" nickname.

By the late 1950s, the automotive look was dominating the cockpits of the Runabouts and Utilities. Not only were automotive steering wheels easy to come by and relatively inexpensive, boat marketers were looking to piggyback on styles made popular by the much larger car industry. *Classic Boating magazine*

the 1958 lineup was at least part of the reason the Riviera-based Capris were shelved. The subsequent poor performance of the Silver Arrow in dealerships—only 92 were ever made and sold over a two-year span—may have led to the revamped 18-foot Capri in 1959.

The smaller Capri would get its remake for the 1959 model year, when it was reintroduced as a variation of the 18-foot Continental hull. Instead of gaudy tail fins, the 18-footer's flashy style was a bit more understated, with blond kingplank and hatch cover. A painted white triangle decorated the aft sides. That same year, Chris-Craft launched its new Chevy small-block-based 283-ci, 185-horsepower V-8 engine, which made the 18-footer into the latest 40 miles per hour Chris-Craft. Some 65 18-footers were built.

By 1960, the year that began with the purchase of Chris-Craft by NAFI, the larger Capri was out of the lineup. The aft deck of the small Capri was stretched and redesigned enough to call it a 19-footer. A total of 119 were made.

The 1957 17-foot Custom Runabout, which by this time had adopted the two-tone finish but maintained the more traditional pointed bow, was made Custom with a chrome stem band, paneled cockpit, and linoleum. *Classic Boating magazine*

Although configured as a Utility with the aft area open, the 19-foot Silver Arrow was sold as a Runabout along with the Capris in 1958. Fewer than 100 were built; however, the Silver Arrow was significant in that it used a fiberglass-over-wood hull, a first (and last) for Chris-Craft.

When the 1961 sales catalog hit dealer showrooms, the 19-foot Capri was the last, lonely runabout among the vast offerings from "The World's Largest Builder of Mahogany Runabouts." Sales material reached back to prewar days to note that the "tumble-home styling of stern area has the look of speed," and a painted white side panel replaced the painted triangle at the stern. A total of 60 would be built. On August 16, the last, hull number CRB–19-0060C, was delivered from the Cadillac, Michigan, plant to Sparta, New Jersey, where it would come to be known as *Miss Mohawk*. It was, by most accounts, the last true wooden runabout built by Chris-Craft.

By then, utilities had usurped the runabouts' throne as the fastest, sportiest boats on the water. The postwar baby boom had made roomier open hulls more popular on the sales floor. Chris-Craft's new owners were already looking ahead to the fiberglass era. According to historian Craig Magnusson's count, Chris-Craft produced 6,337 runabouts in the postwar period 1946–1961, a small number compared to the thousands of boats it and others built during that time. Who knows, the end of the wooden runabout era may have been one reason the Smith family agreed to sell in 1960. Chris-Craft would go on, but the day of the wooden runabout was done.

CHAPTER 3

CRUISERS
The Image of Success

Among the first cruisers built by Chris Smith and his sons were those built during their association with Gar Wood from 1916–1922. Designed by Napoleon Lisee, these performance cruisers were called Flyers and were virtually an oversize version of their successful runabout designs powered with light weight and powerful Liberty engines. These 50-foot runabout-hulled cruisers were capable of remarkable performance and speeds in the 50-mile per hour range.

When the Smiths struck out on their own in 1922, they focused initially on runabouts and successfully established their reputation as stock recreational boatbuilders. By 1928, several custom

Chris-Craft's first successful standardized Cruiser was the 1929 38-foot Commuting Cruiser, commonly called the Commuter. Its all-varnished mahogany hull resembled the appearance of a large runabout. *Karine N. Rodengen*

The popular forward cockpit of the 38-foot Commuting Cruiser offered the owner the option of ordering it with a second set of controls to operate the craft like a Runabout. *Classic Boating magazine*

boatbuilders and a growing number of standardized builders were offering fast sport cruisers, known as commuters. John Hacker's custom-designed commuters were creating quite a stir, and firms such as Robinson, Consolidated, Elco, and Wheeler all began to offer a stock model to fill the need for this new style.

Naturally, the Smiths wanted to expand the Chris-Craft line into the small cruiser market as well. The goal was to build an attractive standardized cruiser that would be fast and reasonably priced, and provide minimum overnight accommodations while providing room for entertaining several people on daytime excursions. The design they came up with could be described as a runabout-style hull configuration with forward flare, modest beam, V-bottom, and enough tumble-home aft to show its heritage. Chris-Craft's new 38-foot

cruiser was a striking beauty with strong ties to the 50-foot express cruisers it built a few years before for Gar Wood.

The Commuting Cruiser model was unveiled as part of the 1929 Chris-Craft fleet, and it would be the first standardized cruiser, built assembly-line style like its Runabouts, marketed under the name Chris-Craft. It was powered with its own 225-horsepower V-8 engine, providing a top speed of 30 miles per hour. The main controls were located in an open bridge with the option of dual controls in the forward cockpit with its own windshield. The hull had all the attributes of an exciting runabout, including a hard chine, the stainless-steel cutwater, varnished mahogany, excellent speed, with berths, galley, and a head. It was an appealing, exciting boat for the Roaring Twenties. For executives who lived on navigable waterways, commuting from home to midtown offices

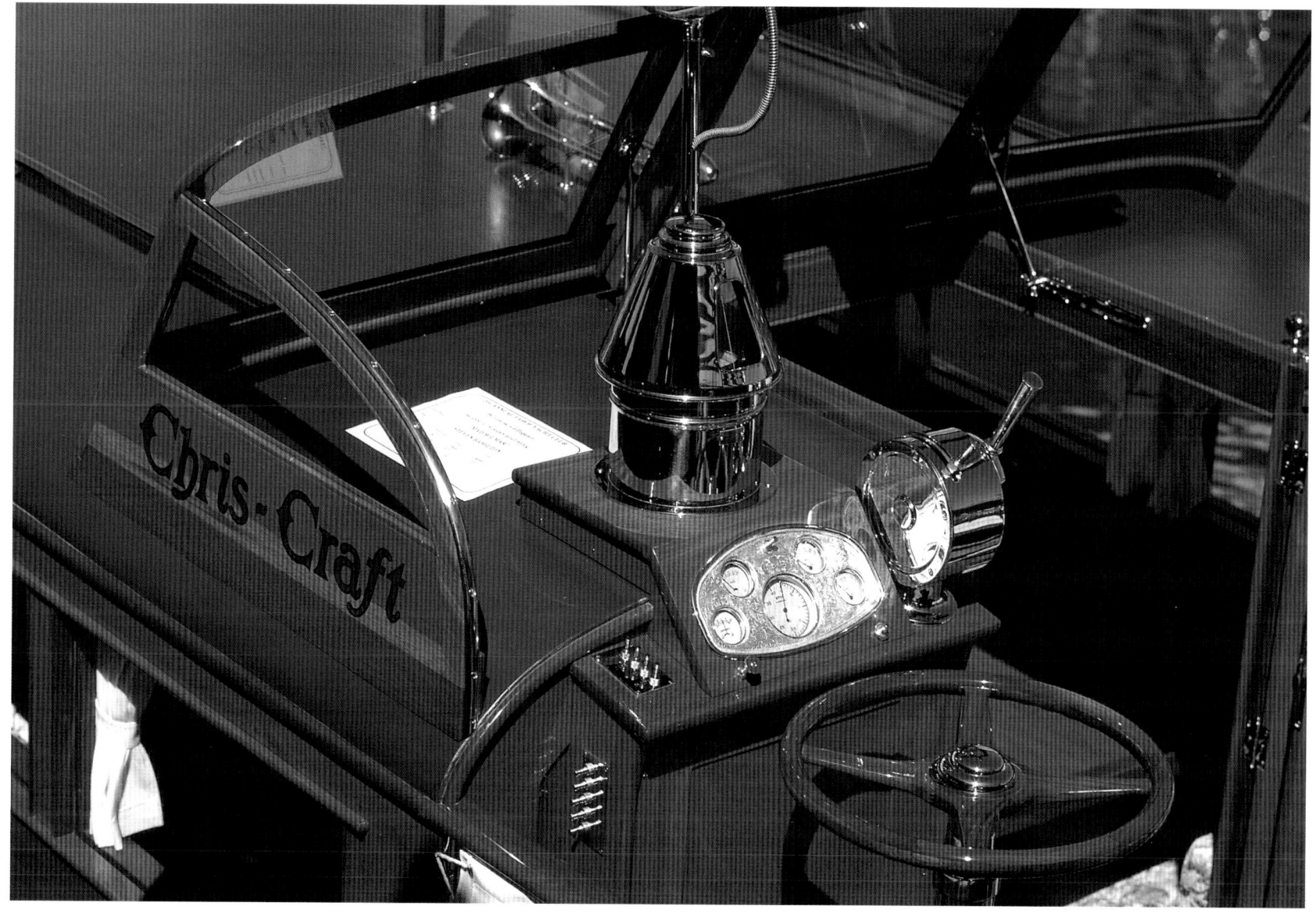

in a sleek high-speed mahogany boat seemed to capture perfectly the new image of success.

Chris-Craft eventually sold some 65 units of the 38-foot Commuting Cruiser, at $15,000 each. The Commuting Cruiser was enough of a success that for 1930 Chris-Craft added two additional stock models to its nascent cruiser fleet. The new 34-foot Custom Commuter offered twin 200-horsepower engines, speed of more than 40 miles per hour and berths for two. The 48-foot Yacht model provided privacy more like a traditional yacht and impressive speed for a larger, comfortable craft. At $35,000, its appeal was limited to fewer potential buyers, but it allowed Chris-Craft to expand its reach across the market.

In spite of the stock market crash in the fall of 1929, many manufacturers were still optimistic and thought that the prosperity would return quickly. Chris-Craft's positive outlook was evident from its full line of family cruisers introduced for the 1931 model year. It would be eight years, however, before Chris-Craft would be able to offer this number cruiser models once more.

The 31- and 36-foot cruiser designs for 1931 offered an interesting variety of cabin layouts and styles for two standardized hulls. Its 32-page Cruiser Sales Catalog for 1931 contained 45 photographs and seven interior layout illustrations. It was a superb booklet with the Chris-Craft coat of arms in full color on the cover. The standard models had hull sides painted French gray with cream-colored cabin sides. The deluxe models had white hull sides and varnished cabin sides. The single cabin models had folding upper and lower berths for four. The double cabin was "much like the single cabin

The location of the helm on the Commuting Cruiser provided excellent visibility for the captain, as well as adequate cabin and cockpit privacy for the owner and his guests. *Classic Boating magazine*

The quick acceptance of the 38-foot Commuting Cruiser prompted the Smiths to confidently introduce this larger, twin-engine 48-foot commuter Yacht model in 1930. *Classic Boating magazine*

with the addition of a cozy private stateroom aft." Four 36-foot cruiser models were offered, including two with aft staterooms. One was the Open Bridge model similar to the 31-foot cruiser. The second was the first Double Cabin Enclosed Bridge (DCEB) model offered by Chris-Craft. It is well worth noting that the first DCEB Chris-Craft made its debut in 1931 and would go through scores of transitions for decades and become its most celebrated design.

The concept of providing several layouts or variations on a standardized hull provided buyers with several options without adversely affecting production. While its cruiser program was sound, the national economy was not. The

34-foot Commuter bade its farewell in 1932, and the 38-foot Custom Commuter was only available on a special order accompanied by full deposit. Most of the cruiser models offered in 1933 were actually products constructed earlier and still in stock.

Before Bill MacKerer was laid off during the darkest days of the Depression, he developed the preliminary design for a small enclosed cruiser with berths for four, a small galley, and an enclosed marine toilet. It would be introduced to the public in late 1933 for the 1934 season. This little cruiser turned out to be so popular that pocket cruisers of this length remained a fixture in Chris-Craft's offerings.

When the 24-foot Family Cruiser model was introduced to the Chris-Craft dealers for the 1934 model year, it marked its first new cruiser in three years. Not unlike the scaled-down utilities offered during these same lean years, the goal was simply to provide a small family with the opportunity for limited cruising in an attractive new boat for under $1,500. A second goal was to keep the cruiser market alive for Chris-Craft and to stimulate interest in family boating and cruising.

In 1935, Chris-Craft offered two hull lengths for its stock cruisers. In the 25-foot size it offered the Utility Cruiser with two berths along with the Family Cruiser and the Streamline Cruiser each with four berths. In the 30-foot length, the Double Stateroom Cruiser with four power options was the only other cruiser offered. The 38-foot Commuter model, called the custom model from 1932 to 1934 (which in this case meant it was built on special order only),

In 1931, Chris-Craft expanded its fleet with four 31-foot models and four 36-foot models. This early 36-foot Single Cabin model fit in with much of what others were offering at the time. *Courtesy The Mariners' Museum*

The 1934 24-foot Utility Cruiser provided all the useable space of a Utility with a small cabin under the deck. This was the forerunner of the popular 25-foot Red and White Express Cruiser. *Courtesy The Mariners' Museum*

The 24-foot Family Cruiser was designed to provide a family of four with all the elements required to enjoy the experience of inland cruising for under $1,500. *Courtesy The Mariners' Museum*

The 1934 30-foot Trunk Cabin Cruiser was another modest and affordable, next (at under $2,500) step-up for those who started with the Family Cruiser. *Courtesy The Mariners' Museum*

The 25-foot 1936 Single Cabin Cruiser was an attractive, small cruiser with outside controls that competed directly with Richardson's popular Little Giant model. *Courtesy The Mariners' Museum*

The 1936 28-foot Enclosed Bridge Cruiser, with the factory-installed hard top over the large cockpit, provided comfortable family cruising as the nation moved slowly out of the Depression. *Classic Boating magazine*

In 1937 the 40-foot Double Cabin Enclosed Bridge Cruiser eliminated the small forward trunk cabin and raised the fore deck to begin years of exciting styling trends for this model. *Courtesy The Mariners' Museum*

was no longer offered in 1935. Still, sales were beginning to pick up a bit and dealers were starting to feel positive once more. By midseason, Jay Smith instructed his son, Harsen, to find Bill MacKerer and bring him back to Chris-Craft. For many employees, the return of MacKerer to his former position was the first solid signal that recovery at Chris-Craft was finally under way.

Anticipating strong sales in 1936, Chris-Craft expanded its cruiser line from 2 standard hull lengths in 1935 to 6 different lengths and 13 discreet styles. It was a major thrust at the right time. Among the model names introduced that year were the Conqueror, Sea Skiff, Semi-Enclosed, Clipper, and Sport Fisherman. Each of these model names would show up several times over the years, and the Sea Skiff name would become an entire Division for Chris-Craft in the mid-1950s.

For many boaters, the Chris-Craft Clipper was their initial cruiser purchase, offering a complete compact cruiser that could sleep four.

One of the most promising designs for the 1937 season was the Double Cabin Enclosed Bridge Cruiser (DCEB). Its nicely balanced exterior design provided a very comfortable interior layout with features usually found on much larger cruisers. To the aspiring new boater, this model seemed like an achievable goal that provided features not found on slightly smaller cruisers. It provided a large, comfortable bridge that resembled a small living room with superb visibility. The bridge had the helm, a drop leaf table, two armchairs, and a large sofa that easily converted to a double bed. Going forward and down a few steps was a large galley, a lavatory, and a stateroom for two. Aft of the bridge was the

owner's stateroom with its own lavatory, built-in dresser, and direct access to the aft cockpit. This design worked beautifully for the typical cruising family because it offered nicely separated spaces that provided a measure of seclusion when necessary. This model became the mainstay of Chris-Craft's cruiser fleet for decades and would become the cruiser style most associated with the Chris-Craft brand name.

One of Chris-Craft's significant rivals for the midsize cruiser market in the late 1930s was the Wheeler Shipyard Company in Brooklyn, New York. Its boats were handsome, rugged craft with superb interior work and custom features incorporated for discriminating owners. The 1938 Wheeler Sales Catalog was an impressive 48 pages and the largest in the industry. It featured 41 standardized cruiser models from 26 to 65 feet. Standard models included sea skiffs, sedans, trunk cabins, sport cruisers, salons, sport fishermen, double cabins, and motor yachts. Located in metropolitan New York on the edge of the Atlantic Ocean, the well-respected Wheeler Shipyard was in the heart of the nation's most prominent boating market.

In 1938, Wheeler's 39-foot Double Cabin Enclosed Bridge Cruiser with power similar to Chris-Craft's 40-foot DCEB cruiser was priced at $11,015, or nearly 10 percent higher. Wheeler's 32-foot enclosed cruiser for $4,860 was nearly 20 percent more expensive than the attractive 31-foot Chris-Craft Enclosed Cruiser at $3,990. There was no question that Wheeler offered traditional interior cabinetry, but Chris-Craft's engaging exterior styling, the security of its convenient dealer network, and more affordable pricing were making a favorable impression on savvy buyers.

Three popular 1937 models—the 26-foot Enclosed Cruiser, the 29-foot Enclosed Cruiser, and the 40-foot Double Stateroom Cruiser, all displaying the distinctive varnished sheer panel. *Courtesy The Mariners' Museum*

The aggression in Europe presented a disturbing contrast to the preparations for showcasing international achievement at the World's Fair in Flushing Meadows, New York, in 1939. Chris-Craft announced an exciting array of cruiser models in sizes from 25 feet to 55 feet, incorporating new levels of luxury. A world-class marina was created to encourage boaters to visit the World's Fair in their own cruisers. In addition, Chris-Craft received scores of new boat orders from customers requesting direct shipment to the World's Fair Marina, where they would accept delivery of their new boat.

Another important milestone for 1939 was the successful introduction of the 55-foot Motor Yacht. A craft of this size required a number of design and construction considerations beyond normal cruiser production. The 55-foot Motor Yacht had full walk-around decks, a beam of 14 feet, and a total displacement of 18 tons, which made it too large to be shipped by railroad flat car and required delivery by water. This yacht was a major undertaking for Chris-Craft, but one that it felt was necessary to maintain its market position.

As it would turn out, the 55-footer needed only a few modifications to become designated as the military "Q Boat"

By 1938 the 25-foot Semi-Enclosed Cruiser was becoming very popular among fishermen, fishing guides, and a wide range of commercial users. The 31-foot Single Cabin Sports Cruiser was an interesting design but experienced only modest sales success. *Courtesy The Mariners' Museum*

The 1939 29-foot Express Cruiser was a classy craft with excellent performance qualities. Every feature of this pocket Cruiser was well planned and so well received that it helped create a market for more Express Cruiser models the following year. *Courtesy The Mariners' Museum*

After suffering through their first labor strike and losing valuable sales opportunities, Chris-Craft was determined to make 1938 a banner year. Model for model, its designs were significantly more attractive than its primary rivals, Richardson, Wheeler, Elco, and Owens. Its hulls showed greater beam, more attractive curves, and more flare forward. Cabin tops were smartly integrated into the total design, and special attention was given to attractive window treatments. Chris-Craft cruisers seemed to provide more speed, as often shown in its exciting advertising illustrations. Optional twin-engine power was encouraged by the images of its cruisers traveling at high speed to the apparent delight of attractive models. With signs of a stronger economy, Chris-Craft was becoming a cruiser builder rather than primarily a builder of small, fast runabouts. Its small boat customers were ready to move up to larger craft and its highly attractive designs were drawing cruiser buyers from other builders. It made good business sense to provide the next step up for boaters who desired to broaden their boating activities from sport boats to cruising.

Sales of larger cruisers also generated far more profit per transaction than small craft. Small runabouts and utilities played an important role in building Chris-Craft's customer base for the inevitable purchase of a larger, more profitable boat. Trading-up became a regular boating activity, and Chris-Craft loved it.

(Quartermaster Craft) during World War II. Since it was already working on defense contracts, the development of the Motor Yacht may have been an anticipated need. Forty-five Q Boats were produced on government contract from late summer 1941 through mid-1943. The exterior lines of the Q Boats were nearly identical to the civilian Motor Yacht, and the interiors were rather Spartan, given that the vessel's prime role was to transport 30 to 40 military personnel.

Chris-Craft added the Deluxe Clipper and the Semi-Enclosed models to the 25-foot line in 1939. A 29-foot Express Cruiser was also added, marking the first return of a high-performance cruiser since the 38-foot Custom Commuting Cruiser was discontinued in 1934. Both 31-foot models were replaced with three 33-foot versions, including a Sport Fisherman model. Both 35-foot models became 36-footers, and the 40-foot was increased to 41 feet and offered in three models.

With its confidence reestablished, this was an excellent year for production and sales. It helped determine an ideal range of standardized models that Chris-Craft would maintain for its wood construction over the next three decades. Another sign of its confidence was its expansion to a second

factory in Holland, Michigan, in 1939. Initially the Holland factory was set up for small boat production, but soon was selected for cruiser construction and became the facility that Chris-Craft could always depend on for superb quality and outstanding efficiency over the years.

The introduction of the 29-foot Express Cruiser was a sign of new models to come in the cruiser fleet. Annually adding a foot or two to the advertised length of the hull was a regular technique to formulate a "new version" of an established model. Several cruiser models added white canvas spray shields providing an exciting look and a functional feature. On the DCEB models, these spray shields created a protected sun deck over the aft stateroom. This provided a unique design feature and increased the styling gap between Chris-Craft and all other cruiser builders.

In 1940 the new 34-foot Express Cruiser again demonstrated Chris-Craft's flair for attractive design. This model was primarily a high-styled boat for fun and entertainment. The cabin interior featured a unique dinette with contemporary art deco styling and special fabric. The large, attractive galley included a bar and beverage cabinet. The interior paneling and all the cabinetry were selected bird's-eye maple finished in a natural blond tone. The forward deck had recessed cockpit seating and could be entered directly from the cabin. The aft cockpit was spacious and partially covered by a unique, removable navy top. This was a marvelous sport

One of Chris-Craft's most interesting designs was the 1939 33-foot Quarter Deck Cruiser. Its ingenious design provided for a double stateroom with full headroom under the aft deck, using a small "doghouse" cabin. This clever feature only raised the cost by $500 above the typical sedan layout.
Courtesy The Mariners' Museum

In 1939 the 36-foot DCEB was the smaller versions of this classic design. The appearance was remarkably similar to the larger models, all providing three separate cabin areas. *Courtesy The Mariners' Museum*

express cruiser and a forerunner to the highly successful Commander series for Chris-Craft. The use of light bird's-eye maple for interior panels, cabinets, and trim was so well received that these attractive hardwoods became the woods of choice for the larger cruisers including the motor yachts. Flame maple, curly maple, and bird's-eye maple made Chris-Craft interiors bright, cheerful, and very appealing.

Making its debut in the 1940 catalog was the "futuristic" 25-foot Express Cruiser, commonly known today as the Red and White Express. In all probability, its special design was motivated by the preparations and enthusiasm generated for the 1939 World's Fair and the quest for the *look of tomorrow* that was sweeping the nation. The sales brochure called it "super-streamlined boat of tomorrow with rakish lines." In reality it was a long deck utility with a large, "speed-lined" V-windshield and a cabin with two berths under a raised deck. The hull was painted white and the cockpit interior and upholstery were fire red. Some of the unique hardware included a modernized combination bow light and burgee flagstaff that looked like the cone of a witch's hat, a streamlined enclosure for a deck siren and a teardrop stern pole for the ensign. The new look included a barrel bow with a split cutwater and the introduction of art deco lettering replacing the traditional corporate logo on the hull sides. It was unique

attempt at incorporating modern concepts into a practical utility with a small cabin enclosure and high-speed capabilities. The Red and White is considered quite distinctive and has become an interesting cult favorite among collectors.

The popularity of the sporty Express Cruisers models resulted in the addition of a 23-foot model and two 40-foot models for the 1941 fleet. The 23-foot pocket Express was modestly priced and very popular with sport fishermen, who appreciated the large cockpit and the convenience of a small cabin. The 40-foot Express Cruiser was a striking craft that in some ways was a modern version of the 1929 38-foot Custom Commuter with its forward cockpit. A clever alternate version of the 40-foot Express was a model called the Challenger. By using the doghouse plan featured on its Quarterdeck cruiser, Chris-Craft provided an inventive aft stateroom in the new Challenger. This feature, along with an attractive hardtop over the helm, was the difference in the two models. Both designs were innovative, exciting, and widely promoted in display advertising. For a buyer looking for the boat that represented the freshest thinking in attractive design in 1941, Chris-Craft, once again, provided wonderful choices.

The 55-foot Motor Yacht was a big step for Chris-Craft into the custom yacht domain for 1939. This model would be in production for five years, with more than 40 built for defense contracts. *Courtesy The Mariners' Museum*

This dashing, high-performance, futuristic design is the 1940 25-foot Express that capitalized on the growing fashion to be modern, largely influenced by the 1939 World's Fair. *Courtesy The Mariners' Museum*

The dashing image of the Express Cruiser seemed to reflect the spirit of the times perfectly. It offered an ideal transitional step for buyers moving up from smaller sport boats on their way to a more conservative cruiser. The economic recovery appeared to be strong and moving ahead as everyone hoped it would. The conflict in Europe still seemed distant, as did the potential for involving America into Europe's battles.

But when civilian boat builders began to receive requests to bid on military craft, the possibility of war needed to be taken seriously. When Chris-Craft published its 48-page 1942 Sales Catalog in the fall of 1941, the first page illustrated four new military craft and warned readers that "defense needs come first with Chris-Craft." These words appeared in print months before the Japanese attack on America at Pearl Harbor. Only a small number of Chris-Craft boats were actually designated as 1942 models, and most were actually delivered in the fall of 1941. Chris-Craft dealers may have received their strongest indications that war was not far off when the price lists for existing models began to increase sharply in the fall of 1940 and throughout 1941. The unspoken message was that pleasure boats might be difficult to purchase with increasing demand to fill government defense contracts.

During the war years, optimistic advertising layouts would appear with futuristic designs anticipating the new postwar models. Independent designer Don Mortrude was commissioned by Chris-Craft to create new styling that would ultimately define the Chris-Craft look in the 1950s. Features such as the double boot stripe, the turtleback bow cap, the bull-nose stem and the Cobra tail fin all came from his drawing board and had impact in developing new elements of style trends.

By August 1945 the Japanese surrender meant the suspension of all government defense contracts. It was time for Chris-Craft's pleasure craft production to begin once more.

Chris-Craft was anxious to provide its dealers with new boats as quickly as possible. The most efficient way to accomplish this was to avoid incorporating extensive design

This limited edition, custom 1940 60-foot Motor Yacht provided an enclosed pilot house and a pleasant canopied deck over the aft cabin along with an aft cockpit. *Courtesy The Mariners' Museum*

changes. It decided to produce the most popular models from its 1941–1942 fleet while using simple and effective styling changes that made the new postwar models appear quite different from their predecessors. The use of an attractive "turtleback" white bow cap on every new cruiser clearly distinguished the postwar models from all prewar models. In one of its 1945 dealer sales bulletins, it announced that the 25-foot Red and White Express would be "put back in production as formerly built in 1942, proving again that it was far in advance of the field when originally built." Among the cruisers one totally new model was the 27-foot Super Deluxe Enclosed cruiser, which had very attractive, modern lines for a small four-sleeper model.

The 1947 postwar catalog illustrated just nine distinct cruiser models. This is probably all that were actually offered in 1946 as well, in spite of the more inspired numbers listed on its early price list. By 1948 Chris-Craft was able to gradually expand its cruiser fleet by adding two very popular sedan cruisers from the prewar fleet with the 30- and 33-foot models. In addition three prewar express cruiser models, the 34-footer, the 40-footer, and the Challenger, were returned to production.

The shortage of mahogany disrupted all boatbuilders in the early postwar years. Builders often had to substitute other wood types. Chris-Craft had always listed each species of wood used for sideplanking, bottom planking, main frames, intermediate frames, bottom frames, keel, chines, etc. This detailed list was not only dropped from the specifications section of its new catalog, there was no mention of wood species

For boaters who loved the convenience of a sedan, the 1941 38-footer was an ideal Cruiser with the deckhouse and cockpit occupying two-thirds of the craft all on one level. *Classic Boating magazine*

This 23-foot Express Cruiser for 1941 was modestly priced and very attractive, and it filled an important void in the market among sportsmen who wanted a small craft with a modest cabin. *Courtesy The Mariners' Museum*

The 1941 34-foot Express Cruiser was a superb boat for entertaining, with its forward cockpit, huge aft cockpit, bird's-eye maple cabin, large buffet style galley and bar, and excellent speed. *Courtesy The Mariners' Museum*

The 40-foot 1941 Express Cruiser was fast, comfortable, and a style leader. It also provided a forward cockpit, a large aft cockpit, and a spacious cabin for extended cruises. *Courtesy The Mariners' Museum*

Wood planned to present totally new boat designs for the postwar market. Their outstanding new designs were sharply different from their very successful prewar models. The effort proved costly and, ultimately, unnecessary for the highly motivated postwar boat buyer. Richardson Cruisers also decided to abandon its traditional models to offer the postwar buyer molded plywood "Cruisers of Tomorrow." This choice was too extreme for the postwar buyer and nearly destroyed Richardson's well-established cruiser business. Even the conservative Wheeler Shipyard was caught up in the craze for sweeping changes with its modernistic Sun Lounger Cruisers, which proved too extreme for Wheeler's loyal followers.

With two major rivals swept away by their own parent organizations and others making radical design changes, Chris-Craft's conservative design refinements provided exactly what the postwar market required. The road ahead looked very promising, and Chris-Craft was prepared to lead the way and travel as far and as fast as this new road to postwar success would lead them.

The beautiful 40-foot 1941 Challenger was an aft cabin version of the 40-foot Express Cruiser with a standard hardtop and a flush aft deck with railings. *Courtesy The Mariners' Museum*

This view of the 40-foot Challenger shows the unique doghouse cabin that provided the headroom for this roomy and private aft stateroom with its own lavatory. *Courtesy The Mariners' Museum*

in the detailed description sections either. It did state, "main frames, intermediate side frames, bottom frames, auxiliary bottom frames, are structurally strong and sturdy. All bottoms are double planked and every hull side is batten seamed." There was no mention of the type or species of the woods used. The best mahogany was saved for the varnished cabin sides and transoms. Decks were more often made with canvas-covered plywood, which was viewed as a more practical decision for cruisers exposed to sun and weather.

By early 1947 one of its major cruiser rivals, Elco, announced its decision to end its cruiser production. Loyal Elco owners were dismayed at the news, which surprised the boating industry. Elco was one of the oldest and most respected builders of fine cruisers and motor yachts. Its new fleet of postwar models was totally redesigned and extremely attractive. Elco achieved fame during World War II as the nation's largest producer of the famous PT Boats. Its new cruisers incorporated many of the construction and design features developed during military production. However, the Elco Boat Company was just a minor division of the huge Electric Boat Company of New London, Connecticut. Although it was a major player in the pleasureboat industry, it was considered a small and inconsequential division of this world-renowned builder of submarines.

The sudden departure of the Elco Boat Division was nearly identical in circumstance and timing to the unexpected closing of another rival builder, Gar Wood. Both firms were small divisions of major industries. Elco and Gar

One of the surprising new models for 1949 was a 21-foot cruiser that appeared so similar to the popular Cruise Along pocket cruiser that it was hard to distinguish one from the other. The Chris-Craft version was offered in standard and deluxe models with engine options to provide speeds to 33 miles per hour. By marketing this appealing little cruiser, Chris-Craft made a clear statement to its rivals that it would not hesitate to replicate any valid concept or model in order to meet market demand and maintain market share.

Four significant models were added to the 1949 cruiser fleet. By employing exciting styling changes, its design staff used the basic hull of the standard 30-foot sedan to create a new Express cruiser that became an instant success. The standard 36-foot hull was used to re-create a new version of its 1941 model 181 sedan with a large entertainment center. This new Salon cruiser featured a stylish deckhouse buffet-style galley along with movable dinette seating, a sofa, and large double-doors that opened to a floor-level cockpit. This unique configuration provided 22 feet of continuous open space in a 36-foot hull aptly suited to gracious entertaining.

The deckhouse interior was finished in light blond Korina that enhanced the feeling of spaciousness.

The unique Quarter deck cruiser reappeared as a standard model looking like a typical sedan style. However, in place of the aft cockpit, the deck was raised to the level of the sheer line, with a modest size doghouse centered just behind the deckhouse. This very clever arrangement provided an attractive, comfortable stateroom as an alternative to the usual cockpit layout. The design was a Chris-Craft innovation and demonstrated its ability to provide maximum potential in limited space.

Mid-1949 marked the arrival of the new 34-foot Commander. It would become one of the most successful cruiser models, combining excellent cruising accommodations with attractive express cruiser design. This model was a contemporary revival of its popular 1936 Conqueror cruiser. With the number of boat owners growing rapidly, Chris-Craft was able to measure accurately the features that buyers favored. Its production technology was so advanced that it was able to meet customer preferences with rapid response time. Chris-Craft cruisers seemed to fit buyers' desires in styling, comfort, and availability. The goals that Christopher Columbus Smith had envisioned while building race boats were being more than realized by the midpoint of the twentieth century.

By 1950, Chris-Craft would offer 27 cruiser styles in 16 hull lengths from 21 to 62 feet. This range of models made it a rival to every other cruiser and motor yacht manufacturer. Chris-Craft literally had a model, style, or length

The 40-foot DCEB Cruiser seemed to achieve perfection in its final design before war production. It provided a superb interior layout of four separate sleeping areas for eight people.

New Chris-Craft 36-ft. Double Stateroom Enclosed Cruiser

And even <u>this</u> picture does not tell the story. For there are 2 complete staterooms forward . . . built-in dinette . . . complete ship's galley . . . you can sleep 6 in solid comfort and cruise where you choose at speeds up to 23 m.p.h. Ready after Victory. See your Chris-Craft Dealer for details. . . . We are 100% on war work now.

Buy U.S. War Bonds Today—

Tomorrow command your own

Chris-Craft

CHRIS-CRAFT CORP., ALGONAC, MICH. ★ WORLD'S LARGEST BUILDERS OF MOTOR BOATS

cruiser for nearly every preference or budget. This posture was in sharp contrast to other boat builders that often specialized in building boats of a particular size range or a special style. In 1950, Colonial, Balzer, and Richardson cruisers primarily favored traditional trunk cabin styling. Owens concentrated on the 27-foot and 33-foot sedan models. Matthews continued to specialize in one basic 40-foot hull size. Even the Wheeler Shipyards narrowed its range of lengths from 36 feet to 52 feet, concentrating on custom features and rather production volume.

The major announcement in 1950 was the addition of the 62-foot Motor Yacht. This luxury yacht with its flush deck provided Chris-Craft with a flagship that could hold its own in company with the vessels of elite custom yacht builders. The 62-footer had a beam of 16 feet and sleeping accommodations for 13. There were four toilet compartments, including two with showers. Quarters for the captain and two crew members were provided forward with their own separate hatchway to the deck. The yacht's interior was bright and refreshing with light blond Korina paneling and woodwork. It had all the luxury features of a custom motor yacht, with the unmistakable attractiveness that had become synonymous with the Chris-Craft name.

In the early 1950s the fleet of cruisers grew to nearly 30 discrete models from 21 to 62 feet. The traditional Chris-Craft stem began to lean forward a bit more in each of the

Independent designer Don Mortrude was responsible for many innovative Chris-Craft designs and special features, many of which are apparent in this concept design.

postwar years. The 1950 52-foot Motor Yacht curved the stem forward and then rounded it back into a massive bow cap. In 1951 the new version of the 42-foot Challenger and the new 47-foot Buccaneer took this feature a bit further and the expression "bull nose" was beginning to become a common descriptor of the new look. This unique stem treatment appeared on the new Holiday series of utility models. This design feature can be traced back to the futuristic concepts by Don Mortrude during the war years and illustrated in the January 1944 *Motor Boating* magazine. By 1953 the bull nose style appeared on one-third of the cruiser models. In spite of continued strong sales, the new look was not universally popular, and the mixed reviews were getting back to the home office. It was time for a new, more universally appealing stem design, and its engineering staff began developing new schemes that would create an attractive new profile and be easily assimilated into their existing hull contours.

One of the conservative cruiser manufacturers still building boats of more traditional style was the Matthews Company of Port Clinton, Ohio. Matthews developed a very efficient, soft-riding 38-foot hull design in 1923 that was so well suited to the choppy wave conditions of Lake Erie that it became its standard hull. Matthews enjoyed the benefits of featuring the same round-bilge, carvel plank hull for sedans, double cabins and sport fisherman models for decades with great success. During the early postwar years, it concentrated primarily on the raised deck sedan model, for which it claimed, "No other stock cruiser runs more level than the Matthews 38." In addition it stated with pride that the Matthews 38 was the heaviest stock cruiser of her size, at 22,000 pounds.

With Chris-Craft annually expanding its fleet of cruiser models, loyal Matthews' customers began to lobby for more additional styles. Using the same "38" hull (which was actually

The new postwar 23-foot Express Cruiser replaced the small cabin port lights with an attractive window and stylish side wing frames from the windshield. The only varnished mahogany was confined to the toe rails and the transom on this model. *Courtesy The Mariners' Museum*

The 26-foot Deluxe Enclosed Cruiser for 1946 was a wonderful starting point for a small family who wanted to try cruising for the first time.

39 feet 11 inches overall) Matthews introduced a Double Cabin Flying Bridge (DCFB) Cruiser. A Sport Fisherman, an Express Cruiser, and a Convertible Sedan followed. The standard sedan also offered five different interior plans to accommodate owner's individual preferences. With this expansion of models, Matthews was clearly attempting to provide an answer to Chris-Craft's extensive cruiser offerings to expand its customer base. Chris-Craft's modern styling and attractive prices were still a challenge to the more traditional and more expensive Matthews cruisers.

Cruiser sales were very strong in the mid-1950s. Chris-Craft's major new entry among its cruiser fleet was the 45-foot Corsair. Its layout was nearly identical to the popular 45-foot DCFB Cruiser, except that it was a full foot wider. This additional foot of beam allowed the Corsair to provide safe, practical walk-around decks with stanchions and lifelines. With standard teak decks, this cruiser offered features usually found on much larger yachts. However, the most significant

change was the treatment of the stem on this new cruiser. Gone was the white bow cap that was the trademark of all postwar Chris-Craft cruisers. It also marked the end of the heavy, massive stem treatment that seemed to be getting out of hand. The stem still had some bull-nose characteristics, but it was being trimmed back and without the heavy bow cap the look was more acceptable. The top of the stem still rolled back at the top to meet a bright mahogany monkey rail, but it was slimmer and attractive. The new treatment was a positive sign that Chris-Craft was heading in the right direction and a more conservative new look was ahead.

It was not uncommon for production cruiser builders to adapt a successful hull design to a variety of cabin configurations. Each configuration would be given a unique name and appear to be a totally new model. In 1954 the 40-foot Express Cruiser and the DCFB Cruiser shared the same hull. This practice was followed with the 36-foot Commander, the Corvette, and the Sport Fisherman models as well as other

The 27-foot Super Deluxe Enclosed Cruiser for 1946 was a totally new postwar treatment that offered fresh styling to a favorite old model. *Classic Boating magazine*

The 33-foot Deluxe Enclosed Cruiser, commonly called the sedan Cruiser, became one of the most popular Cruisers in the early postwar market offering good looks and plenty of room for extended cruising. *Classic Boating magazine*

models. The practice assured the company that it was starting with a proven hull configuration. It also reduced overhead and provided more time to focus on the development of attractive design features. Its ability to produce wooden boats in volume was only surpassed by its ability to introduce attractive new models with innovative styling features year after year. Competitors found it difficult to keep pace with the Chris-Craft innovations, and many of them began to simply incorporate Chris-Craft features into their styling.

By 1951 two major competitors, Richardson and Owens, introduced new models that were clearly aimed at capturing Chris-Craft's success. Richardson introduced a 27-foot enclosed cruiser that was very similar to Chris-Craft's 27-foot Super Deluxe Enclosed Cruiser. This model was a departure from the traditional Richardson style. At

the same time, Owens introduced a 30-foot Express Cruiser that was aimed directly at the same potential buyer as the Chris-Craft 30-foot Express Cruiser. There was no question that the competition was frustrated, and rivals were using similar designs to cash in on Chris-Craft's appeal. Owens offered its express cruiser with a varnished mahogany hull and a cozy interior plan that could sleep six. These were two features that Chris-Craft didn't offer, and it became a formidable alternative. In 1952, Owens followed with an all-new 35-foot express cruiser aimed right at the 35-foot Chris-Craft Commander.

By 1954, Chris-Craft offered 20 cruiser models with flying bridge controls. Its powerful advertising emphasized the excitement of operating your new cruiser from a helm outside the cabin in the company of family and guests. Cruising with

Chris-Craft was being promoted as a stylish and invigorating activity for people who enjoyed good times and fresh air. The 60-page sales catalog had a full color cover featuring its Showboats for 1954. The catalog illustrated 35 new boats from 17 feet to 63 feet, showing 224 people smiling and enjoying their adventure in a new Chris-Craft—nearly 80 percent of who were young, attractive women, though the men were nearly always at the helm. Chris-Craft understood the power of attractive display advertising and the value of motivational sales brochures better than any of its competitors.

The 35-foot Sport Fisherman was a serious new entry into this specialized market. It was a rugged craft featuring painted cabin sides and standard teak decks for easier maintenance. It also provided wide side decks for easy access to the fore deck, and dual controls with the required standard fishing

bridge. Its claim on this husky craft was that, "quantity building saves about half the cost of a custom-built boat of this type." The claim had merit, and it was clear that Chris-Craft was making a serious venture into the sport fishing boat market, which had thus far been the domain of specialty builders.

The 1955 sales catalog announced the new Freedom Fleet. Its follow-up line was, "*The new Chris-Craft Freedom Fleet brings you a new kind of freedom–the freedom to enjoy life fully. And you start, right away . . . the moment you step aboard a new Chris-Craft.*"

The 1955 cruiser models abandoned the postwar turtle-back bow cap feature that had served so well since 1945. In its place was an entirely new treatment that was simple, practical, and very yacht-like—the stem itself and the area where the stem joins the deck used husky attractive mahogany

The 25-foot Express Cruiser was virtually unchanged from its prewar styling, due to its advanced design as the "boat of tomorrow" when it was introduced as a World's Fair model. *Classic Boating magazine*

quarter round shear rails that converged at the stem. This new design was universal for the entire cruiser fleet, providing a distinctive new look. The treatment is virtually the same one that was introduced with the 1954 Corsair. The pleasant new design was well received by dealers and new buyers, reflected by strong sales records for 1955.

Nearly all of the 1955 cruisers adapted a consistent design technique. Chris-Craft designers made greater use of the cabin roof line, extending it to create a sun deck on the 42-foot Commodore and a deeper, safer cockpit enclosure on all of the Commander models. This styling feature on the Commanders required an integrated coaming door to access the cockpit through the higher surround treatment. Every model seemed to embrace this styling feature to partially enclose the open areas with graceful extensions of the cabin roof and cabin sides.

In 1955 the Roamer Boat Company of Holland, Michigan, builders of high-quality steel cruisers and commercial craft, was purchased by Chris-Craft. Harry Coll, who had been in charge of the Holland factory, was named by Harsen Smith to head the new Roamer Division as corporate vice president of the western Michigan group. At the time of acquisition, the Roamer Boat Company was building 34-foot express cruisers, 41-foot DCEB cruisers, and 45-foot steel tugs for the army. The Roamer line would expand to include aluminum hulls and models up to 73 feet.

The 1955 "Freedom Fleet" introduced a new series name, Constellation, to its exciting new cruiser lineup. The Constellation name for 1955 was assigned to the flush deck version of the 53-foot Conqueror. The Constellation provided a huge, inviting, single-level deck that was designed for entertaining guests and large groups safely. The Constellation models would be expanded over different lengths and become Chris-Craft's most celebrated series.

For 1956, Chris-Craft embraced the term Showboats once more and expanded its regular advertising to include 16 of the nation's most influential periodicals. Beautiful full-color, full-page ads appeared regularly in *Holiday, Esquire, Motor Boating, Rudder, Skipper, Yachting, Lakeland Yachting, Boats, Fortune, Sports Afield, Outdoor Life, Sports Illustrated, Sunset, Field and Stream, House and Garden,* and the *New Yorker.*

One of the company's most striking new designs was announced in a series of attractive full-page ad layouts beginning in the 1956 season. It was a special model presumed to come from the drawing board of independent contract designer, Don Mortrude, who had provided Chris-Craft with some of its most inspired designs. The new model was the 33-foot Futura Sports Express Cruiser. This new cruiser provided full teak decks and teak cockpit as standard issue. It

In 1948, Chris-Craft reintroduced the exciting 34-foot Express Cruiser with its sporty forward cockpit. This attractive model would soon give way to the improved 34-foot Commander. *Classic Boating magazine*

featured wide walk-around decks with lifelines and rails around the entire craft. It was the only cruiser in 1956 to provide standard height lifelines all the way to the bow. The cabin roof formed a smart visor overhang over the forward edge of the roof. The graceful curve of its exquisite clipper stem foretold the new look that would remain with Chris-Craft's wooden Cruisers to the end of production. The Futura also introduced use the corporate double "C" scroll as the forward-most extension of the hullside rub strake. It would be four years until this script was uniformly used on all cruiser modes. By 1962 the design became a triple "C" scroll with an arrow running through each letter "C."

The 1956 cruiser fleet also offered Cruisers with the choice of black-finished hull sides as a standard option. The 42-foot Corsair and the 54-foot Constellation were illustrated in the sales catalog with their black-finished hulls. The interiors of many of the cruiser models continued to use blond Korina paneling. The new cruisers with painted interiors incorporated new color schemes, including shades of pink, coral, turquoise, and other designer colors used by mid-1950s automobile manufacturers.

The innovations previewed on the 33-foot Futura in 1956 gradually began to appear on selected cruiser models

The new 34-foot Commander for 1949 would be offered with an open fly bridge or with a standard hardtop as illustrated. It provided two cabins for six and a large one-level cockpit. *Florida State News Bureau*

The Semi-Enclosed Cruisers were fast, spacious, good looking and growing rapidly in popularity through the 1950s. This 1951 27-footer was a good example of their good looks.

the following year. The new Sport Fisherman Cruisers featured the Futura's new style clipper stem design. Other features began to appear, including the prominent use of lifelines, bow pulpits, teak decks, and the simplified, triangular windshield wings. By 1958 every cruiser roof extended beyond the forward windscreen to form a protective visor over the forward cabin glass.

These were examples of how Chris-Craft would incorporate styling changes without causing production delays. As a new model was introduced, it often included a few design innovations. Dealers evaluated and, if well received, they began to appear on established models as the year progressed. If they are as successful as anticipated, they become part of the new look for model changes over the following season.

Among the additions to the 1958 cruiser fleet were two new 25-footers, a Semi-Enclosed Cruiser and the sporty Cadet, with a fly bridge and berths for four. In addition to reviving the Cadet model name from years past, Chris-Craft decided to draw upon the term "Commuter" as the model name for its new 26-footer. This new model reached 36 miles per hour with optional twin power. Using the same hull as the Commuter, it reintroduced the Sports Express

Another variation of the popular Commander series was the 36-foot Corvette that provided a unique, private aft cabin arrangement. Once again, Chris-Craft scooped the competition with this special compact feature. *Classic Boating magazine*

By 1955, Chris-Craft was offering an abundance of Express Cruisers in nearly every length. This smart 27-foot model offered speed to 34 miles per hour with twins for sportsmen in a hurry.

model—another generation of the famous Red and White Express that would also hit 36 miles per hour.

The major new models for 1958 were two variations of the new 65-foot hulls: the Motor Yacht and the Constellation. These two models would mark the largest standardized hull lengths for Chris-Craft yachts. Previously, in 1950, the 62-foot Motor Yacht was introduced and provided an exterior that was similar to the new 65-foot Constellation.

The 65-foot Motor Yacht was a breakthrough design for Chris-Craft. This motor yacht, with its pilothouse, was aimed directly at the offerings of the luxury yacht builders, such as Trumphy, Burger, and Grebe. In most cases these yacht builders' customers often preferred to employ captains to operate their large craft and desired more privacy with their guests. This was one of the advantages of providing a pilothouse layout for a captain. The description of this new yacht emphasized this position stating:

Never before have shipbuilders produced a more magnificent tribute to their art than the

65-foot Chris-Craft Motor Yacht. Designed for the discriminating yachtsman, it reflects the spaciousness, luxury and appointments of contemporary trilevel living. The pilothouse offers a clear view around the horizon; the wide forward deck is ideal for sunning; and the canopied aft deck offers ample room to relax with friends. Indoors, the fashionable deckhouse salon has the gracious appointments which contribute to casual, easy-going shipboard living. There's a complete galley and separate dining salon; owner's stateroom and two guest staterooms, each with private toilet; a captain's cabin, crew's quarters and dining area.

The 33-foot Futura Express Cruiser was illustrated in the 1959 sales catalog in its final production year. Its superb hull configuration can easily be identified on two new models in the same catalog, the 33-foot Sport Fisherman and the 33-foot Sports Sedan. The Sport Fisherman proved to be very popular with its rugged and sea-kindly hull remaining in production for four more years. The influence of Futura clipper stem design continued to prevail, as 12 of the 16 cruiser models adapted this more graceful configuration, and the bull-nose stem rapidly faded into the past. Chris-Craft continued to introduce new styling ideas on selected models, such as new console control stations and the limited use of curved glass on windshields.

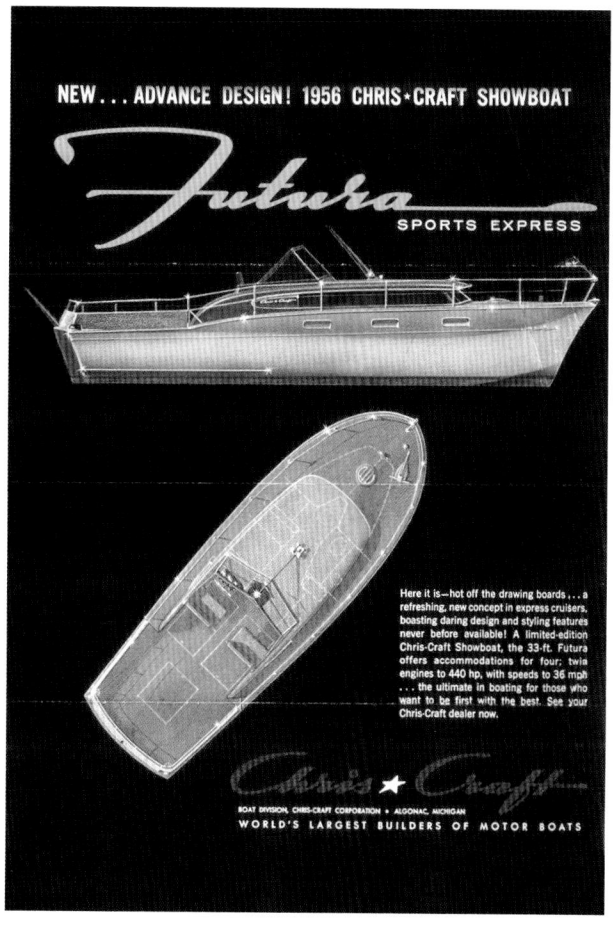

NEW... ADVANCE DESIGN! 1956 CHRIS·CRAFT SHOWBOAT

Futura
SPORTS EXPRESS

Here it is—hot off the drawing boards...a refreshing, new concept in express cruisers, boasting daring design and styling features never before available! A limited-edition Chris-Craft Showboat, the 33-ft. Futura offers accommodations for four; twin engines to 440 hp, with speeds to 36 mph ... the ultimate in boating for those who want to be first with the best. See your Chris-Craft dealer now.

Chris ★ Craft
BOAT DIVISION, CHRIS-CRAFT CORPORATION • ALGONAC, MICHIGAN
WORLD'S LARGEST BUILDERS OF MOTOR BOATS

In 1955 the name Constellation was introduced and became Chris-Craft's most popular series. This 1956 38-footer was offered with either a four- or six-sleeper layout. *Classic Boating magazine*

With the new cruiser line for 1960, the bull-nose stem design that made its initial appearance on the 1950 Conqueror was no longer present on any Chris-Craft cruiser. It was a feature only a dominant builder such as Chris-Craft could have used successfully, because Chris-Craft convinced the market that it represented attractive styling. Gone, too, were the attempts at using curved glass to transition the windshield into the side glass. The sales success Chris-Craft enjoyed with the attractive 1960 cruiser fleet didn't mean that its designers were prepared to rest. Styling improvements and modifications were ongoing, and even the most successful models were updated regularly. Their total sales from all divisions exceeded $40 million in 1960, which was more than three times the sales of its closest competitor, the Owens Yacht Company of Baltimore. Chris-Craft produced more than 8,000 boats that generated a profit exceeding $2.5 million. It was this success that attracted the attention of potential corporate buyers, and in February 1960 the Smith family, owners of Chris-Craft since it was founded, made the decision to sell to National Automotive Fibers, Inc.

The new ownership introduced major styling changes for the 1961 season. All cruisers except the two Sport Fisherman models were given new treatments that tied them together superbly and distinguished them from their rivals.

Wide walk-around side decks with lifelines were present on every cruiser over 28 feet. All cabin rooftops were made of molded fiberglass with bench seats styled into the forward end on the larger cruisers. A wide, dark blue sheer stripe extending to the hull side rub rail became the standard trim. The forward-most portion of the deckhouse was styled with a large port light, which became another distinctive trademark. The large reverse trapezoidal window glass on the cabin sides terminates with special aircraft metal trim. All of the larger cruisers are equipped with modern chrome and teak yardarms.

Natural finish interior paneling for 1961 was offered in light, medium, and dark stains with satin varnish. Another noteworthy change was the new three "C" corporate scroll design that would replace the double "C" scroll that had been in place for the previous six years. The new styling changes once again created even more enthusiasm than the solid success that the 1960 cruiser fleet received. But even more it was a reflection of corporate president Harry Coll's desire to always keep Chris-Craft "at least two years in front of its competition."

There were few changes in the cruiser line-up for 1962. One exception was the 37-foot Tri-Cabin Constellation. This unique model demonstrated Chris-Craft's ingenuity for interior space while still providing an attractive and balanced exterior profile. It featured a large aft deck, three separate sleeping areas, and two lavatories inside the spacious cabin. There was a wonderful owner's stateroom aft, a large main salon, and in the forward section, a generous, private guest stateroom.

Another addition to the fleet was the 60-foot Motor Yacht, which was a redesigned version of the 65-foot Motor Yacht introduced in 1958. The new version, although a bit shorter, provided an excellent interior layout with better

The 42-foot Constellation was an important concept, providing the stately appearance and spaciousness traditionally associated with much larger motor yacht designs. *Classic Boating magazine*

The Motor Sailer

Shortly after the Smith family sold Chris-Craft to NAFI, the new owners expressed their desire to explore the growing popularity of fiberglass cruising sailboats as a new potential market for Chris-Craft. Cornelius Shields, a well-respected and highly skilled sailor, was a principal figure in the purchase of Chris-Craft. Shields & Company was now the majority stockholder of Chris-Craft. It would be Shields who predicted a bright future for a line of fiberglass sailboats, and in September 1962, Chris-Craft announced plans for the production of a 35-foot fiberglass sloop-rigged cruising sailboat. It would be the first of eight special fiberglass models ranging in size from 26 to 42 feet. The sailboat program produced some outstanding models and lasted until 1976, when the market for this type of sailing craft weakened, and it was decided to discontinue the program.

allocation of space that was far more suitable for superior guest accommodations.

In 1963 the most obvious change in the cruiser line was the lowering of the blue sheer stripe to an area about one plank below the shear plank. By lowering the stripe, designers could incorporate within its width the porthole openings. This had a very interesting effect on the overall appearance, because the characteristic porthole openings seemed to vanish in the new treatment, providing a cleaner, uninterrupted appearance. Once again Chris-Craft stylists created a new image to their well-designed cruiser fleet with a simple idea that was effective and attractive. With the discontinuation of both Sport Fishing models, all the cruisers except the two large motor yachts and the 42-foot Conqueror carried the Constellation model name.

At the same time that the sailboat program was under way, a new Research and Development Center was opened in Pompano, Florida. The main function for this new center was to advance its study of fiberglass boat construction. The Hatteras 41-foot and 34-foot DCFB all-fiberglass cruisers along with their Sports Cruiser versions, introduced in 1960, continued to make impressive gains in the market. Their success, along with Bertram's fiberglass cruisers, was creating pressure at Pompano to answer the call for fiberglass cruiser

In 1955, Chris-Craft offered an innovative marketing idea by offering several Cruiser models with black finished hulls. The 55-foot Constellation is an excellent example of this dramatic look. *Courtesy The Mariners' Museum*

The 35-foot Constellation for 1958 was the modern Express Cruiser reborn, with sporty good looks, excellent speed, and large aft deck to accommodate several day guests. *Classic Boating magazine*

In 1964 the 37-foot Constellation incorporated more use of fiberglass to fabricate components such as the forward cabin seat, hardtops, cabin roofs, and other suitable units. *Classic Boating magazine*

The 36-foot Constellation sports a wide navy-blue band just below the sheer from stem to the stern provides an interesting new styling feature for the 1960 models. *Classic Boating magazine*

construction. In 1962 a highly secretive fiberglass cruiser project was begun in the Holland, Michigan, plant. In a new addition to the main plant, Bill MacKerer and Fred Hudson focused their full attention on the development of a superior all-fiberglass cruiser project.

With so much time, effort, and attention given to the development of new fiberglass projects, it becomes more understandable now why the advancement of the traditional wooden cruiser fleet simply remained in a holding pattern when compared to the frequency of model changes that characterized this division in the past. The wooden cruiser fleet was advanced beyond the competition of other wooden boat builders, and it was felt that it could hold its own while further study on the application of fiberglass construction was under way.

The 37-foot Tri-Cabin and the 42 Conqueror were removed from production in 1964. The 34-foot Constellation

The 46-foot Constellation for 1964 proved to be a popular model, with twin General Motors diesels for speeds to 20 miles per hour at a cost just a bit over $60,000. *Classic Boating magazine*

By 1965 the popular Double Cabin Flying Bridge model was called the Constellation Salon. At 38 feet overall, it was the latest form of this model, which had been in Chris-Craft's Cruiser fleet since 1931. *Classic Boating magazine*

was offered with an enclosed bridge as a sedan model. This version offered a larger galley and a much larger lavatory with room for an optional shower. The optional shower in a cruiser of this modest length was considered a very attractive feature. The 60-foot Motor Yacht was replaced by a 65-foot Constellation. Another significant lineup change was the addition of three new Challenger models at 36 feet and 38 feet as an express cruiser, a sedan, and a double cabin fly bridge cruiser.

Prior to the 1964 National Motor Boat Show, the Owens Yacht Company announced its new 33-foot all-fiberglass Sport Fisherman along with a 19-foot sport boat. Chris-Craft's dealers were showing concern that the competition was moving ahead quickly. At the 1964 New York National Motor Boat Show in January, Chris-Craft surprised everyone by unveiling its new 38-foot all fiberglass Commander Express Cruiser. The new craft was priced just under $30,000, to compete favorably with rival builders of wood, fiberglass, and metal cruisers of similar size. In addition to the Express model, the fiberglass Commander was offered as a sedan and a Sport Fisherman model.

In its first full year of production, 50 fiberglass Commanders were sold, providing all the success necessary to continue to develop more new models. In 1965 a 27-foot four-sleeper express cruiser version was introduced as the first

The 65-foot Constellation by 1963 was a magnificent motor yacht, with all the features offered by the finest custom builders. *Classic Boating magazine*

effort to expand the line, which was still part of the Chris-Craft Division.

The Roamer Cruisers and Yacht were given much-needed styling improvements to make them appear more like the attractive Commanders and Constellations. It was difficult to distinguish the 37-foot steel Roamer Riviera from the 37-foot mahogany Constellation or the 38-foot fiberglass Commander when viewing them from a modest distance. With the choice of metal, fiberglass, or wood hull, and the construction of many cruiser models by the same builder at prices that were surprisingly close, the traditional preference for wood became a bit harder to justify. However, Chris-Craft's national advertising continued to work hard helping those buyers who preferred wood construction to feel secure in their choice. Full-page national ads provided 11 reasons why selecting a mahogany Constellation was still a wise choice for boaters.

In 1966 the broad Constellation hull stripe was changed to a deep, attractive shade of maroon. Molded fiberglass was used for cabin sides, hardtops, command bridges, and super-structures, permitting more creative design features while reducing maintenance on areas that often require frequent attention. There was very little varnished wood left on the exterior, reducing the need for perpetual upkeep. Hatteras Yachts expanded its all-fiberglass fleet of cruisers to 11 distinct models from 28 feet to 50 feet. Hatteras and Bertram both presented their messages in very compelling and attractive six-page, full-color, trifold advertising layouts in the show issue of *Motor Boating*.

In a strange twist of fate, the major competitors for the diminishing number of wooden cruiser buyers turned out to be the individual boat divisions of Chris-Craft. With the creation of separate production divisions, Chris-Craft also divided dealer franchise agreements by divisions in the mid-1950s. Chris-Craft dealer franchises were awarded by Division according to a dealer's ability to carry inventory and sell boats. The cruiser divisions in 1966 included Sea Skiff, Corinthian, Cavalier, and the premier Chris-Craft Division. As the market for wooden cruisers began to shrink, the cruiser divisions provided a potential buyer four interesting variations of a similar wooden cruiser from the same organization.

In 1967 the 28-foot Constellation, the 37-foot Constellation, and the 38-foot Tri-Cabin Cruisers were dropped from production as more models were added to the fiberglass Commander fleet. It was evident that fiberglass was becoming a popular choice and Chris-Craft's Commander fleet was attractive, rugged, and affordable. In 1967 there were nine Commander models available. The Roamer Division would offer five models from 33 feet to 57 feet in either steel or aluminum. The sale of mahogany cruisers began to decline rapidly, as dealers found their customers becoming increasingly intrigued by the advantages offered by metal and glass boats over wood for the long term.

One of the great advantages Chris-Craft possessed was skilled woodworkers, and their talents helped to provide luxurious wooden interiors on their growing fleet of nonwood hulled cruisers and yachts. The interior appointments were so tastefully planned in rich, natural woods that their fiberglass and metal cruisers provided all the attractiveness of their wooden counterparts.

In the summer of 1970, Chris-Craft ended boat production at the Algonac, Michigan, factory. It was an event that the workers and residents of Algonac thought would

never happen as long as Chris-Craft was in the boat-building business. After 48 years of boat building in Algonac, it was finally over. It was reported that the final wooden cruiser built by Chris-Craft was a 57-foot Constellation that was sold to Pete Rozelle, commissioner of the Nation Football League and member of the Chris-Craft Board of Directors in 1972. It was fitting that the final wooden Chris-Craft was built at the highly regarded Holland, Michigan, factory, where the reputation for quality and efficiency was considered the finest among all their locations every year.

Fifty years of wooden boat construction came to an end with the delivery of the last 57-foot Constellation. It was magnificent craft that commemorated the end of an era dominated by Chris-Craft. It was a nostalgic moment, but Chris-Craft was still on top of the marine industry. A whole new era in pleasure boating was about to be redefined with new materials, new designs, and new prospects eager to participate.

This 60-foot Motor Yacht incorporated many nice traditional motor yacht features usually found on much larger models, such as the separate pilothouse and a large formal dining salon.

This magnificent 57-foot Constellation, reported to be the final wood Chris-Craft built, was delivered in 1972 to the commissioner of the National Football League, Pete Rozelle.

Chris-Craft's 40-foot Sport Fisherman of the early 1960s had all the rugged qualities this off-shore sport traditionally requires of the boats.

CHAPTER 4

THE UTILITY
A Boat for All Reasons

The sudden and cruel economic depression that swept away the nation's financial confidence was particularly harsh on boatbuilders. By 1932 half of the nation's pleasure-boat industry was forced to close or was just barely hanging on. The Smith family and its new Chris-Craft enterprise narrowly survived this brutal period. The family understood how to make adjustments during hard times; they were resilient, hard workers endowed with prudent business intuition that had served them well before. However, their rapid success and subsequent growth would leave them far more vulnerable at this point than during any previous time as boatbuilders.

The most exciting new design developed in late 1950 was the sensational 23-foot Holiday that transformed the notion of basic Utility into an entirely new styling concept. *Classic Boating magazine*

Surviving this challenge would require adjustments to every phase of their operation including the very style of the craft they were building. One of the designs to emerge from this depressed economy would be a boat identified simply as the Utility. The prototype for the Utility was a modified 22-foot standard Runabout with most of the deck removed and the engine enclosed in a simple mahogany box. It was initially developed to provide a modestly priced, multipurpose craft that would appeal to a wide range of marine applications. While it was fashioned primarily by the economy to maintain some level of production, the Utility also furnished a boat that was ultimately more useful, and its name provided potential owners with justification that their new boat could be considered a practical acquisition.

In the runabout configuration, passengers traveled in attractive cockpits with fine upholstery. The new Utility model offered a large open area with a short deck forward of the controls and one or two bench seats. In order to keep the price of the Utility boat modest, it was devoid of upholstered seats and had little hardware and no trim. In stark contrast to the sporty runabout, the Utility was so plain that it appeared to be a workboat. However, the utility boat style

In 1934, Chris-Craft offered a full line of Utility boats, starting with its basic 15-1/2-foot Model 65, with a simple tiller attached to the rudder for steering at $495 and a 32-horsepower inboard engine. *Courtesy The Mariners' Museum*

This wonderfully preserved 1934 18-foot Utility model, with its original style folding top and rolled-up side curtains, is a perfect representation of the early Utility types. *Don Babcock*

provided room to walk around the boat's interior for fishing, carrying cargo, enjoying water sports or transporting a number of passengers.

By early 1932 it was clear that the economic downturn was widespread, and even those who were not directly affected were cautious about spending money unnecessarily. Boat sales dropped sharply and the Smiths needed to reevaluate the types of craft they were offering in order to keep production moving at some reasonable level. They needed to offer a boat that was modestly priced and provided a more appealing approach to enjoying a full afternoon on the water. Speed and spray were an exciting part of boating, but there needed to be more than that to attract buyers. The utility type of boat could provide the additional appeal.

The first consideration was to provide more interior space without making a bigger boat. By removing much of the deck covering and placing the engine inside a box, they were able to provide more usable space while reducing the cost. In early 1932, Jay and Bernard Smith decided to produce a few boats with this different configuration in order to measure their appeal among local sportsmen. They selected one of their standard 24-foot runabout hulls for the prototype. It was essentially a runabout with a shorter fore deck, a bench front seat, a motor box, and a short deck over the fuel tank. It was simple, with no bright trim, no upholstery, and remarkable interior space. The reduction of material cut construction cost, saved weight, and resulted in a revolutionary approach for boatbuilders.

The largest Utility of the 1934 Chris-Craft fleet was the 21-foot model 73 with a 70-horsepower engine, good for 28 miles per hour. It was also offered with a shelter cabin for $200 additional. *Courtesy The Mariners' Museum*

The model classification, utility, made sense, but it certainly lacked the marketing pizzazz of the term *runabout*. But in those desperate times, the excesses of the previous decade had lost favor and practicality and utility were in.

Chris-Craft prepared for boat's official introduction in the fall of 1932 for the 1933 model year. The first production

The big news for 1936 was the introduction of the luxurious 24-foot Sportsman and its speed of 40 miles per hour. With the Sportsman, Chris-Craft offered a Utility equal to its most elegant runabouts. *Courtesy The Mariners' Museum*

model would offer two standard engine options with the 85-horsepower providing speeds to 30 miles per hour and the 125-horsepower for 35 miles per hour. The modest advertising for the new 24-foot Utility model would focus on how well suited it would be "for fishing, cargo carrying and harbor work."

The new 24-foot utility model showed enough promise in its first year that plans for 1934 would include three new utilities. One would be the least-expensive Chris-Craft of them all, the 15-1/2-foot Model 65, which it would offer at $495. New 18- and 21-footers also debuted, using new hulls designed as utilities rather than using a converted runabout

Introduction of the 17-foot Utility in 1937, offered in both Standard and Deluxe models, was a new length for this series. At $795 with the 55-horsepower engine, the Standard was still aimed at attracting first-time buyers. *Courtesy The Mariners' Museum*

For 1938 the 15-1/2-foot Runabout and the 15-1/2-foot Sportsman were virtually identical. The only difference was that the Sportsman eliminated the rear seat to provide more space.

configuration. The new hulls were generally beamier and carried the full width aft to provide more interior room all the way to the transom. The original 24-footer completed the 1934 utility fleet.

In 1935 Chris-Craft increased the length of the entry-level utility to 16 feet in order to justify boosting the price to $595. It was still a great deal, and they successfully generated a lot of attention by advertising the fact that it was now possible to own a genuine Chris-Craft for less than $600.

It wasn't long before the Smiths' trial runs with the open-style utility-runabout created some interest from their neighbors at Gar Wood's Boat Division. Almost immediately Gar Wood modified a stock 22-foot Gar Wood runabout in a similar manner to Chris-Craft, but held off bringing it to market in order to evaluate the reception of Chris-Craft's Utility. By the fall of 1934, Gar Wood decided to follow Chris-Craft's lead, and offered a 20-foot Utility at the 1935 National Motor Boat Show in New York. When it turned out to be Gar

Wood's best-selling model at the show, they knew that Chris-Craft was clearly on the right track with this new model.

In 1936, Chris-Craft's nearly exclusive hold on the utility market would be challenged by other boatbuilders eager to latch on to the optimism of recovery. Always on the leading edge of marketing its products, Chris-Craft tried to ease away from the utility classification and introduced the name "Sportsman" to provide greater dignity to its version of this popular craft. Initially it used this attractive name for its most deluxe model, the 24-footer that featured the luxurious appointments usually found in only the finest runabouts. Some of these features included fully framed V-windshield, leather upholstery, full dash instrumentation, abundant deck hardware, mahogany paneled interior, and a wide range of engine options. With this special model, Chris-Craft announced to the boating world the arrival and celebration of its most deluxe Utility. The new name worked, and this particular model would always be known as the *Sportsman*.

The most innovative feature was the rear-facing aft seat in the new 19-foot Sportsman in 1939. The styling differences between Utilities and Runabouts were becoming less apparent. *Courtesy The Mariners' Museum*

Aria is a superb example of the popular 1938 21-foot Deluxe Utility. With the 110-horsepower engine, this Model 805 could reach 34 miles per hour; it sold for $1,790. *Classic Boating magazine*

By 1938 the enclosed or cabin Utility was becoming a very popular alternative to the open 21-foot Utility model, for just an additional cost of $275. *Courtesy The Mariners' Museum*

As the American economy slowly recovered, new preferences began to emerge among the boat buyers. The utility design was becoming a popular choice among recreational boaters who enjoyed fishing, swimming, aquaplaning, and water skiing. Boaters found it easier to spend a full day on the water with the more accommodating utility style than with the confined cockpits of a runabout.

Another pleasant variation of the open utility design was introduced in 1937 with the optional streamlined cabin. An attractive, permanent enclosure was installed over the middle third of the boat using the same hull as the open utility model. This practical variation, with full ventilating windows, allowed the owners to have the best of both worlds—a large open cockpit as well as a shelter in case there is a sudden change in the weather.

The cabin version of the utility became so popular that it often outsold the open utility models, in part because the open style of the utility provided easy, direct access to the cabin interior. There was no need to traverse a slippery deck, over the engine hatches to then descend a narrow opening to enter the cabin enclosure. The cabin utility provided shelter along with the comfortable feeling that it was easy to exit the enclosure. In the older limousines an emergency escape seemed difficult, and it often required a measure of courage to ride inside their snug enclosure.

Chris-Craft also offered an optional, nonfolding, canvas navy top on the 21-foot and 22-foot utilities as well as the 24-foot Sportsman. This "navy top" option required a special factory-installed mahogany windshield to provide more headroom and better visibility for this early top. It became a popular option, providing for use of the boat in a wider range of weather conditions.

Nineteen thirty-eight featured several design innovations that would influence new styling trends. The utilities showed increased beam, pronounced flare, and more freeboard, resulting in engaging hull shapes and improved performance. The enclosed utility models provided attractive, streamlined cabin enclosures with pleasing roof contours and attractive window openings, drawing upon the most positive automotive design features. These new treatments began to influence rival builders as Chris-Craft captured more of the boating market. Using its strong advertising program in a large number of popular journals, Chris-Craft became the popular trendsetter in popular boating. Soon the vision of what people aspired to own when it came to the boat of their dreams was the image of a Chris-Craft. While Chris-Craft and its rivals at Gar Wood already understood the vast appeal of the utility-style sport boats, Century Boat Company was far less certain. Century cautiously offered three standard utility models in lengths of 17, 18-1/2, and 20 feet. Its reluctance to fully endorse the style was delivered by its advertising copy's apologetic tone with this description as late as 1940:

> While all of us approve of and enjoy the many refinements of deluxe fittings and equipment, it is nevertheless true that expensive adornments and complete panoply of trim are not at all essential for the wholesome enjoyment of sport afloat. Nor, in every case, are those refinements practicable; it is very true that rough service and considerable "banging about" fall to the lot of many craft, and under such conditions the extra fittings and trim would be a wasteful luxury. Standard utilities are particularly adaptable to the requirements of hunting and fishing expeditions and for use under conditions where baggage, luggage and bulk supplies dictate plenty of space and great weight-carrying capacity in a boat.

By early fall of 1939 full production began in the first factory branch in Holland, Michigan. By mid-January 1940, 48 15-1/2-foot utility-runabouts were ready to be delivered to dealers who were getting anxious to stock their showrooms. Chris-Craft executive Larry McDonough described the preparations and activities at the new plant

The flagship of the Utility fleet was the 24-foot Sportsman that claimed speeds to 41 miles per hour with its powerful 212-horsepower engine. There were several engine options offered, including twin 95-horsepower units.

this way: "The formula initiated at Holland involved the permanent transfer of one or more experienced boatbuilders from the Algonac Plant, along with temporary key Algonac veterans to train personnel in each department. This included complete tooling for the selected model, consisting of stall, assembly jigs, fixtures, and patterns: detailed shop drawings, cutting bills and lumber details, material specifications. All of this was essential to build the boat and to ensure that it contained only the already tested and approved materials, and that it was built to the firmly established Chris-Craft standards."

In January 1941, Chris-Craft worked out an arrangement with the city administration of Cadillac, Michigan, to acquire an additional 125,000 square feet of production space in an available structure. In less than five weeks after the deal was made, production of 18-foot and 22-foot utility boats was under way. This aggressive expansion program was, in part, motivated by the need to meet the rapidly growing demand for its boats.

Chris-Craft signed its first military contract to supply marine engines for boats built by another company in February 1941. This contract was followed by an order for 27 standard 22-foot utilities for the U.S. Army Air Corps to serve as rescue boats for downed aircraft. In May 1941, three

The cabin version of the 24-foot Sportsman provided a fast and comfortable small commuter for boaters who preferred this type of transportation. *Courtesy The Mariners' Museum*

slightly modified Chris-Craft stock cruisers promptly filled another government purchase order.

Numerous styling refinements were incorporated on Chris-Craft cruisers and runabouts between 1938 and 1942 that strengthened their popular appeal. The runabouts with "barrel" styling and folding windshields, and smartly styled cruisers with white canvas spray shields, flared windshields, and creative cabin window shapes set them apart from the competition. At the same time, the utility fleet in four basic lengths remained virtually unchanged, and they dominated the field.

Although war seemed inevitable, Chris-Craft prepared for all contingencies and created its 1942 sales brochure in

October 1941, even as the factory was receiving contracts from the Defense Department. On the inside cover of its new catalog it displayed aerial photographs of its three factory locations in Algonac, Holland, and Cadillac, Michigan. On the opposite page appeared illustrations of four special military craft in production with the following statement, ". . . We are building and have built boats for the United States Army, United States Navy and for other departments as rapidly as ordered. Defense needs come first with Chris-Craft. The new models, shown on the following pages, were designed and built without interrupting our defense activities. Production may be limited by defense demands on our facilities."

Then after December 7, 1941, the nation was at war. Chris-Craft's modest inventory of 1942 boat models was sold promptly, marking the end of its pleasureboat production for the next four years.

During the war the use of creative advertising promised many new, unusual, and futuristic boat designs as soon as peace returned. Independent designer Don Mortrude published concept designs for *Motor Boating* magazine that illustrated the precise bull-nose stem that became the distinguished new feature for the postwar Holiday and Continental models. His wartime concept boats illustrated the pronounced rounding of the covering boards, extreme flare forward, and the continuous flare over the entire length of the hull.

Chris-Craft artists turned out several interesting modernistic designs during the darkest days of the war, but while anticipation for these exciting postwar designs was nearly universal, Chris-Craft decided not to incorporate wholesale model changes immediately. Meeting the demand for new boats quickly was more critical than making time-consuming changes. The small craft were restyled with new windshields. Larger models and cruisers featured an attractive turtleback bow cap that was the single, most prominent change and distinguished the postwar models from the otherwise similar prewar models.

By 1939 the 21-foot Deluxe Cabin Utility grew in popularity among sportsmen who enjoyed extending the boating season into the chilly spring and fall months. *Classic Boating magazine*

The big 29-foot Sportsman was the open Utility version of Chris-Craft's new Express Cruiser, introduced in 1939. Records show that only four 29-foot Sportsmen were produced. *Courtesy The Mariners' Museum*

Competition for the early postwar utility boat market came mainly from Chris-Craft's long-standing rivals at Gar Wood and Century. When Gar Wood completed its defense contracts early, it made an adventurous decision to redesign every model completely for the postwar market. Their new postwar line of boats was considered by many to be the most attractive in the industry. However, this decision to redesign every model was costly in lost time and increased prices. Redesigning required extensive retooling. Gar Wood Jr. frequently commented, "The new Gar Wood models redesigned the company right out of business." Gar Wood Industries ultimately closed its Boat Division shortly after the 1947 National Motor Boat Show.

Richardson was another example of a boat-builder that decided to make total design changes for the postwar market. Its new designs were costly and too extreme for most traditional buyers. Richardson nearly lost everything. It was able to recover by returning to its more traditional styling.

Chris-Craft's more prudent approach kept its costs under control and provided a running start that it would not relinquish for decades.

There was a severe shortage of quality mahogany in the United States at the conclusion of the war, as boatbuilders resumed pleasureboat production. Many craft that traditionally featured all-varnished mahogany hulls were forced to

substitute cedar planking for scarce mahogany. Since the appearance of cedar was not as attractive as varnished mahogany, the hulls were painted rather than stained and varnished. The flagship of the utility fleet, the 25-foot Sportsman, used so much mahogany that it was temporarily discontinued from late 1946 until 1948.

In 1948 the Chris-Craft catalog illustrated three models, the 16-foot Deluxe Utility, the 22-foot Sportsman, and the 22-foot Custom Sedan, each with white painted hulls. Absent from the catalog specifications was information on the types of wood used by Chris-Craft. Its prewar catalogs specified Philippine mahogany for main frames, auxiliary bottom frames, bottom planking, keel, battens, and decks. With the shortage of mahogany, other woods were often substituted. In most cases it appeared that clear cedar was used on hulls that were intended to be painted and on all the bottom planking. Cedar was a reasonably good substitute but lacked the brilliance necessary for varnishing. Mahogany was precious and used for decks, transoms, and selected models with varnished hulls. The interior panels or sealing boards in the utility models with painted hulls consisted of clear, light-colored woods such as spruce, aspen, or maple as a mahogany substitute. Finished with varnish, these light-toned woods provided a modern and rather attractive appearance for the

A pair of popular 22-footers for 1941, showing the open Utility model alongside the Streamline Cabin Utility. The cabin option was available for an additional $225.

The 18-foot 1941 Deluxe Utility offered good speed at 34 miles per hour. It proved to be one of the most enduring Utility models, remaining in the line virtually unchanged through 1954.

The 25-foot 1946 Sportsman had several new refinements, including the attractive mahogany bow cap, the wider amidships deck, and the superb windshield design. *Classic Boating magazine*

utility interior. The 16-foot SR Rocket (1947–1948) was the only runabout planked with cedar and painted. However, the Rocket, listed as a runabout model, was by definition a utility boat because its engine was covered by a motor box rather than decked over.

In 1949 the 16- and 18-foot Deluxe Utility boats would share the name Sportsman with the 22- and 25-foot models. This would mark the first time that all four Utility models were officially identified as Sportsman.

In 1950 the 16-foot Sportsman's length (16 feet 5 inches) was increased by 10 inches and its beam by 3 inches, transforming it into the 17-foot Sportsman. The other Sportsman models stayed essentially the same. Chris-Craft's ability to acquire more mahogany improved, and all the Sportsmen models featured varnished mahogany hulls for the first time in the postwar production period. However, the use of light-toned ceiling boards was attractive and remained standard in the 17-foot and 22-foot Sportsman until the 1951 models.

For the first time in 11 years the 25-foot Sportsman model, originally presented in 1936 (as a 24-footer), was not being offered. In its place was an entirely new generation of utility craft that would challenge every competitive builder of sport craft. It featured extreme styling that would change the look in open cockpit wood sport craft forever. The new series

The 22-foot Sportsman was the most popular postwar model. The hulls were planked with cedar and finished in white, due to the shortage of premium grade mahogany in 1947–1948. *Classic Boating magazine*

would be called the Holiday models. To many devotees of Chris-Craft, the introduction of the Holiday models was the official presentation of the long-awaited, postwar dream boats with exciting, futuristic styling. Granted, the 20-foot Custom Runabout in early postwar years was a totally new hull configuration accented with blond mahogany right into the transom. However, rounded covering boards and the barreled bow were common treatments on some prewar runabouts. Even the folding V-windshield on the Custom Runabout was identical to the final prewar style windshield. The Custom Runabout was an important postwar model, but it did not make the radical statement or have the influence of the remarkable 23-foot Holiday.

Introduction of the spectacular Holiday series made the term "utility" inappropriate when referring to Chris-Craft's new models. At the same time, the runabouts' styling advantage

over utility types vanished with the arrival of the 23-foot Holiday. It was the design of the future with incredible spaciousness and marvelous performance. The Holiday design concept came directly from Don Mortrude, who began designing for Chris-Craft in the 1940s. Mortrude was responsible for many of the firm's most interesting and innovative designs, including the Capris, the Continentals, the Cobra sport boats, the Silver Arrows, and the Futura cruisers.

Although the changes reflected in the 23-foot Holiday were extreme departures from existing designs, the timing was right, and the total package was so well executed that it didn't immediately offend traditionalists. Virtually everything was new—it was unprecedented for a standardized production craft to incorporate so many changes all in one boat. Once aboard and given the opportunity to enjoy its generous room and superb level riding performance, even

By 1949 the availability of premium mahogany allowed the 22-foot Sportsman models to return to their traditional all-varnished hulls. The 145-horsepower option provided 36-mile-per-hour performance at $3,330. *Classic Boating magazine*

skeptics began to accept the Holiday. Among the extensive list of creative innovations featured on this superb show-stopper was a huge curved aft seat, the absence of an aft deck, steering column shift lever, extreme windshield angle, bull-nose stem, teak cockpit floor, fully rounded covering boards, blond mahogany sheer plank, continuous flare all the way to the transom, and the most creative transom design in the industry.

With the 23-foot Holiday, Chris-Craft presented consumers with a boat that fulfilled the promise of the advanced postwar design that everyone had anticipated. While it was more expensive than other utilities, this was a boat that attracted attention everywhere and was a superb handler as well. With Gar Wood's departure from boat-building a few years earlier, the more upscale market for small craft was wide open for Chris-Craft to cultivate as it wished. A 28-foot Holiday was listed on an early price list, but was not illustrated in the sales catalog and presumably never in production.

Beginning in 1951, the Kit Boat Division offered a 21-foot Sportsman along with other utility types. As the stripped-down utility models of the 1930s graduated to the top of the class in style and price, the plywood Kit Boats, and later Cavaliers, fulfilled the role of entry-level boats.

In 1952 the 17-foot Sportsman was restyled to become the Special Sportsman, and a 20-foot version of the Special Sportsman was added to the lineup, bringing the total to seven distinct models in the utility group. This array of models provided Chris-Craft with a price range for the utility line that started at $2,100 for the 17-foot Special Sportsman and increasing to $5,500 for the fastest version of the 23-foot Holiday. This offering of utilities provided potential buyers with everything from basic models to the traditional utility designs to the spectacular models that were the ultimate in the utility concept. This line-up stayed nearly the same through 1953 except for modifications to the 23-foot Holiday. The beautifully rounded transom with its forward rake was quietly redesigned. The new transom design became a bit more conventional, raked aft, rather than forward. This change was made to lower the cost of construction by reducing labor time and keeping the transom treatment more in line with the balance of the Chris-Craft fleet. The length was changed slightly to make it the 24-foot Holiday. Another change was the return to a more conventional dashboard, with the instruments elevated to a more traditional location. Upholstery was a soft green, reminiscent of the leather color used in the classic Sportsman models.

A new "hardtop" version of the 20-foot Sportsman introduced in 1953 was nearly identical to the design developed by Eddie Kaunitz of the Gar Wood Boat Division in 1945. This unique top required a wood-framed, ventilating windshield that supported the forward edge of the top. Two curved stainless-steel supports running from the windshield frame aft to the covering boards provided lateral support. This particular landau-style top did not include glass along the sides of the enclosure. This top employed snap-in transparent panels that, when removed, provided a very pleasant, wide open appearance. It was a simple top to construct, weighed less that the traditional sedan-style enclosure, and provided an attractive way to enclose a small craft without creating a claustrophobic interior space for passengers.

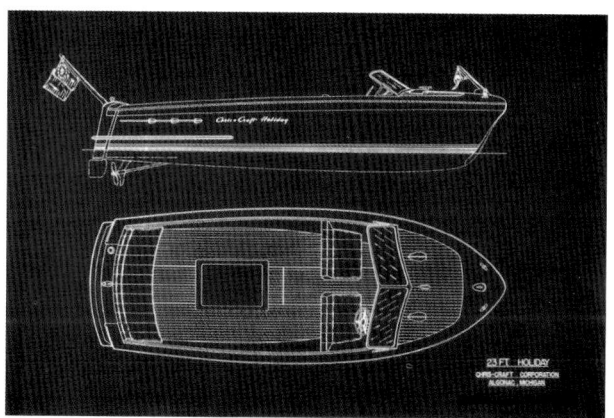

The flush blond bow cap, the fully rounded covering boards, and rakish windshield left no doubt that the 23-foot 1951–1952 Holiday had little interest in following traditional appearance. *Classic Boating magazine*

121

The new 60-page catalog proudly announced, "Showboats for 1954" as the new theme for the year. Chris-Craft's popularity soared as eager buyers enthusiastically embraced its attractive new models. One noteworthy milestone for the utility models was the option of diesel power in a stock utility for the first time. The more conventional 19-foot Holiday had become a 20-foot model. The fact that its photo is missing from the catalog provided a clue that a major model change might be in the wind.

By 1955, Chris-Craft customers had come to expect annual changes in the lineup, and the highly successful utility fleet was no exception. Two of its longest-surviving standard utility models, the traditional 18-foot and 22-foot Sportsman, would be discontinued. The 17-foot Sportsman would continue as the basic, entry-level utility for the next four years. New for 1955 was the Continental series, the next generation in the Holiday concept. These early Continentals were a refined version of the original Holiday models and lent themselves to easier construction resulting in easier maintenance. The Continentals eliminated some of the more costly Holiday features such as teak flooring, blond sheer plank, full-rounded covering boards, varnished sealing panels, and the blond bow cap. These changes created a new design leader among utilities for the next several years, as the Continental's popularity was exceptionally strong.

The 25-foot Continental would also be offered with twin 105-horsepower engines for speeds to 43 miles per hour. It was a wonderful year for the utility enthusiast, with eight of the nine models offering the modern hull configuration that had been introduced in 1951 with the first Holiday.

In 1956 the 20-foot Sportsman returned to the utility line. Both the 17-foot and 20-foot Sportsman were nearly unchanged except they now featured unframed, rather unattractive, curved Plexiglas windshields. The 25-Holiday was dropped from production, and the 22-foot Holiday and Continentals each became a foot longer, as did the 25-foot Continental. The Holidays and Continentals also had the option of a hardtop sedan version with a special ventilating windshield arrangement.

In 1957 the catalog once again touted the "Showboats" of Chris-Craft. The only change to the Utility fleet was the addition of a blond mahogany kingplank on the forward deck of the two Sportsman models. However, the big news for 1957 was the introduction of the all-new 21-foot Continental with automotive-inspired tail fins and a curved glass windshield similar to the type used on the Capri Runabouts. This new model offered speeds to 45 miles per hour, making it the fastest Chris-Craft and the fourth utility for 1957 to exceed 40 miles per hour. Nearly all of the utility models exceeded the Chris-Craft runabouts in overall speed. The era

Though Utilities were born of the Depression years, they soon rivaled top-of-the-line Runabouts. The 1938 catalog, for example, featured Utility models, Runabout models, plus hybrid "Utility" Runabouts," including this 19-foot Sportsman featuring a rear-facing seat and two single seats on either side of the engine box. In the 1950s, Utilities would ultimately usurp the Runabouts as the sportiest boats of the Chris-Craft lineup. *Robert Bruce Duncan.*

The new premium series of Utilities called Continentals was introduced in 1955 to take over the status held by the Holidays. This 23-foot 1956 Continental could do 41 miles per hour with 285-horsepower Cadillac power. *Classic Boating magazine*

of choosing a runabout for overall speed and thrilling performance was over. In 25 years, the Depression-era workboat had risen to become the fastest sport boat in the Chris-Craft fleet.

The radically designed Silver Arrow, the "sports car of the waterways," debuted in 1958 as Chris-Craft's first fiberglass boat. Sales promotion claimed, "fresh, daringly new styling, from one-piece, reinforced deck to the sleek canted fins, give the Silver Arrow a look of action even when standing at the dock." Chris-Craft had been uncharacteristically

slow to embrace production of fiberglass boats, and when it finally did introduce the Silver Arrow, it was in fact a 19-foot wooden boat constructed and planked with 7/16-inch spruce, which was then fiberglass covered from the chine up. The deck, however, was one piece of reinforced molded fiberglass. The Silver Arrow ultimately had only limited sales appeal with fewer than 100 units produced over two years. Its purpose, however, was to provide Chris-Craft with an immediate experience with fiberglass construction, and to that end it was a success.

With the introduction of the 19-foot Silver Arrow in 1958, Chris-Craft curtailed production of the 20-foot Holiday and the 20-foot Continental models. Buyers shopping for a utility in this size range could select from three—the exciting new 21-foot Continental, the conservative 20-foot Sportsman, or the fiberglass Silver Arrow. Even though two Utility models were being discontinued, it was clear that boaters preferred the room provided by the "utility" styling.

Chris-Craft was delighted with its new 21-foot Continental, for which their ads quipped "Has fins, will travel." The Continental incorporated the tail fin feature, that was so popular with automobile designers in this period, along the aft section of the covering board down to the bottom of the shear plank. In 1958 this model was also equipped with a fiberglass, aircraft-type sliding hardtop that was similar to the style developed by the Century Boat Company, its chief competitor in the sport boat market. Automobile styling was the rage in the mid-1950s, and Chris-Craft wanted to cash in on the enthusiasm buyers seemed to show this new styling. The use of fiberglass provided designers with the latitude necessary to incorporate features that wood construction could not.

The radical departure from traditional utility designs, with the introduction of the Holiday series in 1951 and followed by the Continental series in 1955, ended forever the workboat image of the original utility. A Chris-Craft customer in 1958 could choose from eight different models of "utilities," compared to just two Capri model runabouts. If maximum top speed was vital to the new buyer, a utility model was the only choice, because they were faster than Chris-Craft's stock runabouts. The sporty runabout was no longer the ultimate Chris-Craft for those seeking maximum speed and attractive style. By 1960, the term "runabout" made its final appearance in the official sales literature, and from that point on the term "sport boats" covers all but cruisers.

There were still more changes in the 1959 utility fleet. As the popularity of boating continued to increase, the utility style was again the most frequent choice of new and experienced small craft boaters alike. Chris-Craft added a 17-foot Ski Boat that appeared very similar to its 17-foot Sportsman. However, it was a new design that was slightly larger in all major dimensions and more ruggedly constructed. The 18-foot Holiday was discontinued, the last of the model that had been introduced in 1951 giving way to the more popular 18-foot Continental.

The 23-foot Continental was also discontinued to make way for a new Sportsman model that would be a favorite among those who still appreciated more traditional styling. This would be a totally new 24-foot Sportsman that provided generous freeboard, a smart clipper bow, a handsome

In 1955 a 29-foot Sportsman was offered, after being absent for 15 years. Again only four 29-foot Sportsmen were produced, making it one of the rarest of all stock Chris-Craft models. *Gerry Pederson*

The controls and instrument panel on the 1956 29-foot Sportsman provide a special treat for the helmsman. *Gerry Pederson*

From 1955 to 1958 the luxurious Continental series shared the same hull configuration as the same length Holiday that had become the basic model.
Classic Boating magazine

This 20-foot 1955 Continental model was offered with all the nice deluxe trim and upholstery.
Classic Boating magazine

mahogany-framed windshield, and enough space under the forward deck for a compartment for storage and room for a marine toilet. The new Sportsman was available with twin engines and offered a maximum speed to 40 miles per hour. It was an ideal combination of classic styling, generous size, and solid performance. Chris-Craft kept a lot of boaters happy with this model and provided the most diverse line of utility models ever offered by a single manufacturer. This was a fabulous year for everyone who enjoyed utility-style boating. There was a model to satisfy every preference, and Chris-Craft dominated the market.

By mid-1960, Chris-Craft's new owners, National Automotive Fibers, Inc. (NAFI), implemented separate dealer franchises for each of the various product lines. Their goal was to allow dealers to specialize in the types of boats most suitable to their client base or the region in which they were located. In this way they could increase sales with more dealers selling boats appropriate to their established operation. In 1960, Chris-Craft presented its Sport Boats in a special catalog that included six utility types and one runabout. The 19-foot Capri was the only runabout being offered. In addition, the plywood Cavalier Division was building an 18-foot Sports Utility and a 23-foot Sportsman. From the customers' standpoint, there were still eight utility-types by Chris-Craft from which to select the model of choice.

This 23-foot 1956 Continental with the Cadillac 285-horsepower engine option could achieve 41 miles per hour. Only the 21-foot Chris-Craft Capri runabout was faster, as the Utilities were overtaking the runabouts for pure speed. *Classic Boating magazine*

The 26-foot Continental in 1956 offered the option of twin 175-horsepower engines to provide this big Utility with speeds to 40 miles per hour and precision maneuverability for tight docking situations. *Courtesy The Mariners' Museum*

New for 1958 was the 42-mile-per-hour 19-foot Silver Arrow, a wood hull covered with fiberglass that was a Chris-Craft experiment with alternative types of construction. *Classic Boating magazine*

The 21-foot Continental was restyled with a trim clipper bow, in keeping with the balance of the fleet, and the fin treatment became a bit more conservative. The hardtop version of the Continental had a restyled fiberglass roof that provided hatches on either side to facilitate entry directly to the front seating area. It was a nice feature that was particularly convenient for the helmsman when docking alone. Sedans could present a challenge for the lone driver when there were no crew members to secure the dock. Some cabin configurations took enough time to exit that getting a line on the dock cleat was often a worry. The new top was very attractive and made this version of the Continental, a very appealing alternative to the open model.

There were major changes made in the utility offerings for 1961. Four models from the previous year were discontinued: the 17-foot Sportsman, the 18-foot Cavalier, the 18-foot Continental and the 23-foot Cavalier Sportsman. Five new models were added. Three of the models were called Open Skiffs in 20-, 23-, and 27-foot lengths. These painted lapstrake hulls were aimed directed at the growing success of Lyman Boats. They were attractive, sea kindly boats that were easy to operate, roomy, and quite rugged. The made ideal commuting and fishing boats and were easier to maintain. In addition, it offered the 23-foot Ranger as the deluxe version of the skiff hull style. The final new entry for 1961 was the 21-foot Sportsman in the Cavalier line with a white-painted plywood hull and standard V-bunks under the forward deck. It was a very attractive craft with 8-1/2-foot beam and speeds to 37 miles per hour. The 1961 model year marked the final production year for a true wood runabout from Chris-Craft after 40 years of continuous runabout production. The utility boat, brought to life by the Depression, survived to become the sport boat of choice.

After considerable testing, Chris-Craft introduced one of its most adventurous sport craft, the 16-foot Ski-Jet in 1962. The hull was similar to its stock 16/17-foot mahogany Ski Boats with its own 185-horsepower V-8 engine. Instead of a conventional propeller shaft, strut, propeller, and rudder below the waterline, the boat had a steerable jet mounted to the transom. A multistage Buehler jet drive took in water through a grill flush with the bottom of the hull. Thrust was achieved by shooting a stream of water rearward at a rate of 3,000 gallons per minute at 4,000 rpm, with enough thrust to reach speeds of 43 miles per hour. The Ski-Jet was offered in 1962–1963 with only modest production of 46 units.

After an absence of three years, the popular Holiday model name returned in 1962 with three new sport designs in 18-, 20-, and 23-foot lengths. The new Holiday featured stems raked forward at a sharp angle, vinyl-covered decks, wrap-around windshields, a concave transom, and a long wide rub from the transom to amidships, where it met the golden

The luxurious 1958 21-foot Continental could reach 43 miles per hour with its 300-horsepower Cadillac engine, a speed that was equal to Chris-Craft's fastest runabout model for the first time. *Classic Boating magazine*

The husky new 24-foot Sportsman for 1958 offered a more traditional appearance. The new design provided a forward cabin area large enough for two berths and a marine head.

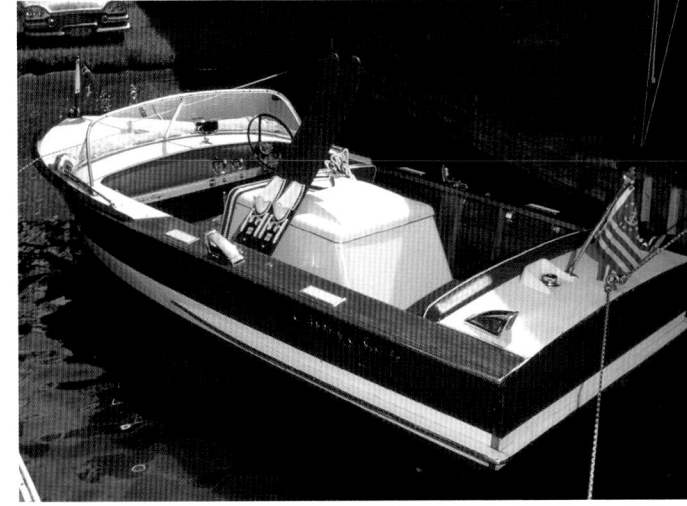

Clockwise from above:

The 1955–1959 18-foot Continental combined a simpler construction style to hold costs down with excellent speed of 40 miles per hour to become a favorite boat for dealers to keep in stock. *Classic Boating magazine*

Sporting tail fins, turquoise upholstery, and a wrap-around windshield, the 1960 21-foot Continental showed a great deal of influence from the styling of the booming auto industry. *Classic Boating magazine*

The 18-foot Holiday for 1962 was a complete sport boat featuring a prominent oversize lower rail that integrated into the transom, nicely mimicking 1960s auto styling. *Classic Boating magazine*

The 17-foot Ski Boat was well suited for water skiing, tubing, and a wide range of pulling sports, with its economical 185-horsepower V-8 and speeds to 41 miles per hour. *Classic Boating magazine*

The 17-foot 1964 Super Sport was a clean, no-nonsense craft with ample vinyl for reduced maintenance and superb performance with speeds to 44 miles per hour. *Classic Boating magazine*

The 20-foot 1963 Holiday gave new meaning to fender rail styling. Its low profile accentuates the tall engine box. This smart sport boat was capable of a sizzling 46 miles per hour! *Classic Boating magazine*

The 1964 18-foot Super Sport clearly shows the modern styling that kept these wood boats in tight competition with fiberglass styling right to the end of wood production. *Classic Boating magazine*

arrow in the CCC scroll design. The 18-footer was offered with the 185-horsepower V-8 for 40 miles per hour; the 20-foot model was powered by either the 185- or the 275-horsepower V-8 for speeds to 47 miles per hour; and the 23-footer could be ordered with the same engine options, with speeds to 41 miles per hour. The 23-footer also had the option of a stylish fiberglass top with gull-wing doors. The most intriguing feature of these hulls was their longitudinal speed stabilizers, for extra stability and control, that the catalog said were "needed to break through waves while going full speed."

A 19-foot plywood Cavalier sport boat called the Golden Arrow was one of seven new models to appear in the 1963 lineup. It was a very attractive, low-maintenance sport design constructed of high-quality 3/8-inch, five-ply marine plywood over solid mahogany frames. In addition to its stylish design, it was easy to operate and remarkably swift. With the standard 210-horsepower V-8, it was rated at 45 miles per

hour, which was well suited for tournament water-skiing. Its nearly seamless bottom made it practical to trail to favorite waterways without concern for time lost for "soaking up." It was a great achievement in plywood boats, with excellent performance and clean lines.

A smaller version of this craft with similar construction was the 16-foot Custom Ski Boat, powered with the 185-horsepower V-8 that provided a good 43 miles per hour with seating for six. The 17-foot Custom Ski Boat was a product of the Chris-Craft Division, with traditional Philippine mahogany planking and weighing nearly 500 pounds more than the Cavalier 16-foot Custom Ski Boat. With the same 185-horsepower V-8, the heavier 17-foot planked model was a bit slower, rated at 41 miles per hour. Both models made extensive use of vinyl on the decks and interior.

In 1963 the popular Sea Skiff line was given the Sportsman model name for all four open models from 18 to 27

The extreme styling of the 1965 18-foot Super Sport demonstrates the energy devoted to modernizing and appealing to buyers who might be attracted to fiberglass sport boats. *Classic Boating magazine*

The 17-foot Super Sport Ski Boat was an ideal performance craft for water skiers, with considerable vinyl to handle tough service. *Classic Boating magazine*

feet. These Open Sea Skiffs were part of a wonderful series for Chris-Craft. This was the last year for production of the Open model Sea Skiffs. They are very tough, sea kindly boats that were built to last a long time. The Sea Skiffs can still be found in large numbers and remain extremely popular with fishing guides and rough water boaters.

There were 10 sport utility models from six separate series offered in 1964. Both the Holiday and Continental model names appeared for the final time, and a new model, the Super Sport, was introduced. The Super Sports adopted sporty features from Detroit's musclecars of the era, including

bucket front seats, extensive use of vinyl, sport steering wheels, and gull-wing doors on tops, fins and exciting instrument panels. Chris-Craft pulled out all the stops to increase interest in sporty wood boats, to keep the inevitable end as far away as possible—even as the new owners were working to develop the company's first true fiberglass hull, a sailboat to be introduced in 1964.

The 18- and 20-foot Holidays remained unchanged from the 1962 versions. The 17-foot Super Sport is similar in every way to the 17-foot Custom Ski Boat, and the 21-foot Continental was reintroduced after an absence of a year. The

In 1968, the final year for wood sport boats, the 20-foot Grand Prix was the top of the line and the fastest Chris-Craft, at 45 miles per hour and selling for $7,725 with a 300-horsepower V-8. *Classic Boating magazine*

21-foot Super Sport was the former 21-foot Holiday model from 1962. The model names were being reassigned, but the boats were basically the same as they were previously. As we look back now on this period, there must have been some major concerns about the direction this industry was heading in the mid-1960s.

In 1965 the 17-foot Cavalier Custom Ski Boat had varnished plywood hull sides stained golden walnut. It was an attractive and a pleasant alternative to plywood hulls that are traditionally painted. This was the price leader in the utility line and the only 1965 model not called a Super Sport. The Super Sports had turquoise vinyl twin bucket seats forward and white vinyl decks. The 17-footer, capable of 44 miles per hour with its standard 210-horsepower V-8, was the most popular model in the shrinking sport utility craft fleet.

The 1960s models were well designed, ruggedly constructed, and excellent performers capable of high speed. The vinyl covering on the decks and interior portions of these boats should help them survive longer than their more vulnerable brightwork predecessors. They also had the advantage of being built at a time when purchasers were aware that wood construction was nearing the end and these might be among the last to be built. Good care was an important consideration for their original owners right from the start.

After three straight years without introducing any new models, and each year showing a steady decline in sales for wood sport utilities, the conclusion spoke for itself. The final year saw the introduction of another famous automobile model name, Grand Prix, as the wood boat division made another brave attempt to capture the interest of sport boaters who could identify with a new name. The wood era for Chris-Craft's small sport utilities would end with the 1968 models. Those fortunate enough to purchase these wonderful craft right to the end of production acquired excellent boats that were carefully engineered and constructed. Many original owners still have these boats, use them every season, and often state that they have no intention of selling them. This special sense of owner pride is one of the fascinating characteristics of classic wooden boat ownership.

CHAPTER 5

KIT BOATS AND CAVALIERS
Value-Packed Chris-Crafts

As the supply problems of the postwar period faded, Chris-Craft was poised to continue its domination of the pleasure-boat market. By 1950, Chris-Craft had left numerous competitors in the higher-end inboard runabout, utility, and cruiser markets behind—witness Gar Wood Boats' exit in 1947. But the Smiths recognized that among the millions of boats registered each year, many were entry-level outboards, hauled on car-tops or trailers by a family-oriented customer base. A young war veteran starting a family as part of the baby boom wasn't likely to have a few thousand bucks to buy a top-of-the-line Chris-Craft, but he was still going boating and needed a boat to do it.

Chris-Craft set out to reach entry-level boaters with plywood Kit Boats in the 1950s, such as this 1952 14-foot Deluxe Runabout. A 1950 5-1/2 horsepower Chris-Craft Challenger outboard motor powers this restored model.

When Chris-Craft published this Kit Boat brochure in 1957, the Plywood Boat Division had grown to include the sales of prebuilt kits as Cavalier models. With the success of the Cavalier line, Kit Boats would be discontinued the following year. Shown on the cover are the 12-foot Meteor outboard and the 19-foot Sports Express Cruiser.

By 1961 the Cavalier Division was well established, offering a value-line of plywood Sport Boats and Cruisers like this 25-foot Express Cruiser. In addition to the aging K engine, buyers could equip their Cavalier Express with the new Chris-Craft 283 V-8 for 33 miles per hour and a bargain price not much more than $5,000. Standard equipment included galley with two-burner stove and a toilet.

Thus began the Kit Boat Division of Chris-Craft, in which consumers could order a variety of small boats that would arrive in a box full of precut pieces for assembly at home.

One long-time suggestion has been that Owen Smith instigated the Kit Boats after watching so many wood scraps end up in the boiler—a story supported by the legendary thrift of the Smith operation. However, with few exceptions, Kit Boats used some mahogany and other hardwoods but were essentially plywood boats. While it's certainly possible that the company had plywood left over from building landing craft during the war, there probably weren't many plywood scraps left over from building planked mahogany boats in 1950.

More importantly, Chris-Craft was simultaneously developing its 5-1/2-horsepower Challenger and 10-horsepower Commander outboard motors. The 5-1/2-horsepower unit was introduced in 1949 and its big brother a year later. It's more likely that the Kit Boats were part of a plan to get more of the entry-level boat market than it could with its basic inboard utilities. According to Antique Outboard Motor Club member John Scheurer, George Smith (son of Bernard) built some small utility class, stock outboard racing boats to use as test beds for the two outboard engines. A stretched version of a 13-foot test boat became the 14-foot Kit Boat offered in late 1950.

Ultimately the outboard motors would be withdrawn from the market after a challenge from Kiekhaefer over patent infringement. But Chris-Craft's strategy seems clear; it planned to build and sell outboard motors, and started the Kit Boat Division to sell boats to hang the motors on. In fact, early Kit Boat catalogs featured pictures of completed boats motoring along thanks to Chris-Craft Challenger and Commander outboards on the transoms. Boats and motors both would have appealed to the growing market of entry-level boaters. The company sought out those new boaters, the do-it-yourself crowd, through the magazines that catered to them—*Popular Mechanics* for example. The kits were also marketed as projects appropriate for kids—fathers and sons—through ads in magazines like *Boys Life*.

Three models were offered in mid-1950, an 8-foot Pram, 14-foot Rowboat, and 14-foot Outboard Kit Boat. But it wasn't long before it expanded the lineup substantially, with models that traded on the popularity of the "real" Chris-Crafts. In 1951 it added a 12-foot Runabout Boat Kit—essentially a car-topper—to go with the 14-foot Runabout, and a Sailing Kit for the 8-foot Pram.

The lineup also included considerably larger boats that were designed to use inboard engines. An 18-foot Outboard Express Cruiser Boat Kit could be configured to use outboard or inboard power. It offered a 21-foot Sportsman Boat

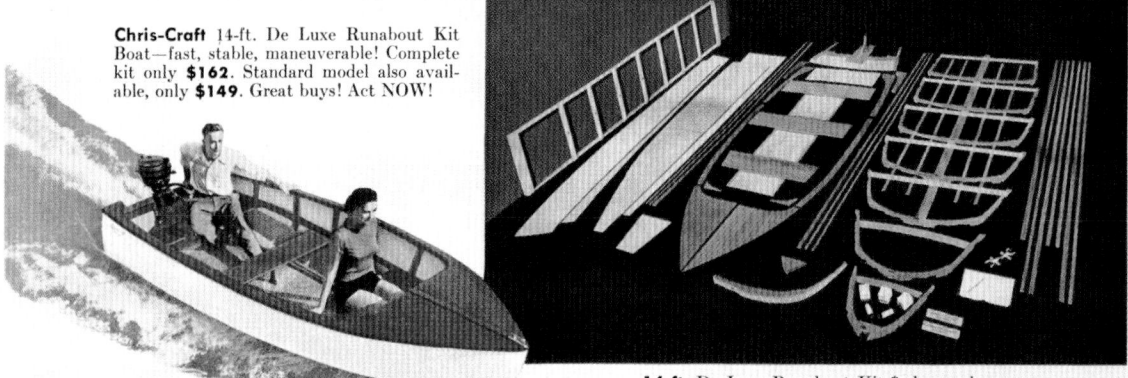

Chris-Craft 14-ft. De Luxe Runabout Kit Boat—fast, stable, maneuverable! Complete kit only $162. Standard model also available, only $149. Great buys! Act NOW!

14-ft. De Luxe Runabout Kit,* shown above.

Dandy 8-ft. Pram Kit Boat. Assemble it yourself for fishing and fun! Kit price only $42. Pram Sail Kit also available, $65.

Fast 12-ft. Runabout Kit Boat—easy to assemble! V-bottom. Sturdy but lightweight for car-top carrying. BIG value at $118.

Rugged 14-ft. Fishing Skiff Kit priced at $111, complete! You can't go wrong! Don't delay! Buy your Chris-Craft Boat Kit today.

$595 buys a kit for this new 18-ft. Outboard Express Cruiser! Tremendous savings! Outboard or inboard power. Truly a beauty!

Big 21-ft. Sportsman Kit Boat with roomy cockpit. A terrific kit buy at $614. Get complete data on all kits. Mail coupon today!

NOW! Own a CHRIS-CRAFT
for as little as $42 full price!

Assemble a new Chris-Craft Boat Kit! Have fun doing it! SAVE ½ or more! They're a cinch to put together! *Only the finest materials available are included in each Chris-Craft Kit: accurately precut Philippine Mahogany parts and Fir marine-plywood panels; brass fastenings; special screw driver; seam compound; decals. Illustrated instructions make assembly EASY with household tools! New Chris-Craft Boat Kits are the greatest values ever offered in the history of the boating industry! Thousands are assembling 'em! HURRY! Buy your Chris-Craft Boat Kit NOW! Mail coupon for FREE folder TODAY!

(Kit prices quoted f.o.b. factory, subject to change without notice.)

Beautiful 21-ft. Express Cruiser Kit Boat brings real cruising pleasure down to rock-bottom price! This kit sells for only $747. Act NOW!

Save thousands of dollars! Buy kit for this sleek 31-ft. Express Cruiser at $1995, *full price!* Mail coupon for FREE Kit Folder NOW!

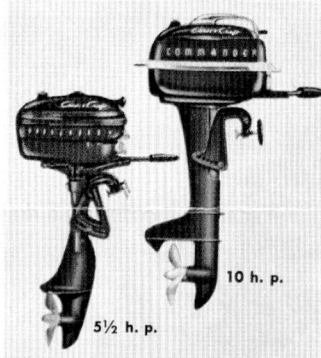

10 h. p.

5½ h. p.

THE CHOICE OF EXPERTS

Two great Chris-Craft Outboard Motors—5½ and 10 h.p.—the choice of experts! New dependability, all-around performance! For every outboard need, buy Chris-Craft!

Chris ★ Craft
CHRIS-CRAFT CORPORATION, ALGONAC, MICH.

MOTOR BOATS • MARINE ENGINES • OUTBOARD MOTORS • BOAT KITS
WORLD'S LARGEST BUILDERS OF MOTOR BOATS

CHRIS-CRAFT CORPORATION, Algonac, Mich.

Send me FREE folder on:

☐ Chris-Craft Boat Kits   ☐ Chris-Craft Outboard Motors

Name_____

Address_____

City_____ Zone_____ State_____

The Kit Boat Division was launched along with the introduction of Chris-Craft's outboard motors, the Challenger and Commander, both promoted in this early 1950s ad. The company advertised the Kits in a variety of magazines, such as *Popular Mechanics* and *Boys Life*, opening up direct mail as a new sales channel and getting kids hooked on Chris-Craft from early on. The 31-foot Express Cruiser shown was the largest of the Kit Boats and featured a double-planked mahogany bottom.

If you couldn't afford a real Chris-Craft Sportsman, there was always the Kit Boat version.

By adding a trunk deck, steering wheel, and throttle, the 10-foot Utility Racing Pram met American Power Boat specifications for outboard racing. Two of the Smith kids were active in the Algonac Racing Association, using the Challenger and Commander outboards on small hydroplanes.

Kit modeled after the extraordinarily popular carvel-hulled Sportsman Utilities in the standard Chris-Craft lineup, and a 21-foot Express Cruiser Boat Kit built on the same basic hull. Buyers purchased the 21-foot hull Kit, then could customize their boats with the Sportsman Windshield Kit, the Sportsman Pilot Seat Kit, the Express Cruiser Cabin Kit, and/or the Express Cruiser Flying Bridge Windshield Kit. The Sportsman

went for $614, the Express Cruiser for $747, plus engine. The kits included decals, with "Kit Boat" included underneath the Chris-Craft logo.

Top of the line in 1951, however, was the 31-foot Express Cruiser Boat Kit, which unlike the rest of the kits featured a double-planked bottom (1/2-inch mahogany planks over 1/4-inch plywood) to go with the 1/2-inch fir

By the mid-1950s, Kit Boats took on tempting model names like this 14-foot Comet. Styling cues on this 1957 Comet included a two-tone look that mimicked the standard Chris-Crafts and tail fins—a feature found on the Capri Runabout and 1958 Silver Arrow.

THE BIGGEST NEWS IN BOATING— *Flite-Speed*

14-FT. COMET

Handsome, Flite-Speed Comet, club-coupe styled and designed for hot performance with high-horsepower outboard motors. Fore and aft seats for 4-6 passengers. Long forward deck, and aft deck with hatch. Storage space for fuel tank and battery. Self-draining motor well. Takes outboards as big as 35 hp, speeds to 35 mph.

Length	13' 4"
Beam	62½"
Depth	29½"
Weight	345 lbs.

Copyright 1957 Chris-Craft Corporation

6

With outboard engines gaining power, Outboard Express Cruisers became popular among boaters looking for a bargain. Chris-Craft used the Kit Boats to compete, offering the Sports and Sports Express Cruisers in 1957.

marine-plywood sides. Builders were provided with the traditional canvas and bedding compound Chris-Craft liked to use between the bottom layers. While the deck was canvas over plywood, the covering boards and cabin front and sides were Philippine mahogany. The cabin could accommodate a dinette, galley, toilet and two berths. The shipping weight of the complete kit was 5,000 pounds, and it

sold for $1,995 (without the engine)—compared with around $10,000 for the 31-foot standard Chris-Craft Express Cruiser—power included.

In 1952 the kits came into their own, having sold well enough to become the Kit Boat Division of Chris-Craft. Alan and Silvia Smith, two of Bernard Smith's grandchildren, were active in the Algonac Boat Racing Association,

Well-kept Kit Boats survive today, such as White Lightning, a 1956 14-footer with the optional windshield kit and modern power.

7

The larger Kit Boats could also be equipped with inboard power. This 1957 22-foot Express Cruiser, once built, was ready for Chris-Craft's 95-horsepower K inline six engine, or single or twin outboards.

141

using the Challenger and Commander outboards with success in the B and M hydroplane classes. No surprise, then, that Chris-Craft offered a 10-foot Utility Racing Pram Kit. It was no hydro but, as the brochure made sure to point out, "with the addition of a trunk deck, steering wheel and throttle, the hull will meet Class JU, AU and BU specifications under the current rules of the American Power Boat Association."

Racing of a different type prompted the introduction in 1953 of a 12-foot Penguin Sailing Dinghy Boat Kit, which met the specifications of the Penguin Class Dinghy Association for competition. It featured a plywood rudder and centerboard, spruce mast and boom, and was designed to carry 72 square feet of sail. As with other kits, the shipping crate was designed to double as a building jig.

Also new was a 14-foot Duckboat Kit, a plywood version of the kind of craft Chris Smith began building more than a half-century earlier. The kit came with materials to create a "conventional double-ender" as well as a transom should you prefer to build it to take an outboard motor.

All in all, the impressive 1953 lineup included 20 models in 10 lengths ranging from the 8-foot Pram to the 31-foot Express Cruiser. The kits were promoted as being easy enough for a beginner to tackle, with "the difficult jobs" already taken care of at the factory—the Philippine mahogany frame was precut and notched for the chine, for example. As one insider put it, "If you cut a piece of wood, you had made a mistake." Kits included detailed instructions, solid brass fasteners and a special screwdriver, a can of seam compound, bedding compound and canvas, and waterproof glue. All the industrious boater really needed was a space in which to build the boat. And, of course, Chris-Craft could help you with power options as well.

With the Kit Boat Division established and a comprehensive advertising plan under way, Chris-Craft introduced a few nonboat kits as well. There was the knotty pine Chris-Craft Gun Cabinet to store your hunting weaponry when you weren't out in your duckboat, and the knotty pine Chris-Craft Treasure Chest that could double as a bench seat. Given that the Kit Boats were reaching the market not

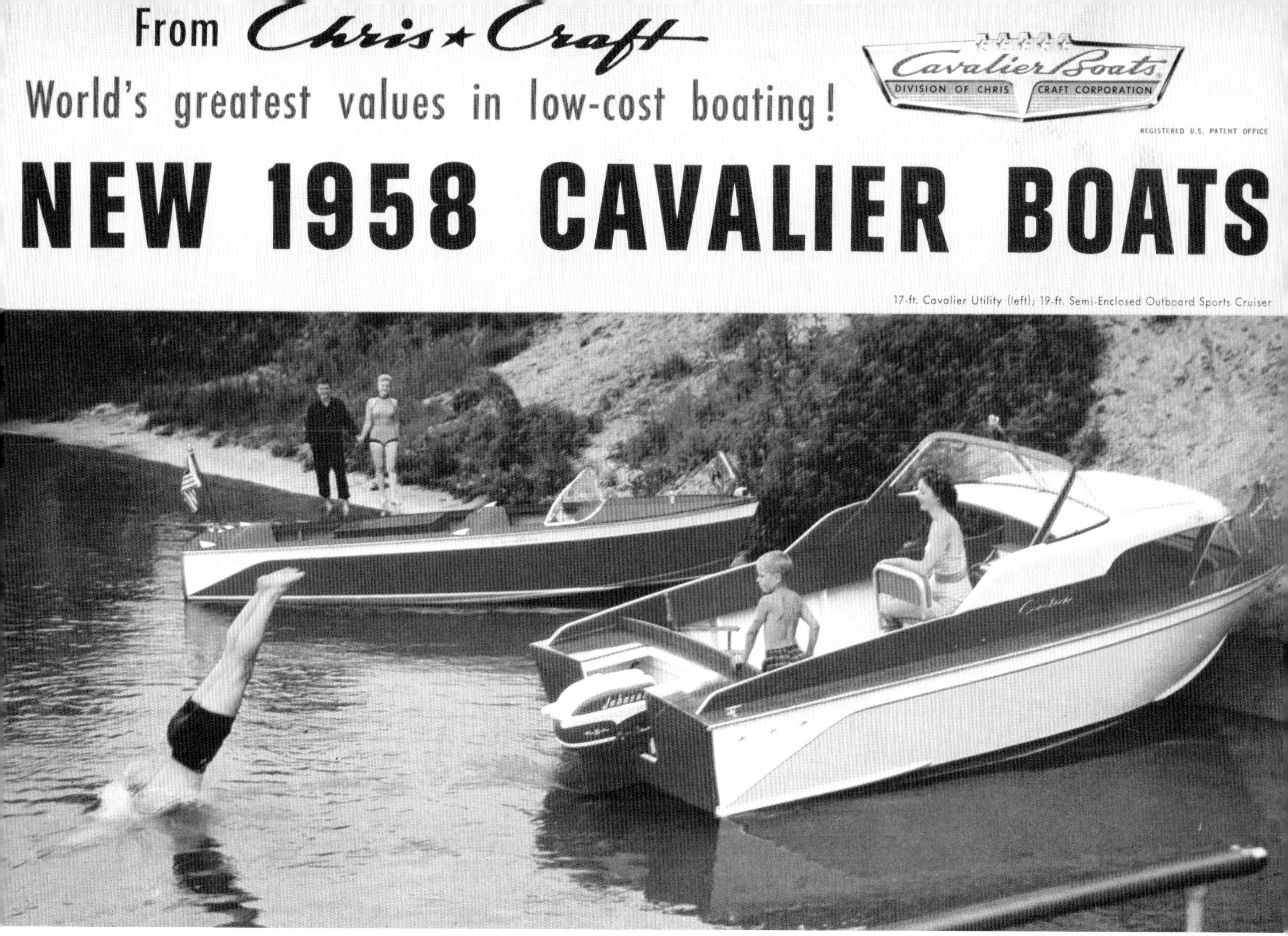

NEW 1958 CAVALIER BOATS

17-ft. Cavalier Utility (left); 19-ft. Semi-Enclosed Outboard Sports Cruiser

just through traditional marine channels but via hardware stores and lumberyards, it made sense to broaden the offerings to the DIY crowd.

In 1954 the Kit Boat Division launched a 14-foot Cruiser that could sleep four. Granted, the single-axle Land Cruiser wasn't meant to float, but rather was a mobile home kit for landlubbers with a wandering soul. Alas, the idea did not catch on, and it was discontinued after a year. No doubt the Land Cruiser was an outgrowth of the Chris-Craft Lifetime Boat Trailers, sold as handy add-ons to haul your Kit Boat to water once it was built. There were four trailer models, CC-300, CC-650, CC-1000, and CC-2200, the model numbers corresponding to the trailers' capacities.

While the conventional mahogany-planked Chris-Craft lineup was undergoing a shakeup in 1955 with the Cobra, Continental, and Capri replacing the Racing Runabout, Holiday, and Riviera, Kit Boat names were jazzed up in 1955. The fleet included the 12-foot, single-cockpit Meteor and 12-foot Utility-style Vagabond, the 14-foot dual cockpit Barracuda with walk-through center deck, the 14-foot Caribbean, Zephyr, and Dolphin, 15-foot Marlin, the 18-foot Fiesta, 20-foot Gay Paree outboard, and 21-foot Monterey Express. Some of these models, like the Gay Paree and a 16-foot Express Cruiser, were simultaneously offered as prebuilt boats, as promoted in *Motor Boating* in 1955. While the 31-foot Express Cruiser was dropped, key models such as

In 1958 the Kit Boats were on the way out, and the Cavaliers would take over the plywood boat line for Chris-Craft. Shown on the cover of this catalog are the 17-foot Cavalier Utility and 19-foot Semi-Enclosed Outboard Sports Cruiser.

143

powerboat industry. In 1955, one of the most remarkable years in Chris-Craft's long history, the Smiths launched the Sea Skiff Division to go head-to-head with Lyman and other long-time lapstrake skiff builders. In addition, it purchased Roamer, a builder of steel-hulled Cruisers located in Holland, Michigan, and also began the Plywood Division as an offshoot of the Kit Boats. Although Chris-Craft had aborted its own outboard motor development in 1953 (leaving behind designs for a 25-horsepower two-stroke and four-stroke V-4), Mercury, Johnson, and others had progressed to where outboards were lighter, more powerful, and plentiful enough to be inexpensive. Between the growth of small outboard runabouts, including an increasing number of fiberglass entries, and small, pocket cruisers, the Smiths once again saw a niche that needed filling.

Early Utilities and Express Cruisers, 1955–1958

Chris-Craft started with five plywood models in 1955, no doubt identifying which of the Kit Boats sold best. Utilities included a 15-foot Cavalier (60-horsepower inboard $1,595) and 17-foot Cavalier (131-horsepower inboard that gave it 40 miles per hour speed, $1,795), and the Gay Paree 20-footer, available configured for outboard or inboard

The 17-foot Cavalier Utility was a popular model in the late 1950s, in part because it could be powered by the sprightly KBL inboard engine, generating 131 horsepower, making it a 38-mile per hour boat for around $2,500. Chris-Craft sold 936 in Utility configuration through May 1959, plus another 104 units in Runabout trim. *Courtesy The Mariners' Museum*

National Automotive Fibers, Inc. purchased Chris-Craft in 1960, and continued to support the Cavaliers. With glassed plywood bottoms a common option, the Cavalier line bridged the gap between wood and fiberglass for Chris-Craft.

the Utilities and Express Cruisers created the foundation of the Plywood Boat Division.

Kit Boats would be revamped again in 1957, with a few new faces, such as the 14-foot Grayling and 15-foot Tarpon. The little 12-foot Meteor and 14-foot Comet grew tail fins, aping the Capris and Continentals of similar vintage in the standard Chris-Craft lineup. A minifleet of 19-footers, including a Sports Express Cruiser, Sports Runabout, and Sports Convertible, all beamy utility-style boats that could be built to carry an outboard or run with inboard power, mirrored the prebuilt Cavalier Express and Cavalier Semi-Enclosed 19-footers in the burgeoning, newly named Cavalier Division. Ditto the new 22-foot Express Cruiser, which was enjoying considerable popularity as a prebuilt Cavalier.

By 1958 it was clear that the Cavalier line was the future for Chris-Craft's plywood boats, and the company began selling the kits at bargain prices to get rid of inventory. That would continue into 1959, when the Cavalier line, as the Plywood Division would be called, came into its own.

Cavaliers

"The World's Largest Builder of Motor Boats" had every intention of staying the biggest, and took several steps in the mid-1950s to ensure its dominance of the recreational

power with speeds up to 25 miles per hour starting at $1,099. Cruisers included a little outboard 16-foot Express Two-Sleeper that started at $699, and a 21-foot Cabin Cruiser—inboard or twin-outboard—with room for a toilet and Cruiser amenities such as icebox, sink, and stove available as options.

The plywood boats were built primarily in the Mississippi River town of Caruthersville, Missouri, and in Salisbury, Maryland, the new home of the new Sea Skiff line. Although the Skiffs were round-bilge lapstrakes, the strakes were made of plywood, so housing the two divisions in one venue would have made sense. To keep prices down on the value-oriented Plywood Division boats, standard equipment was kept to a minimum—lights, bow and stern poles, and windshield. Options available for a price included instruments such as ammeter, oil pressure gauge, and tachometer, and auto bailer, dock lines, lifting rings, seat cushions, and even the shipping cradle.

The Cavalier models would expand to include a 20-footer in 1956, with advertising promoting "The Three Cavaliers," which were "Value-packed Chris-Craft plywood boats for 1956." Two of these three models would prove tremendously popular in the early Plywood Boat days. The

15-foot Cavalier Utility sold 1,096 units from early 1955 through mid-1959, with another 128 going out the door as Cavalier Runabouts. The 17-footer sold 936 in Utility configuration and 104 in Runabout trim during that same period. It was popular since it could handle the 131-horsepower six-cylinder inboard, making it a 38-mile-per-hour boat for $2,585 as a double cockpit forward Runabout. The larger V-20 Utility could also take the bigger engine, but was less successful, with 40 built over a one-year period.

Overall, these were impressive numbers, rivaling and even outperforming unit sales of traditionally planked boats. For example, Chris-Craft sold 1,532 carvel-hulled 17-foot Sportsman models during the same period, a boat that sold for $2,970 equipped with the 131-horsepower engine, or about $500 more than the plywood 17-footer. The 18-foot Continental, priced at $4,100 with the same engine, sold only 484 during more or less the same time frame. Clearly customers were responding vigorously to the new "value-line."

These early Utilities would lend their Cavalier model name to the Plywood Boat Division starting in 1957. After its disastrous attempt at marketing small fiberglass Runabouts by purchasing Lake 'n Sea in 1957, Chris-Craft would concentrate on positioning its Cavalier plywood boats as competition for upstart fiberglass boat companies. Cavaliers could be ordered with their plywood bottoms glassed over as

In 1961, Express Cruisers were a stalwart of the fleet. There were 21-, 23-, 25-, 30-foot models offered.

1962 *Chris-Craft* CAVALIER

EVERYTHING'S NEW IN THE VALUE FLEET— STYLING, PERFORMANCE, FEATURES, LUXURY!

As happened with Utilities in the 1930s as well as Sea Skiffs, the value-oriented Cavalier lineup had established its brand and began offering more luxury. The cover of the 1962 Cavalier catalog featured the new 26-foot Custom Four-Sleeper, precursor to the Futura Cruisers. A handrail surrounded the flush-deck cockpit, and the carpeted cabin featured a galley, convertible dinette, wardrobes, vee-berths, and a toilet. *Courtesy The Mariners' Museum*

an option, and they were considered good boats for the money in their time.

The plywood Cruiser lineup expanded as well in 1956 with the addition of a 22-foot Four-Sleeper Express Cruiser with Flying Bridge, which could also be configured for one of two inboards or with room for two outboards. The 22-foot Four Sleeper would sell 406 units through 1958, plus another 303 in Two-Sleeper configuration.

In 1957, when all the prebuilt plywood models took on the Cavalier brand name, the 21-foot Cabin Cruiser would lose favor (after selling nearly 300 units) to a newcomer, a 19-foot Cavalier Express, which sold for $3,350 when powered by the 95-horsepower K engine that gave it 30 miles per hour. It was also offered as the VS-19 Cavalier Semi-Enclosed starting a year later—combined sales for the 19-footers was

272 units through 1959. A revamped outboard 16-foot Cavalier Semi-Enclosed Sports Cruiser was introduced as well, selling for $1,025—plus $19 for the cradle and $10 to load the boat onto the cradle. Or, the same hull was available as a Sports Utility, though far fewer were sold this way. If your budget was lower still, the Cavalier models continued to be offered as Kit Boats as well in 1958.

Express Cruisers, 1959–1962

But the best was yet to come in bargain cruisers as the 1959 Cavalier lineup was revamped, dropping the 16-, 19-, and 22-footers to launch a whole new fleet. It was a time of transition at Chris-Craft—having moved world headquarters to Pompano Beach, Florida, two years earlier, the Smiths named Harry Coll president of Chris-Craft, the first non-family

member to head the company. Harsen Smith, as chairman of the board, was focusing on preparing the company to be sold, appearing on the cover of *Time* magazine that spring.

The Cavalier Division's new 1959 Express Cruisers came in three lengths, promising "luxury boating with complete family cruising accommodations at a sensational new low price" with the 23-foot Two-Sleeper, 25-foot Four-Sleeper, and 30-foot Six Sleeper. All three were available with the new 185-horsepower Chevy-based small-block V-8 engine marinized by Chris-Craft. Featuring the "New V-8 Power," the 23-footer claimed 35 miles per hour and sold for $4,380; the 25-footer, 33 miles per hour for $5,245; and the 30-footer, 26 miles per hour for $7,880. The 30-foot Express could also be equipped with twin V-8s, gaining another 10 miles per hour, for $9,695. Standard equipment on the Express Cruisers included a galley with stainless-steel sink and two-burner alcohol stove, vinyl-covered cushions in the berths, toilet, and even the instruments. Options included a companion seat, curtains, pilot seat, stern pole and ensign, and windshield wiper. The 30-footer was described as having "a long, sleek silhouette. A gracefully tapering style-line extends full length of the hull, terminating in a bold, stainless steel band—creating a look of motion."

The 23- and 25- footers would be offered into 1961, selling a combined 1,676 units. A 21-foot Express Cruiser Two-Sleeper model appeared in 1961 and 1962, selling a modest 140 units. The 30-foot Cavalier Express Cruiser sold 388 units from 1959 through 1961.

For customers interested in the growing Cavalier line but wanting a bit more luxury, the 26-foot Custom and 30-foot Custom Cruisers were offered starting in 1961. The 26-footer was a Four-Sleeper that found a ready market—880 were sold. These were the precursors to the Futura Cruisers that would sell well in various lengths through the 1960s.

Cavalier Sports Utility, 1959–1962

Also new to the 1959 Cavalier lineup was an 18-foot Sports Utility, which joined the 15- and 17-foot hulls as the three utility-style boats in the Cavalier fleet. Both the 17- and 18-footers could be purchased with the new 185-horsepower V-8, turning them into 40-mile per hour boats at the bargain prices of $2,770 and $2,885, respectively. Most of the 18-footers were sold as the Custom V-8 Sports Utility, which included a glassed bottom, instrumentation, seat cushions, and vinyl flooring as standard and sold for $3,025.

185-horsepower V-8, and roomy enough for a good-sized family. It had a two-sleeper cuddy with a ventilating hatch and paneled interior, and could be equipped with a folding top and an optional head. This was the vinyl era at Chris-Craft, and the Sportsman was no exception, sporting vinyl-covered forward deck, vinyl cockpit flooring, and two-tone vinyl seats. The 23-foot version sold 111 units for 1960, and the 21-footer sold 125 units over the following two years.

Custom Ski Boat and Golden Arrow, 1962–1968

Skiing was one of the various reasons that the enclosed-cockpit Runabout style fell out of favor. Chris-Craft competitors like Century and Correct Craft had established good reputations by offering performance-oriented ski boats, and Chris-Craft would respond. In 1959 it had introduced a 17-foot planked-mahogany Ski Boat—a version of the 17-foot planked Sportsman hull—that sold for $3,620, powered by the small-block V-8. In 1962–1963 it offered the 16-foot Ski Jet that used the 185-horsepower V-8 attached to a Buehler jet drive. And while the inboard Cavalier Utilities were no doubt being used for water skiing, it was time for the Cavalier Division to bring a Ski Boat model to market.

The 19-foot Cavalier Golden Arrows were offered in 1963–1964 as an offshoot of the popular Cavalier Ski Boats. The Golden Arrow featured bucket seats, vinyl decks, and floors with namesake gold-and-white color scheme, and speeds to 45 miles per hour when equipped with the new 327 V-8. Chris-Craft purchased Thompson in 1962, making it possible to offer a transdrive version of the Golden Arrow as well. *Courtesy The Mariners' Museum*

The Cavalier Division began offering its own lapstrake-style boats in 1964, such as this 24-footer, and called them Seastrakes. The hulls were the same as those in the Futura lineup, but featured lapstrake sides from the chine up, as well as interior paneling. *Courtesy The Mariners' Museum*

No doubt in 1960 when the new owners of Chris-Craft, National Automotive Fibers, Inc. (NAFI), compared the sales figures of the wide array of models offered by Chris-Craft, they saw sales trending toward utilities and value-boats and away from the traditional planked Runabout. The 19-foot Capri Runabout was offered with the new V-8, selling for more than $4,200 in 1961 while offering lower top speed than the 18-foot Cavalier Sports Utility. Consequently, it was no surprise that the Capri sold only 162 units in 1960–1961, compared with 709 units for the three years of the Cavalier. The Capri would be the last of the traditional Runabouts, helped out the door by the upstart plywood Cavaliers.

Cavalier Sportsman, 1960–1962

Chris-Craft had used the Sportsman name for higher-end utilities since before World War II, and the now-famous postwar U-22 Sportsman was one of the company's best sellers. The Kit Boat Division had sold a 21-foot hull as a Sportsman that also could be made as Express Cruiser, and Cavalier continued that strategy in 1960 with a 23-foot Sportsman based on the 23-foot Express Cruiser hull, following it in 1961 with a 21-foot Sportsman based on the 21-foot Express Cruiser.

Although they enjoyed only modest sales, the Sportsmen were considered good boats by more than one Cavalier dealer. They were fast enough for skiing at 35 miles per hour with the

Thus one of Cavalier's longer-running models, the 16-foot Custom Ski Boat, was born. It debuted in 1962, and stayed in the lineup through 1966, selling 565 units. It was one of the Cavalier models built and sold in Italy as well. Powered by the 185-horsepower V-8, the little boats could scoot right along. In 1966 an 18-foot Custom Ski Boat—a version of the 18-foot Utility and Custom Utility that sold so well in 1959–1962—was added to the fleet, taking the place of the 19-foot Golden Arrows that were built in 1963–1964. The 18-footers were similar in style, but could handle the 327-ci, 210-horsepower V-8, which gave them a top speed of 45 miles per hour. And in 1967–1968, the 16-footer and 18-footers were dropped in favor of one model sold as a 17-footer in modest quantities.

While the sales of the Ski Boats and Golden Arrows didn't set any records, they were quintessential Cavaliers, offering plenty of boat for the money. Moreover, they were no doubt in the lineup to hold off the encroachment of small fiberglass boats from other makers that were beginning to take over the small boat market in the mid-1960s. Chris-Craft's new owners had purchased Thompson in early 1962 and subsequently introduced the Corsair fiberglass Runabouts

and Express Cruisers, introduced a fiberglass sailboat and the fiberglass Commander in 1964, and were working on improving fiberglass technology, especially for Cruisers. They were, nevertheless, behind the curve. The Cavalier "value-line," especially the Ski Boats, would keep them in the game until they could catch up. The all-fiberglass deep-V hull Lancer Sport Boat was introduced in 1966, and once it was established in the market, the glass-over-plywood boats would be phased out.

The 19-foot Golden Arrow was introduced in 1963 as a larger version of the 16-foot Cavalier Ski Boat, named for its gold-and-white color scheme. Like the 18-foot Custom Ski Boat, it was rated at 45 miles per hour with the 210-horsepower 327-ci engine, making it a good ski boat, though only 170 were built over two years, not including those made in Italy, through 1964.

Custom Yacht

The 35-foot Custom Yacht took over the top of the Cavalier line in 1962, offering multiple cabins, 31-miles-per-hour speed from twin V-8s for just under $19,000. In comparison, that same year, Chris-Craft had reintroduced the Motor Yacht to the planked Cruiser line, a 60-footer that sold for nearly $150,000, and the popular Chris-Craft Constellation line of Cruisers included a 36-footer selling for around $23,000.

The 22-foot Dory and the 22-foot Cutlass (shown above) were related to the Seastrakes. With plywood bottoms and lapstrake sides, they were introduced in 1964. The Cutlass continued into 1968 with 355 units sold. *Courtesy The Mariners' Museum*

The 16-foot Cavalier Ski Boat debuted in 1962 and stayed in the lineup through 1966, when it was replaced by an 18-footer that could handle the 327-ci 210-horsepower engine. Still, this 1965 16-footer could reach 43 miles per hour powered by the 283 V-8, more than enough to handle family water skiing chores. *Courtesy The Mariners' Museum*

The 35-foot Custom Yacht proved to be a steady seller, with nearly 300 units sold in the first three years of production. It was boosted to 36 feet starting in 1965, and sales were slower—perhaps due to the introduction of the planked Crusader line that same year— averaging around 50 units per year through 1968.

Cavalier Dory and Cutlass, 1964–1966

These 22-foot fishing boats were like the Seastrakes that appeared in the Cavalier line-up in 1964 in that they featured lapstrake sides, using plywood strakes. The bottom was still plywood, with fiberglass overlay optional. Introduced in 1964, they were typically powered by the 185-horsepower V-8. They were open-hulled boats, with a stern seat over the

gas tank, helm seat covering the forward section of the motor box, and forward seat. A bow locker provided storage. The Dory stayed in the Cavalier lineup through 1966, selling 130 units, while the Cutlass enjoyed more success and survived into 1968, selling a total of 355 units.

Futuras and Seastrakes, 1963–1968

The Cavalier cruiser lineup was refined further for 1963 as changes instigated by the new owners were beginning to reach the boats on the sales floor. The Futura, as the plywood cruiser fleet would be called, was a familiar name to Chris-Craft cruiser enthusiasts—it was the model name of a planked 33-foot Express Cruiser in the conventional Chris-Craft lineup for nearly five years starting in 1956.

The first Futuras—in 26-, 28-, and 31-foot lengths, took the place of the Express Cruisers and Custom Cruisers. A 24-footer called the Fiesta—a name from the old Kit Boat Division—was also offered in 1963.

The Cavalier Futuras would continue to represent the value-line for Chris-Craft as the traditional Cruiser Division was making the move to fiberglass. The 38-foot Commander, an all-fiberglass Express Cruiser, was introduced in 1964. With competitors like Owens offering fiberglass cruisers as well, it was simply a matter of time before the "glass over ply" Cavaliers would get the axe.

Until then, however, the 1964 Cavalier Futura fleet featured hulls in five lengths, starting with the 24-foot Four-Sleeper that had been the Fiesta model previously. Other versions included the restyled 26-foot Custom, and a newly introduced 27-foot Four-Sleeper with beam of 10 feet, 2-1/2 inches that made for a 8x16-foot cabin. The 28- and 31-footers would last only two years in the lineup.

In general, styling was modernized, hardware upgraded, and the hull strengthened. For example, the cockpit floor was made thicker to keep noise levels down—a matter of ongoing concern with the plywood hulls. Planking on the sides and bottom was upgraded to a stronger fir inner ply. The engine ventilating system was improved as well. Chris-Craft promoted its plywood hulls as superior to competition in 1964 due to the use of transverse framing members and longitudinal battens that extended the full length of the bottom. The plywood sheets were fastened to the battens with rubber sealant and silicon bronze screws to support the hull evenly without relying on the frames alone. Hullsides continued to have "an exterior surface of phenolic resin overlay"—which was a generic way to say the bottoms were glassed over the plywood. No "Chris-Craft Grade Fiberglass" here.

Colors and trim were in tune with the 1960s, as described by Cavalier Division sales manager Bruce Donaldson in a memo to his dealers:

V-berths and dinette are covered with durable golden fleece vinyl and give a bright modern décor. A new deep pile moss green carpet adds an extra touch to the quality look of the new Cavaliers. Nomad gold vinyl on the icebox and storage door accent the white high pressure laminate working surfaces. Instrument panels have been redesigned with a rearrangement of gauges, switches, throttle and clutch controls. . . . Relocation of cockpit rails on the 26-footer provide better access to the cockpit. Aluminum anodized moldings have been added to the transom corners to give a welcome protection and good looks to this area. Silver blue cabin rounds and

cabin side vents are accented by a black sheer stripe. . . . Aircraft gull vents give a look of motion to the new styling. A Fiesta red boot top crowns a new "showroom" gold TBTO antifouling bottom paint.

Seastrakes used the same basic hulls but used lapstrakes for the sides from the chine up to the sheer line. According to long-time Chris-Craft dealer Charles Cross, the Seastrake versions were far stronger than the Futura models as a result of the lapstrake hulls. In addition, interior paneling was added, which may have made for an even quieter ride. Seastrakes were available in the 24-foot and 27-foot lengths in 1964, then were expanded to include a 25-footer, 30-footer, 33-footer, and 36-footer in 1965.

When Chris-Craft established a plant in Stratford, Ontario, (Canada) in 1965, the Futuras and Seastrakes were among the models built there through 1968, as was one of the more curious offerings in the Cavalier Division, the Crusader.

Crusader 1965–1968

When the all-fiberglass 38-foot Chris-Craft Commander was introduced at the New York Boat Show in 1964, the long-term fate of the wooden-hulled cruiser was sealed. But there was still a small market for wood-lovers, and just

Although Cavaliers were plywood boats, the planked-mahogany 28-, 30-, and 36-foot Crusaders were new for 1966 out of the Cavalier Division. This 1966 30-footer was advertised as offering live-aboard facilities for six, with vee-berths, convertible dinette and lounge, complete galley, and enclosed lavatory. It could be powered either by a twin 185-horsepower or a single 210-horsepower V-8.

The Fiberglass Revolution

The Smiths were astute business people and boatbuilders of unparalleled experience. But they were also, at heart, believers in the wooden boat. Yes, they acquired Roamer, a builder of steel-hulled Cruisers in 1955, but that was more a matter of serendipity—the company was located in Holland, Michigan, where Chris-Craft was already established. When it came to fiberglass, they were slow to advance.

Chris-Craft's first noticeable use of fiberglass was on the golden deck lid and dorsal fin of the Cobras in 1955. It was little more than a decorative application of the new material, and just over 100 units made it to the market. In 1957, in the midst of moving the headquarters from Algonac, Michigan, to Pompano Beach, Florida, Chris-Craft acquired Lake 'n Sea, a maker of small fiberglass outboard Runabouts. However, the technology Lake 'n Sea used had enough problems that Chris-Craft soon gave up and sold the company.

Much ado was made of the Silver Arrows in 1958, in which the hulls included fiberglass. But in fact, the bottoms were traditionally double planked, and fiberglass was only used from the chine up, helping form the decorative dual fins. In addition, the resin did not contain pigment, but was painted.

Chris-Craft did, however, recognize the growing market for small, inexpensive inboard and outboard Sport Boats that fiberglass was destined to fill. For the Smiths, the Cavalier division was created in part to fill that niche. And, unlike the Cobra or Silver Arrow, a Cavalier could be purchased with its plywood bottom overlaid with fiberglass, an option that was offered through the end of the Cavaliers in 1969.

Harsen Smith, Harry Coll, and others who led Chris-Craft in 1959 must have recognized the tremendous challenge that lay ahead. The company had millions invested in jigs, tools, and employee training, virtually all of it geared toward wooden boat construction. If fiberglass was the material of the future for pleasureboats, Chris-Craft would need to undergo a massive retooling effort requiring extensive capital, ongoing energy, and—more to the point—a fierce dedication to fiberglass. Faced with this vision of the future, the Smiths decided to sell the company, and did so in early 1960 to National Automotive Fibers, Inc. (NAFI).

Over the course of the next decade, the new owners—aided by long-time Chris-Craft employees such as President Harry Coll, Bill MacKerer, and others, would oversee the conversion of Chris-Craft from wooden boat-builder to fiberglass boatbuilder. In 1962 it acquired Thompson, a company that offered not only the transdrive inboard/outboard engine but had low-price 16- to 20-foot fiberglass Sport Boats on the market. The Thompsons would evolve into the fiberglass Corsair lineup.

NAFI also opened a new Research and Development Center in Pompano Beach in 1962, where the focus was on developing and improving fiberglass technology. It announced that same year plans to build a 35-foot all-fiberglass sailboat.

By 1969 the Cavalier line had done its duty in attempting to hold off the all-fiberglass competition. The introduction of the 19-foot Commander Super Sport, an all-fiberglass Sport Boat capable of 50 miles per hour, marked the end of the days of glassed-over plywood. It was also the first Runabout-style boat offered by Chris-Craft after the Capri was discontinued in 1961, and was available in late-1960s versions of green, blue, and red. *Courtesy The Mariners' Museum*

The Motor Sailer was on the market for the 1964 model year, and sales were headed up by Bruce Donaldson, whose primary responsibility was the Cavalier line. Also in 1964, and ultimately more significant, Chris-Craft introduced an all-fiberglass 38-foot Commander Cruiser, which had been developed at the Holland, Michigan, plant. By 1966 the fiberglass revolution had reached the lapstrake Sea Skiffs, and the Corsair division launched the first of the deep-V hull Lancer Sport Boats designed by Jim Wynne.

In early 1968, Herbert Siegel would cap his takeover of Chris-Craft Industries by being named president and chairman of the board. A year later, Harry Coll would retire, and the Cavalier line would come out with its last sales catalog.

Also in 1969, the fiberglass Commander line, which had grown year-by-year since 1964, would include a 19-foot Sport Boat, the Commander Super Sport. Described as a high-performance fiberglass speedster, the fiberglass Super Sport was powered by a 302-ci engine and boasted a top speed of 50 miles per hour. Unlike the Utility-style wood Super Sports in the Chris-Craft lineup earlier in the decade, this was a double-cockpit forward Runabout, offered in green, blue, and red with a contrasting kingplank "racing stripe," reminiscent of the 1950s. The revolution was complete. Nearly 50 years after the founding of Chris-Craft, the company was once again offering a fast Runabout, only this time in fiberglass.

when the traditional boat enthusiast thought it might be all over for planked mahogany hulls, Chris-Craft introduced the Crusader line, sold through the Cavalier Division. Crusaders were built with double-planked bottoms and board-and-batten sides, using solid mahogany, not plywood. There were offered in 28-, 30-, and 36-foot cruiser configurations.

Why would the plywood division introduce a planked boat as a new model? By the mid-1960s, the difference in retail price between a planked Constellation and plywood Yacht of similar lengths was less than $1,300, as plywood construction offered fewer cost-savings. Double-planked bottoms used plywood for the inner layer by this point, minimizing the difference between the plywood and traditionally planked hulls. And since the mid-1950s, Chris-Craft's various divisions were often their own competition, as dealers were offered franchises by the division.

The 28-foot Crusaders were powered by the 185-horsepower V-8 and sold for $7,790, or they could be ordered with twin-engine power for $9,535. The Crusader line did reasonably well, given that the boats were introduced in the midst of the industry's fiberglass revolution. Some 435 units were built among all three hull-lengths through 1968.

The plywood-based Cavaliers would be phased out after 1968, as the fiberglass revolution had finally prevailed at Chris-Craft. The Cavalier line had served its purpose not only entry-level boats, but as a bridge from the old to the new while Chris-Craft underwent radical changes—in ownership, corporate structure, and technology—from the late 1950s to the late 1960s. The Cavalier name would be reborn at Chris-Craft nearly 20 years later, during the Murray years, to promote a value-line of 17- and 19-foot Sport Boats, including an entry-level 17-foot outboard. In a way, it was a fitting return to its outboard roots.

The top of the Cavalier line was the Custom Yacht, offered initially in 1962 as a 35-footer, and gaining an extra foot in 1965. This model was from 1968, the last year of production. Featuring a double-cabin flybridge design, it could sleep six in three private cabins with two enclosed lavatories. Carpeting, draperies, paneling, and headlining were standard, and it was powered by twin 327-ci V-8 210-horsepower engines to speeds of 31 miles per hour. *Courtesy The Mariners' Museum*

153

CHAPTER 6

SEA SKIFFS

Lapping the Competition

A long the New Jersey shore, Hubert L. Johnson and Henry Luhrs understood the inherent strength and the sea-kindly qualities that lapstrake construction provided for their small "Jersey sea skiffs" in choppy seas. On the south shore of Lake Erie, the Lyman Boat Works in Sandusky, Ohio, mastered the building of lapstrake boats that would handle the choppy waves of this large but shallow Great Lake. Fishing guides on the St. Lawrence River also grasped this construction technique to provide sport-fishing parties with comfort and safety for daylong journeys in pursuit of great catches. Experienced boaters and sportsmen who placed more interest in secure, comfortable performance rather than slick design features often preferred boats of lapstrake construction.

By 1962 the image of the Chris-Craft Sea Skiffs had improved significantly and dragged the competition into greater respectability with models like this fast 20-foot Sportsman. *Classic Boating magazine*

But for the first 30-plus years of Chris-Craft, the Smiths had stayed with their traditional carvel-hull construction for all their pleasureboats, with double-planked bottoms and single-plank-and-batten sides. By using high-quality mahogany with a fine varnish finish, the company had defined for the public the traditional look of the runabout.

Following World War II, the increasing popularity of lapstrake hulls was initially viewed as a nostalgic throwback rather than a growing trend. However, as interest in boating spread, the soft riding, sea-kindly qualities of sea skiff–type hulls gained favor. In addition, the sea skiff tradition of all-painted exteriors meant less maintenance—a welcome bonus. And, like other utilities, the practicality of the sea skiff style was gaining a significant following among new and veteran boaters.

Century, one of Chris-Craft's traditional rivals for the runabout and utility market, moved quickly to prepare a lapstrake utility skiff for its 1952 production schedule. Century frequently demonstrated its ability to introduce a new design with remarkable speed. It realized that there was an opportunity to market a practical sea skiff type of craft and decided to more forward. Chris-Craft, claiming to be the world's largest builder of motorboats, continued to study the market, even as it began work on its own prototype round-bilge boats.

As early as 1949, reports at Chris-Craft's dealer meetings indicated that some of their merchants made strong appeals for the addition of a small lapstrake boat to offset sales that were being lost to aggressive Lyman dealers. The frequency of these reports fueled interest in Algonac regarding the popular appeal of lapstrake construction. The accomplishments of Lyman and the multitude of Jersey Shore lapstrake builders interested Bill MacKerer and Harsen Smith.

In spite of its enormous size, Chris-Craft always expanded very carefully. It worked internally with its New Model Planning Group to consider any new changes or additions to its well-organized production plans. The Group was made up of midlevel representatives from each department involved—sales, engineering, manufacturing, cost, and purchasing—who worked out the details, made the decisions, and moved the project forward for final approval and implementation. The introduction of new models always required significant supporting data to reduce the chances of failure to an absolute minimum.

Chris-Craft began to acquire a few lapstrake boats manufactured by well-regarded sea skiff builders for careful scrutiny and study. MacKerer and Smith put them through rigorous tests to validate the reports of their performance characteristics. In addition to water tests, they had each boat disassembled in order to examine construction methodology for possible ways to make improvements or to introduce changes where appropriate. It was a regular technique used by Chris-Craft to keep aware of the competition and maintain its position of leadership in the industry.

Its extensive tests provided positive information on performance at a wide range of speeds, with surprising roll resistance attributed to the overlapping planks and keel. Even the construction technology was smoother than anticipated. The

Planning Group concluded that the popularity of this style was well founded and appeared to be very promising. The group was also confident that it could introduce a superior version and, in time, become a dominant factor in this market. The Planning Group finalized details and costs, prepared working shop-drawings and advertising. Preparations were begun to open a new Sea Skiff Division to build round-bilge, lapstrake boats in a variety of popular lengths. Prototype Sea Skiffs were built in Algonac and then at the Cadillac factory for their initial testing in 1953. The 22-foot open Sea Skiff was the first production model actually delivered to dealers.

By early 1954 construction was under way in Salisbury, Maryland, for a new factory designed exclusively for the production of round-bilge, lapstrake boats to compete head-on

The 22-foot Open Sea Skiff was actually the first model offered to Chris-Craft dealers while other models were still in production. *Classic Boating magazine*

The 1957 26-foot Enclosed Fly Bridge Cruiser is a four-sleeper model using the same basic hull as the Open model Sea Skiffs. With twin 105-horsepower engines, it would make 27 miles per hour. *Courtesy The Mariners' Museum*

with the established builders of this style boat. It would be the start of the Chris-Craft Sea Skiff Division, under the leadership of W. S. Vance. Using technology gained from its experience building plywood landing craft during World War II, Chris-Craft planned to use a new adhesive sealant called Thiokol to bond the contact surfaces of the overlapping plywood strakes on the Sea Skiff hulls. It was a remarkable product that would create an extremely strong bond, remaining intact under stress. In the tradition of "Chris-Craft grade" mahogany, Chris-Craft went so far as to rename Thiokol *Chris-Craft Sea Skiff Sealer.*

The following announcement quietly appeared in *Motor Boating* magazine:

A new Sea Skiff Division of the Chris-Craft Corporation has been formed to produce a complete line of round-bilge, lapstrake boats. The first

model, a 22-footer, is already available in dealer showrooms in many parts of the country. Features include a big open cockpit, a private compartment forward and a choice of either 60- or 95-horsepower engines. A special synthetic-rubber planking compound is applied to the area of the planks that are to overlap. Planking is drawn up tight with copper clout nails and brass screws.

A subsequent advertising blitz then helped Chris-Craft hit the market at full stride for the 1954 season. The inaugural advertisement appeared in the January 1954 Boat Show Issue of *Motor Boating*. The heading read, *It's New! It's Fast! It's Versatile!* Below the bold heading a full color photograph of the first 22-foot open Sea Skiff was shown running at full speed with the words, "with rugged round-bilge, lapstrake design." The ad continued:

Presenting the big, brawny, all-new 22-foot Sea Skiff – built by Chris-Craft – the finest round-bilge, lapstrake boat in the world! This great, new Chris-Craft has everything you desire in a clinker-built boat: attractively rugged appearance; power to carry big loads at speed; exceptional maneuverability, seaworthiness and soft riding qualities at *all* speeds, even in rough water; and an unusual degree of comfort and convenience in a husky boat built for hard use, year after year after year.

The 22-foot Sea Skiff was priced attractively at $2,990. However, nearly every usual standard item was listed as an extra to keep the advertised price as low as possible. Such items as seat cushions, a fire extinguisher, and even the windshield were listed as optional accessories. The planking on this skiff was 3/8-inch, 5-ply marine-grade fir plywood, with decking of marine-grade mahogany plywood; the transom was Philippine mahogany, the frames white oak and Philippine mahogany, and the stringers Philippine mahogany.

Shortly after this announcement appeared, Century's new lapstrake model, the 19-foot Viking, won top honors in the Second Annual Around Miami Beach Marathon Race, beating 71 entrants in high and choppy seas. It was a significant accomplishment and served notice that Chris-Craft had a bit of catching up to do as it entered this new market. By midseason, Chris-Craft's Sea Skiff orders eclipsed its production capacity at the huge Salisbury, Maryland, factory. It was immediate proof that its decision to build Sea Skiffs was on the mark. It was also a signal to the competition that Chris-Craft's would become a formidable lapstrake boatbuilder.

The 30-foot Semi-Enclosed Sea Skiff Cruiser was big and rugged with a huge open aft cockpit that would make 30 miles per hour with optional twin 130-horsepower engines. *Courtesy The Mariners' Museum*

The 1957 40-foot Semi-Enclosed Cruiser was capable of offshore fishing assignments and 30-mile-per-hour speeds with twin 200-horsepower engines. The raised deck provided a roomy cabin area. *Courtesy The Mariners' Museum*

In the decade that followed the hull design and styling features of lapstrake craft from Chris-Craft and its competition would advance dramatically. Chris-Craft made regular design improvements every model year, as would Lyman and Century, to the delight of new buyers. They were moving away from the traditional workboat appearance and were creating their own new style with massive windshields and widely flared hulls. The sea skiff style has aged gracefully and their strong, painted, plywood hulls seem to resist rot stubbornly. The sea skiff hull shape provides a smooth, well-controlled ride in waterways that are often plagued choppy

The forward stateroom in the 40-foot Sea Skiff shows the unfinished style of the early model Cruisers. As Chris-Craft became a force in the lapstrake skiff market, the standards quickly elevated for Sea Skiffs. *Courtesy The Mariners' Museum*

An interior shot of the dinette area in a 1957 40-foot Sea Skiff Cruiser. Chris-Craft initially introduced the typical Spartan interior style before offering some luxury inside. *Courtesy The Mariners' Museum*

This close-up view of a 1958 26-foot Open Sea Skiff shows the large, attractive windshield and side wings that helped provide needed headroom under the folding navy top.

conditions created by heavy boat traffic. It is not uncommon to observe 50-year old Chris-Craft, Lyman, or Jersey sea skiffs still performing their designed activities for fishing guides or family touring, and then showing up at a local Classic Boat Show. The lapstrake sea skiff types may turn out to be the most durable wood-constructed service craft ever offered.

When Chris-Craft opened the Sea Skiff Division in 1954, its goal was to appeal to a wide range of prospects that were considering midsize, round-bilge, lapstrake open models. Its first production model was the popular length, 22-foot Open Skiff. This was followed by an 18-footer aimed directly at the Lyman Islander and the Century Viking models. Buffalo-based Jafco Marine also began producing a similar 18-foot lapstrake utility that was heavily promoted and attracting a sizable following.

Chris-Craft followed the 18- and 22-foot models with a big 26-foot open model and two semi enclosed 30- and 35-foot cruisers that were targeted at the market occupied by East Coast skiff builders such as Zobel, Hubert Johnson, and

Luhrs. In 1954, Lyman's largest inboard model was its modest 18-foot *Islander*. By August 1954, the complete Chris-Craft Sea Skiff line was illustrated in full color on the fourth cover of *Motor Boating* magazine.

A year after the launch of the new line, the January 1955 Show Edition of *MotorBoating* ran this press release:

> The rise in popularity of Chris Craft's round-bilge lapstrake Sea Skiff line has seen it grow from a single 22-footer, just a year ago, to an entire fleet including low-cost open sea skiffs and husky, twin-screw, full-fledged cruisers.

From a compact 18-foot Sea Skiff to a big 35-foot semi-enclosed cruiser that sleeps four, all have round-bilge hulls that provide smooth, soft-cushioned ride and embody a new technique in lapstrake construction. Chris-Craft uses a special synthetic rubber sealer that is applied to the planks and joints, in a glutinous state. Once the sealer is applied, the planks of marine-grade fir plywood are drawn tight and secured with brass screws into the frames, and rivets or copper clout nails in between. The compound penetrates into the pores of the wood, and as it cures, sets up a long-lasting, nonhardening bond.

In the very next column in the same magazine appeared the announcement of Lyman's new boats for 1955 in which it quickly made the point that it had been committed to lapstrake construction since 1875 and were "specialists in clinker construction." Sensitive to Chris-Craft's intrusion into their domain, Lyman announced a faster version of its popular 18-foot Islander with speeds to 33 miles per hour. It also answered the competition by making a few slight changes to its standard Islander model and calling it a runabout model. It also introduced a 20-foot runabout model with 7-foot, 4-inch beam and a Gray Marine 13-horsepower engine, providing speeds to 35 miles per hour. The marketplace for lapstrake boats was heating up, and the likely customers benefited from the increased competition.

At the 1955 National Motor Boat Show, Chris-Craft provided visiting prospects with a creative handout entitled, "A factual report on lapstrake boats." The report clearly made a strong case for the superiority of their sea skiffs over those of all its rivals. This powerful handout made it clear to all traditional skiff builders what they should expect from Chris-Craft as it sought to dominate this special boating niche. For the next 15 years, marketing skiffs would be a whole new ball game.

Chris-Craft's "factual report" emphasized the superiority of Thiokol, a.k.a. the trademarked Sea Skiff Sealer, and described the construction process:

Seams and joints of Sea Skiffs are reinforced with Chris-Craft's synthetic-rubber-based Sea Skiff Sealer. It is both a tenacious adhesive and watertight sealer. It makes Chris-Craft Sea Skiffs far stronger than ordinary lapstrake boats, provides them with a new kind of long-lasting water tightness, and it adds strength. Tests showed that a pull of 32 pounds per square inch separated the seams in ordinary lapstrake hull construction—clout nails with putty or compound filler. A pull of 130 to 150 pounds per square inch (more than four times the force) was required to tear apart Chris-Craft strakes fastened with copper clout nails and Sea Skiff Sealer. Even then, the seams held but the wood around the seams shredded!

Sea Skiff Sealer is elastic. A block of wood, bonded to another block with 1/16-inch thickness of Sea Skiff Sealer, can, with considerable force, be moved transversely about 1/4 inch across the bonded surface of the second block without losing adhesion. When pressure is released, the two blocks return to their original relative position. This quality allows the strakes to "work" without affecting the bonding seal. A Sea Skiff using this special sealer *without* copper-clout-nail fastenings was subjected to severe rough-water tests at high speeds. After months of testing, the hull remained completely intact and watertight.

This sealer is highly resistant to the effects of water, weathering, fuel and oil. A test patch, exposed to sun and weather continuously for over eight years, showed no tendency toward brittleness or cracking.

"The result is that Chris-Craft Sea Skiffs are far more durable, far more watertight than other boats of this type. The sealer is used in all seams and joints from keel to seat risers in 18-, 22-, and 26-foot models and from keel to sheer in the 30- and 35-foot models.

The whole tone of the report was to convince interested buyers that the Chris-Craft Sea Skiff was superior to the product that other veteran builders had been producing for years. They pointed out every feature that was better in the

The 23-foot 1962 Sportsman Sea Skiff provided a roomy cuddy cabin forward with two berths and plenty of good storage room for all-day fishing trips. *Classic Boating magazine*

In 1963 the 18-foot Sea Skiff was replaced with this husky 19-footer that was capable of 37 miles per hour, which could provide enough speed to satisfy serious water skiers. *Classic Boating magazine*

new Chris-Craft versions including dependable worm-and-pinion, rod-to-rudder steering; the well-ventilated bilge; the fuel tank mounted below aft deck and vented overboard; the importance of fuel shut-off valves at tank and carburetor; a skeg and bronze shoe to protect the propeller; and water-cooled copper exhaust pipe. Chris-Craft quality was evident throughout the Sea Skiff line. The external design features, however, were purposely similar to the traditional lapstrake utilities and small cruisers of the veteran builders.

By 1957, Century Boat Company had expanded its lapstrake utility-skiff line to four models. There was the Nordic 19, The Viking 19, the Raven 22, and the Nomad 16, which was primarily an outboard model. Lyman also expanded its fleet of inboards to include a 23-foot model starting at $3,595 to complement its $2,640 18-foot runabout model, prices that were competitive with Chris-Craft. The lapstrake market had become a marketing battleground.

Looking to build on its initial success, Chris-Craft bolstered the lineup in 1957, adding a new model in the popular

22-foot line-up, the Ranger, which featured greater beam, more freeboard, and deluxe features such as interior carpeting, varnished mahogany paneling in the cabin, and cabin headliners. as standard equipment. With greater dimensions all around, the Ranger offered V-berths under its broad fore deck. The V-berths became a very popular feature providing a welcome accommodation for owners wishing to stay aboard overnight or take a quick nap in comfort.

Equally big news for the Sea Skiff fleet was the addition of an attractive 40-foot semi-enclosed cruiser. With the installation of the optional fishing bridge, this model was ready for some serious sport fishing adventures.

As Chris-Craft established a leading position among the builders of lapstrake round-bilge boats, it also began to include the unique features that traditionally set its boats apart from the competition. The Sea Skiffs were offered in six attractive hull colors at no extra cost. Cabin interiors were trimmed with varnished mahogany to provide a less Spartan appearance than commonly found on craft of the sea skiff type.

Chris-Craft continued a relentless advertising program, pointing out the special features of its Sea Skiff line. Each ad would present facts and details that appealed to the more practical buyer, who would be inclined to consider this type of craft. In July 1958, the heading for their double-page advertisement in *Motor Boating* read, "WHY *YOU* SHOULD BUY A NEW CHRIS-CRAFT SEA SKIFF NOW." The copy in the ad made it clear that sales of 1958 Sea Skiffs were the most impressive in their short Sea Skiff history and the reasons were listed for readers to peruse along with testimonials from current owners. Fifteen models were listed along with their prices and a subtle warning that prices might never be this low again.

By 1959 it was becoming clear that Chris-Craft's success with the Sea Skiff line was a major influence on the entire lapstrake skiff segment of the boating industry. Lyman decided to rework its 23-footer so it, too, could offer V-berths, calling its version the "sleeper" model. But it still only offered its inboard models in 19- and 23-foot lengths. Other builders were catching on to Chris-Craft's success and their lapstrake versions began to take on some of the features of Chris-Craft's styling with a larger more attractive windshield treatment, increased freeboard, greater hull flare, attractive sheer lines and attractively paneled interiors.

The Owens Yacht Company of Baltimore, family-operated boatbuilders who competed heavily with Chris-Craft in the cruiser segment, finally jumped into the fray with three lapstrake models in mid-1959. In a clear attempt to cash in on the enthusiasm for this style, an ad for Owens sea skiffs appeared in late 1959 that claimed that Owens was "laps ahead of any other lapstrake in her class!" Its ad claimed, "The new Owens sea skiff design is as different from old-style round-bilge boats as a liner is from a barge!" Its claim was based on a special feature of its new design. Owens used a smooth bottom and a hard chine that it said provided less friction, less roll, and better handling in rough seas. The result is "performance capability no traditional lapstrake boat can match." The three models Owens introduced in 1959 to earn its share of this popular market were the 21-foot Semi-Enclosed Sportsman for $3,845, the 25-foot Sea Skiff Express for $5,195, and the 27-foot Sea Skiff Express for $6,747.

By 1960, Owens was part of the Brunswick Corporation and established its own Sea Skiff Division. A 35-foot Sport Fisherman was added to its growing seven-model lapstrake fleet. As buyers' enthusiasm for lapstrakes continued to build, other boat builders, such as Wheeler Yacht Company and Richardson Boat Company, announced the production of sea skiff–type craft.

Chris-Craft was on a roll, as well as in the midst of being sold to NAFI. It kicked off the 1960 season with a spectacular

The 1964 24-foot Ranger two-sleeper model Sea Skiff was a superb-looking craft with all the traditional sea worthiness required of a working boat. *Classic Boating magazine*

trifold, five-page ad at the front of *Motor Boating's* January 1960 Boat Show issue. One of the most striking, full-color advertisements in the annals of boating, it featured not only a two-page spread of the 66-foot Constellation, but six Sea Skiff models among 17 new boats overall.

In 1960 the 22-foot Open Skiff was replaced with a new 23-foot hull that shared dimensions and structure with the 23-foot Ranger. The Ranger was the deluxe model while the 23-foot Open Sea Skiff was the basic version of the same hull. The 27-foot Open Sea Skiff replaced the 26-footer with a totally new hull that provided greater beam, significantly more freeboard fore and aft, a smartly raked stem, and concave hull flair. Modest changes in the other sea skiff hulls were also made as the models were becoming far more attractive in the tradition that made Chris-Craft so popular with consumers. In 1954 it entered this market carefully with designs that were very similar to the styling used by the established builders of sea skiffs. Now it was ready to introduce more features that reflected the Chris-Craft styling touches that had been its strength for four decades.

In response to the numerous boatbuilders entering the sea skiff market, Chris-Craft declares that its approach was "the one correct total skiff hull design! Round bilge with permanently sealed, lapped planks on sides *and* bottom not only doubles the hull strength, but cushions the hull against wave *pound* and permits smooth banking on turns without side slip. Lateral *air cushioning* action minimizes pitch and roll. Result: More speed, softer, drier ride, greater seaworthiness in all kinds of water conditions!"

In 1961 the Sea Skiff Division introduced the innovative 42-foot Custom Cruiser, featuring a totally new concept in sea skiff styling. The flybridge windshield and the forward cabin windscreen had a surprising reverse rake. The inward slope of the windshields was parallel to the angle of the stem, a radical styling departure that caught everyone off guard. It was, perhaps, a show of great confidence and a statement to the industry that Chris-Craft was becoming the leader in the sea skiff field and in a position to experiment with bold, new design concepts.

The 23-foot Sea Skiff provides excellent visibility for the helmsman with its level ride and nicely positioned front seat and excellent windshield height.
Classic Boating magazine

The Sea Skiff Division felt that it was a time to verify its leadership by offering finer interior treatments to those willing to pay a bit more. The only exterior difference between the Hardtop and Custom midsize 30-, 32-, and 36-foot cruisers was the treatment of the trunk cabin. The front of the trunk cabin was significantly improved from the original pair of port lights to full glass, which provided an abundance of natural light as well as excellent forward visibility. On the interior, however, the Custom sported full carpeting, drapes, and all natural mahogany-finished interior, and it looked much more like the traditional interiors of the Chris-Craft cruisers. Promotional material favored the Custom versions, which were "for boating families who prefer luxury along with seaworthiness," while "standard models are still available." As for performance, the 36-foot Sea Skiff's twin 275-horsepower engines could push her to 36 miles per hour.

Chris-Craft kept the pressure on the competition when it presented its 1962 Sea Skiff models, introducing the Corinthian line in the 30-, 32-, and 37-foot lengths. This new line would be the successor to the Custom line of the previous season. The Corinthians featured natural walnut paneling throughout the cabin interior and restyled treatment of cabin windows. The cockpit railings, cabin roofs, and hardtops were also restyled, moving closer to the well-established Chris-Craft look.

The transition from the conservative Jersey sea skiff utility cruiser in 1954 to the upscale Chris-Craft version was virtually complete. In less than eight years, Chris-Craft had taken a very traditional, sea-kindly design and fashioned into it into an attractive, popular craft without losing any of its outstanding performance features. It was an accomplishment without equal in an industry in which change can be sternly rejected. Looking back on this period, it is surprising that well-established builders, like the Lyman Boat Company, did not move faster to offer a wider range of models. Lyman was an excellent builder and the freshwater leader in lapstrake construction long before Chris-Craft, Century, Thompson, Cruisers Incorporated, and so many others entered the lapstrake niche. Lyman created the market, built excellent boats, and then seemed to sit back for too many years while other boat builders capitalized on its specialty.

In 1962, Century expanded its lapstrake line with the new 26-foot Raven with single or twin engines. While maintaining its established construction and design style, Century added features such as a hardtop and bow rail options. Surprisingly, Lyman's inboard lapstrake fleet was still lagging behind its competition, offering only 20- and 24-foot models, while its 18-footer was available only as an inboard-outboard type. However, the 20-footer did feature the relatively new and innovative inboard-outboard engine. In 1963, Lyman finally expanded its line, adding the 28-foot, twin-engine Islander Day Cruiser with galley, dinette, and sleeping accommodations for four. It was an attractive sport boat that would turn heads at 35 miles per hour.

Buyers eagerly anticipated Chris-Craft's Sea Skiff styling changes each year, as the new models appeared in the fall issues of boating magazines. In September 1963, for example, the new Sea Skiff Corinthian began to appear showing new features and increasing the overall length on several models. The new 38-foot Sea Hawk was its largest model, with a sleek hull and a smartly styled cabin profile. The deckhouse doors folded back to create a large open area from the helm to the transom. The Sea Hawk and the Corinthian became the standard of design excellence for buyers who wanted the solid performance of a Sea Skiff hull with attractive design features and luxury appointments. Among the important standard features of the 38-foot Sea Hawk were a full-size General Electric refrigerator, electric three-burner stove with oven, dockside wiring, hot and cold water system, shower, electric toilet, walnut finish paneling, plus bow and side rails. Power choices included 275-horsepower V-8s or diesel engines. As the Sport Fisherman model, the boat included dual controls, icebox for bait, cutting board, and separate cockpit sink. It was a well-thought-out design that made a hit with serious sportsmen.

The rest of the 1963 Sea Skiff line remained constant, except for the addition of 1 foot to the overall length to the 31- and 34-foot Corinthian and the addition of a Ranger version of the 21-foot Sportsman model.

The popularity of lapstrake hulls continued into 1965 as Owens, Century, Lyman, Trojan, Pembroke, and many others continued their commitment to this construction style, even as fiberglass boats gained market share. At Chris-Craft, other than making the 21-foot Sportsman 1 foot longer, the Sea Skiff fleet continued with the same models as 1964. Lyman's 28-footer was selling well, and it prepared an open utility version called the Sportsman, a special name cherished by Chris-Craft since it first used it in 1936. (Before the end of the decade, Lyman would also use Sea Hawk, another Chris-Craft model name.) The Lyman Sportsman had two berths and a marine head under the fore deck, plus a galley

Thompson Boats: Outboard Lapstrakes

Behind the scenes, Chris-Craft was preparing a plan to acquire the Thompson Boat Company of Cortland, New York. This acquisition could provide a convenient way for Chris-Craft to increase its presence in the outboard boat market after closing the Kit Boat Division. It might also provide a prudent way to expand its highly successful lapstrake line to smaller craft with a quality builder that enjoyed an excellent reputation for good design and performance. It could instantly provide Chris-Craft with a modern, quality boat factory and a skilled labor force. But most of all, Thompson had an experienced technical staff that was making excellent progress in the development of rigid fiberglass hulls and the successful inclusion of contemporary outdrive propulsion.

In January 1962, Chris-Craft completed the purchase of the Thompson Boat Company. Thompson would operate as a wholly owned subsidiary of Chris-Craft under the name Thompson by Chris-Craft. The new owners expanded Thompson's fiberglass program, including a new facility designed especially for fiberglass construction.

By acquiring this well-respected boatbuilding firm, Chris-Craft was able to offer a full line of proven lapstrake outboard models from 16 to 20 feet to its dealers immediately. With this new facility Chris-Craft could quickly enter the substantial outboard boat market with a quality product. With only slight styling changes, the attractive Thompson lapstrake boats were a perfect extension of Chris-Craft's Sea Skiff line. The new factory in Cortland would also provide Chris-Craft with an excellent facility to build its new Corsair fleet of fiberglass hulls. In the 1963 Boat Show press release, Chris-Craft called the Cortland fiberglass operation the Corsair Division, while the wooden lapstrake models became the Thompson subsidiary of Chris-Craft. Two of the Thompson brothers, Bob and Ted, remained with Thompson in charge of these two operations.

Thompson promoted its new Sea-V hull design that provided a deeper entry forward, resulting in a more comfortable ride as well as a more attractive hull shape. All the Thompson hulls for 1964 were painted charcoal gray, providing an engaging contrast with white vinyl decks and flared aluminum windshields. However, in 1964 another era ended, as Thompson ended its wood hull production. In 1965 its entire production at the Cortland factory would be fiberglass hulls under the *Corsair* model name. By 1970 the Corsair Division became part of the Sport Boat Division.

The 38-foot Sea Hawk, introduced in 1963, provided all the rugged characteristics of a lapstrake hull in a Cruiser that was superbly styled.

By 1966, Chris-Craft was finally starting to catch up in the fiberglass revolution, and suddenly there was a new look to its models. The 18- and 20-foot Sea Skiff Sportsman had fiberglass hulls. The 18-footer had 150 horsepower stern drive and the 20-footer had a 210-horsepower inboard. The balance of the sea skiff line still used wood construction, but time was running out for wood as the material of choice among major boatbuilders.

However, in another surprise move, Chris-Craft expanded its wooden hull skiff offerings at the very time it was also introducing fiberglass at both ends of its lines. Chris-Craft officially introduced a new line called the Corinthian carvel skiffs at the 1966 National Motor Boat Show. The Corinthian name, previously used for the lapstrake Sea Skiff cruisers, belonged to a new series of smooth-sided, solid-planked Philippine mahogany cruisers called carvel skiffs, rather than lapstrake plywood-planked sea skiffs. The 32-, 35-, and 38-foot Corinthian carvel skiff cruisers had overlapping stabilizing strakes on the bottoms, and the 43-footer had a double-planked bottom. The bottoms were flattened out aft to reduce roll. The hulls had a full-length quarter foil just above the boot top to knock down spray and keep passengers dry in heavy seas.

Still, lapstrake Sea Skiffs would not disappear without a struggle. Reaching back to the marketing strengths that got Chris-Craft Sea Skiffs started, advertisements promoted the advantages of wooden lapstrake construction that had been its trademark for more than a dozen years.

and dinette in the cockpit, an interesting arrangement for a sport boat. With speeds to 35 miles per hour, it became a popular choice for those seeking a small multipurpose craft. It took Lyman a long time to answer the call, but it seemed to be on track.

At the same time, the Cavalier Division of Chris-Craft, specializing in plywood boats, introduced its new Sea Strake line. The Sea Strakes were a lapstrake version of its traditional smooth-sided Cavalier Cruiser hulls. This was an interesting way to offer lapstrake performance at a lower price than the Sea Skiff line, further challenging the competition.

The cover of the May 1965 issue of *Motor Boating* magazine featured a beautiful color photo of the 38-foot Sea Hawk Sport Fisherman running at full speed on a beautiful day. Five months later a similar 38-foot Sea Hawk Sport Fisherman Cruiser appeared once more on the October cover. It may have been coincidence, but it may also be a vivid example of how attractive and how popular this stylish boat appeared to marine photographers and to publishers selecting outstanding cover images. Chris-Craft elevated the sea skiff to a new level of status and performance in the boating world, just as it had done with so many other craft over the years. However, in the early spring Chris-Craft introduced two new Corinthian cruiser models with "smooth-planked sides and a round bottom with stabilizing strakes." The two models were 35 and 38 feet long with a profile similar to the lapstrake Sea Skiff models. These new boats caused a stir and some wondered if they were prototypes for possible fiberglass cruisers.

A round-bilge, full lapstrake boat is unbeatable for fast, smooth, dry riding in offshore waters. Overlapping strakes act as steps to cushion the waves, and round-bilge construction is strong enough to withstand the pounding of heavy seas. The inner keel on the Chris-Craft is tough, stringy Philippine mahogany flanked by main stringers of seasoned fir. The ribs are white oak and are bolted to the outer keels, which are stout oak. On the cruisers, the ribs extend past the keel to the opposite side of the hull, resulting in double framing and extra strength. The strakes are five-ply marine grade plywood because of its tremendous strength. It's also just flexible enough and it doesn't split when fastened (a common problem in lapstrake boats using solid planking). Chris-Craft uses copper, silicon bronze, and brass fastenings to prepare each boat for a lifetime of salt water service, rather than "clout nails," common among other builders. Each strake has its own size and shape in order to fit without stress. Between each strake is the highest quality poly-sulfide sealant made. It's expensive and hard to work with but, once bonded, seams between the strakes can stretch to twice their size without breaking. This sealant is impervious to gas, oil, temperature and never becomes brittle.

The side strakes have an outer ply of Philippine mahogany with a phenolic resin overlay, which protects and seals the wood to provide a perfect base for smooth paint finishes. Chris-Craft quickly changed the Spartan interiors so common in the traditional sea skiffs into pleasant, attractive and inviting cabins.

The 25-foot Sea Hawk Clipper presented an interesting variation of the Sportsman hull with a short raised deck cabin enclosure and a flybridge windshield. The snug cabin provided room for a small galley, a marine head, and two bunks, making this multipurpose craft an overnighter, a roomy fishing boat, a ski boat, or a fast runabout. At the same time, it offered the soft-riding quality of a lapstrake hull in a new configuration at an attractive price. Both Century and Lyman jumped on this design and turned out their own versions on their existing 26-foot hulls. Lyman called its model the Offshore, and Century named its the Buccaneer.

The number of Sea Skiff offerings shrank from 13 individual models in 1967 to just 8 models in 1968, in seven different lengths.

It was a time of transition in the boat industry, as materials other than wood became accepted and appreciated for their special qualities. When Chris-Craft began to use materials such as plywood, steel, aluminum, and fiberglass for its boats, it sent a message to consumers that these materials were legitimate options that they could consider. Owens and Century offered wood and fiberglass versions of their most popular designs to provide their customers with a choice. Lyman, on the other hand, continued to build wood boats exclusively. Lyman ads justified its devotion to wood by pointing out that 75 percent of the inboard cruisers delivered in 1967 were built of wood. Lyman, once more, refused to recognize a growing preference among new boaters, even after its major rivals had accepted the value of developing hulls of new materials. By May 1969 deliveries of fiberglass cruisers exceeded those of wood by a two-to-one margin. Owens, Luhrs, and Pembroke stopped wood production entirely, and Pacemaker announced that it will not build wooden boats under 32 feet in length. The boat industry was in transition and many new builders were emerging with new techniques, innovative ideas, and interesting designs. The new boatbuilders also seemed to be free from any lingering nostalgia for wood construction. Traditional

boatbuilders, in many cases, found that their workers could not successfully make the transition from wood construction to fiberglass fabrication. In some situations, the problem was so severe that the difficult transition resulted in total failure of the business.

As the end of wood construction approached, the Sea Skiff line shrank further to two popular cruiser sizes, the 30- and 33-foot models. In 1970, Chris-Craft grouped all of its wooden cruisers into a special catalog called Custom Wood Cruisers. The catalog contained the 26-, 30-, and 36-foot Futura models; the 31-, 38-, and 57-foot Constellations; and the two Sea Skiffs.

The final Sea Skiff catalog copy belied the trends in the industry. "These are the true value cruisers of this or any other year. Wood boats in the classic tradition of the sea, designed and styled for the modern family, represent an unbeatable combination of seaworthiness, performance, and cruising comfort. Hulls are fast, tough and made to stand up to rough seas. Throughout the world, Chris-Craft is acknowledged as the leader in wooden hull construction."

Thirty years after the final lapstrake Sea Skiff rolled from the Chris-Craft factory, they are still sought by boaters who enjoy the pleasure of cruising in a comfortable and attractive wooden boat. The Sea Skiffs are well designed, superbly constructed, and have survived the test of time. A Chris-Craft Sea Skiff that is 30 or 40 years old still provides sea-going comfort and attractive styling with reasonable maintenance requirements. The Chris-Craft Sea Skiffs are one of the great success stories of classic wood construction and performance.

The 1961 42-foot Custom Cruiser was a radical departure from tradition, with its reverse windshield rake. It created quite a stir, but never started a strong movement in this direction.

169

CHAPTER 7

ENGINES
The Power of Chris-Craft

As the world's largest builders of mahogany boats, Chris-Craft was also one of the largest users of marine engines. No surprise, then, that within five years of its beginnings as volume builder of standardized runabouts, it would become a builder of marine engines.

Cost and inventory control were among the advantages of building engines in house. Rather than being held hostage by other engine manufacturers' ability to generate a reliable supply of the engines, Chris-Craft could regulate its own supply chain. It also allowed it to offer a variety of engine options, assembling the engines based on advance

When the Smiths brought the 22-foot Cadet to the market in 1927 with plans to build as many as 500 units a year, they needed a fresh supply of appropriate engines. Among the engines offered initially was a Scripps F-6 100-horsepower, as seen in the foreground of this view of the Chris-Craft exhibit at The Mariners' Museum in Newport News, Virginia. By May 1927, the Chrysler Imperial marine engine, developed for Chris-Craft, was the stock motor for the Cadet. Boats in the background include Era Past, a 15-1/2-foot Model 65 Utility (left), and Sue, a Model 27 19-foot Double Cockpit Forward Runabout powered by a 92-horsepower Chrysler Crown, one of 53 made in 1935. *Courtesy The Mariners' Museum*

Jay W. Smith (center) relied on help from Chief Engineer Elmer Jasper and Engine Plant Supervisor Otis Corrie to help develop the A-120 engine, shown in various stages of completion on the shop floor. The cylinders of the big V-8 were cast in pairs that added up to a mighty 824.67 ci of displacement, developing 250 stock horsepower. *Courtesy The Mariners' Museum*

orders. The company could also save money, passing savings on to the consumer while maintaining its profit margin—a distinct competitive advantage.

Moreover, by specing out its own engines, Chris-Craft could build engines to suit the boats rather than the other way around. In designing and engineering a powered boat there are always compromises to be made. By having control over the design of both the hull and the powerplant, Chris-Craft had more freedom to emphasize performance, reliability, ease of manufacturing, or cost, depending on the model and market for the boat.

Life with Engines

Smith family legend suggests Chris Smith was tinkering with marine engines before 1900, in the days of naphtha. Jeffrey Rodengen writes that Chris and Hank purchased a naphtha engine around 1894 and adapted it to one of their launches. In 1896, they acquired a used Stintz single-cylinder, two-horsepower, two-stroke gasoline engine from a fellow Algonacker, Isaac Colby, who couldn't get it to run well. Chris had little more luck with it until, as Jay W. recalls in

the famous *Time* magazine article, "Charles Stintz showed up two years later with a gadget he called a carburetor." According to the same article, based on the 50-year-old recollections of Jay and his brothers, the Smiths adapted the crude gasoline engines of the early 1900s successfully enough to push 26-footers to 18 miles per hour as early as 1906, and "beginning in 1908, Chris Smith built about 36 racers a year, sold them for $550 apiece."

There's no doubt that Chris—and perhaps more importantly for the future days of Chris-Craft, Jay W. and Bernard—were working with and learning about marine uses of gas engines from early on. By the time Chris signed on to build boats with John "Baldy" Ryan, his and his sons' knowledge of the internal combustion engine would have been intuitive. The Smith-Ryan Boat Company was making a point of advertising the benefits of a marine four-stroke. "Engine trouble is forever ended, for we have replaced the uncertain 'go-if-I-please' two-cycle popper (the 'Ogre' of all motorboat enthusiasts) by a steady, *4-cylinder, 4-cycle Engine*—sure as the flight of time." Jay W. was in his 20s when he joined Ryan in the cockpit of their *Reliance IV* raceboat,

When Chris Smith & Sons Boat Company was founded in 1922, its efforts to provide stock runabouts for Everyman were aided by a low-cost supply of Curtiss OX-5 aero engines left over from World War I. The Smiths marinized the water-cooled V-8 engines, adding a transmission and electric starter. The resulting Smith-Curtiss OX-5 generated 90-horsepower at 1,400 rpm. *Classic Boating magazine*

powered by 75-horsepower six-cylinder Van Blerck engine. The pair awed the speedboat world and smashed records in St. Louis in 1910 by averaging more than 37 miles per hour over 20 miles.

The period from 1905 to 1915 was marked by substantial improvements in the weight-to-horsepower ratio of marine engines, and the Smiths were in the thick of it, learning with and from a variety of mechanical minds. Joe Van Blerck was a Dutch immigrant who worked for Henry Ford in Detroit before opening his own engine shop in Detroit in collaboration first with John Hacker, then later with Charles Page in Monroe, Michigan. According to Stan Grayson in *Engines Afloat*, Chris Smith was likely an early supporter of Van Blerck, who would go on to become a leader in marine engine design and manufacture in the late 1910s.

The Smiths also benefited by joining forces with Jack and Martin Beebe. The Beebe brothers were experienced boatbuilders from Marine City, Michigan, who at one point teamed with Napoleon Lisee in Algonac before they all would end up on the Smiths' payroll. Jack's specialty was engine work, and he knew well another dominant marine engine of its day, the Sterling. Among his accomplishments,

Beebe is credited with coaxing the speed the Smith-built *Miss Detroit* would need—powered by a Sterling eight—to win the Gold Cup in 1915.

Because the Smiths were given the opportunity to work with budgets that only spendthrifts like Ryan and his friend J. Stuart Blackton could afford, they were exposed to leading edge internal combustion technology of the day in the effort to build the fastest boats in the world. By 1915 they would have been well grounded in converting horsepower to speed when they agreed to partner with Gar Wood to build and race unlimited hydroplanes on the world stage.

Race-bred Apprenticeship

For Jay W. and Bernard, brothers who would later be the driving force behind Chris-Craft, the Smith family's partnership with Wood only enhanced their knowledge and experience developing and applying internal combustion technology to the water. After all, the boats they built and raced were little more than engines and a propeller that were surrounded by a few bits of well-placed wood.

While Jay and Bernard Smith worked with Wood, World War I and the new phenomena of airplanes gave

Developed with the Smiths for use in the Cadet, the Chrysler Imperial six-cylinder marked the entry of the automaker into the marine engine market in 1927. This 101-horsepower Imperial was and is the original power in a 1929 Cadet, *The Laker*.

Needing an in-house V-8 to replace the aging OX-5, the Smiths developed the A-70 in 1927. Number 328, one of 367 A-70s built before it was superseded by the A-120, still powers Hull Number 3117, a 1929 Model 14 28-foot upswept-deck Runabout named *Why-Not*. The A-70's 225 horsepower pushed the big triple-cockpit to 42 miles per hour, which original owner Jack Rutherford put to good use racing in the 825-ci Class in the early 1930s.

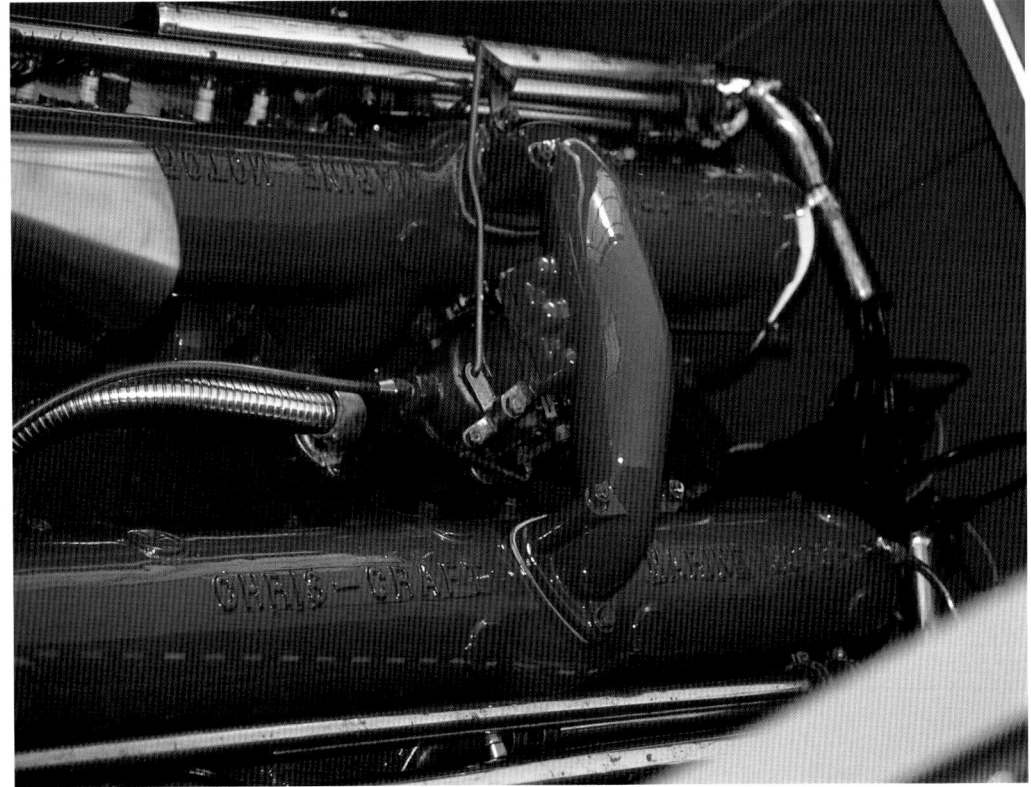

rise to the development of still lighter, more powerful engines. Jesse Vincent of the Packard Motor Company—for whom the Smiths would later build racing Runabouts called the *Packard Chriscrafts*—and John Hall led the development of the V-8 and V-12 Liberty aircraft engines. More than 20,000 Liberty engines were built by Packard, Ford, Buick, Cadillac, Lincoln, and Marmon—nearly 12,000 more than ultimately would be needed for the war effort.

While it was Wood who bought trainloads of Liberty engines for use in his own Baby Gar Runabouts, the Smiths were no less familiar with the V-12. The famous Smith-built *Miss Americas*, piloted to Gold Cup fame by Wood, used twin Smith-Liberty powerplants. The C. C. Smith Boat and Engine Company would market surplus "Grant-Liberty" engines (marinized by Howard Grant) for $4,500, and one of Smith's early stock Runabouts sold through Central Marine Service Corporation featured the Liberty-based "Smith Marine Twin-Six" engine. All of this would serve Jay and Bernard well when it came time to start their own company in 1922. The 12-cylinder Liberty would even surface as late as 1933–1934 as Depression-era power for Chris-Craft's 27- and 31-foot Custom Runabouts.

The Curtiss OX-5

The development of the Curtiss OX-5 V-8 aircraft engine that was used in the Curtiss JN, or "Jenny," biplane, was vitally important in the early days of Chris-Craft. As Jim Wangard noted in *Classic Boating*, the OX-5 was the latest in the line of Model O V-8 engines originally created by Curtiss as early as 1909. Once the OX-5 design was approved by the U.S. military in preparation for the war, some 7,000 units were built by Willys-Morrow and Willys-Overland. Like Van Blerck's Twin Six introduced in 1916 as well as other marine engines, the OX-5 was an overhead valve configuration that weighed 400 pounds wet and was rated for 90 horsepower at 1,400 rpm. At 4 pounds per horsepower, it was a strong engine in its day.

Once again, thanks to Gar Wood, the Smiths were familiar with Curtiss engines. Before the end of the war, Wood acquired from Glenn Curtiss a prototype V-12 aero engine, which the Smiths successfully marinized for use in *Miss Detroit III* in 1918.

As with the Liberties, once World War I ended, surplus engines were readily available and relatively cheap—the Smiths reportedly bought a number of them for $50 a unit. Given that the engines were on the market for $1,000 in 1919, and still available as late as 1928 for $250, the $50 figure may be simply part of the legend. Or, Wood may have been able to pull some strings for Jay and his brothers in order to get a friendly price. In any case, while other boatbuilders were using more expensive Hall-Scotts and other purpose-built marine engines, the Smiths capitalized on an available, low-cost supply of the surplus OX-5s, which they marinized themselves. Dubbed the Smith-Curtiss OX-5, this engine was an important part of the Smiths' ability to start their new company, manufacturing stock Runabouts.

The OX-5 powered the Smiths' early 26-foot Standardized Runabouts for the first few years of production, and the surplus engines helped them price their product competitively. But by 1926, unit sales and production volume at the Smith plant were expanding rapidly, and the OX-5s were getting long in the tooth. As of 1926, the Smiths began discounting the 26-footer equipped with the OX-5, dropping the price to $2,900, while simultaneously offering the same boat with either of two Kermaths, a 150-horsepower at $3,500 or 100-horsepower at $3,200.

With the planned 1927 launch of their second model, the 22-foot Cadet, the Smiths would need a fresh supply of engines for that boat at a cost that would let them continue to produce the best boat for the money. They would also need a replacement for the OX-5 to power the 26-footers and larger models that would be introduced in the near future. Other makers—Dodge in particular—were driving prices

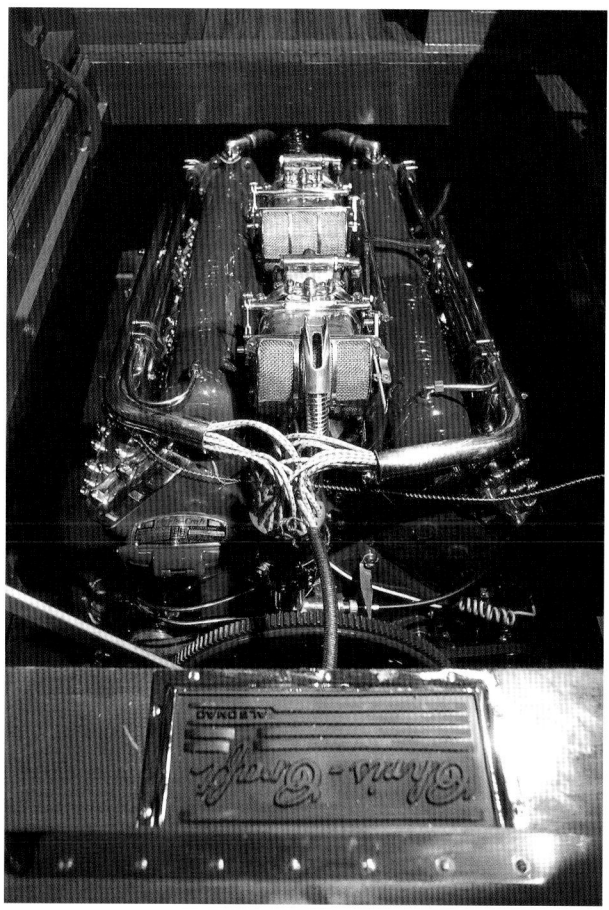

The A-120A featured dual caarbs, high-compression copper heads, and high-lift cams generated additional horsepower over the stock A-120 V-8. This example powers a rare 1929 38-foot Commuting Cruiser, Mad Wilmar. *Classic Boating Magazine*

With the Depression came the need for economical power. Chris-Craft started its long use of Hercules engine blocks with the four-cylinder 132.7-ci Model B in 1934. The little 450-pound flathead developed 55-horsepower in its early years. It remained in use following World War II, then was reintroduced in 1954 as a 60-horsepower engine. It would end up as the longest-running Hercules block engine in the Chris-Craft armory, even serving as steady inboard power on the 35-foot Motor Sailer sailboat in the 1960s.

After introducing the first generation K engines in 1937, Chris-Craft fitted the 221.4-ci Hercules block with triple downdraft Zenith carburetors (left side), a lighter flywheel and high-performance cam to boost horsepower to 121 horsepower in the KB engine. Note the bottom of the fin-like carb cover cut into the engine hatch cover, a stock configuration on the 16-foot Racing Runabout in 1940. This particular KB was bored out, boosting it to 130-horsepower.

down, making it all the more necessary to find good engines at the right price. And with the hiring of sales manager Jack Clifford, it was time to display at the New York Boat Show, which meant having a marine engine.

First Generation V-8s

The Smiths embarked on a two-pronged approach to the challenge. Knowing, perhaps, that they would be hard-pressed to ramp up their own engine-building efforts quickly enough to satisfy the astounding growth in demand for Run-abouts, they worked a deal with Walter Chrysler to offer the new Chrysler Imperial 100-horsepower marine engine in their new Cadet. According to *The Legend of Chris-Craft*, the development of the 835-pound Imperial was a joint project between Chrysler and the Smiths. Chrysler would benefit from immediate credibility in the marine industry through its association with Chris-Craft, and the Smiths could promise service and parts to hundreds of buyers who needed only to journey to their nearest Chrysler dealer.

Meanwhile, Jay and Bernard—who by 1926 had more than 20 years' experience with marine engines each—led the development of a larger engine, to be built on site in

Algonac. The A-70, a 200-horsepower V-8 listed at 1,450 pounds with 824.67-ci displacement, was the first engine to come out of the factory doors. It featured a 12-volt electrical system that used Delco-Remy generator, starter, distributor, and coils. So-called Siamese cylinders were cast in pairs with cast-iron liners. The engine was offered first in the 26-foot Runabouts, then later in the 28-foot Customs and 30-foot Custom Commuters.

Improved carburetion in 1929 boosted the A-70's horsepower to 225, and the 1929 sales catalog promoted the fact that "it speeds a 38-foot cruiser along at 30 miles an hour, day after day," which was "only a hint at its power and performance." With the A-70 installed in the 26-foot Runabout, it promised 45 miles per hour. For 1930 the A-70 was modified to accept Holley DD-5 downdraft carbs, increasing horsepower to 250 while keeping 5x5-1/4-inch bore and stroke the same. According to engine restorer and historian Earl Sheehan, some 356 A-70 versions of the V-8 were built. A race version could also be made, using aluminum high-compression heads, aluminum flywheel, racing camshaft, and dual intake manifolds, with the resulting A-70-A racing motor capable of 325 horsepower at 2,400 rpm.

Following World War II, Chris-Craft brought out a longstroke version of the standard K engine, the KL. The additional displacement (to 236.6 ci) added 15 horsepower to the K. Except for the spark plug wires, this KL is as it was originally, still powering a 1949 Deluxe Runabout.

It was rarely long before Chris-Craft would introduce a performance version of a new standard engine, and the KL was no exception. In 1951 the KLC put out 120 horsepower at 3,800 rpm, with lighter flywheel, high-performance cam, and higher compression.

As Chris-Craft's engineers continued to refine the in-house V-8, the A-70 would be superseded by the A-120, which featured virtually identical specifications, though the engine had gained weight, listing at 1,750 pounds. It could be made into A-120-A racing engine with dual carbs, high-compression copper heads, and high-lift camshafts, which boosted it to 350 horsepower. The Racing A-120-A was fitted to the rare 26-foot Special Race Boat in the mid-1930s, but no doubt more than one stock A-120 owner tweaked his engine as well. In 1935, Chris-Craft built a special race motor for H. Mendelson, boring the A-120 out to 845.418 ci and installing copper heads with some valve work, resulting in 348.4 horsepower at 2,850 rpm. The conversion cost $558.18 more than the stock motor.

Although the Depression would force consumers and Chris-Craft to look for more economical engines, the A-class V-8s stayed in production until World War II. By that time, they were considered old-fashioned gas hogs, the Chrysler straight eights were considered a better eight-cylinder alternative in the marine industry, and Chris-Craft had moved on to the inline sixes. Some 615 A-class engines were built overall, some of those still hanging around and sold as inexpensive leftovers following the war.

The most powerful of the K-series inline sixes was the KBL, a longstroke version of the KB that put out 131 horsepower. Introduced in 1948, the KBL would last into 1956, when it was replaced by the KFL model that featured dual updraft carbs. This KBL powers a 1952 Riviera. *Classic Boating magazine*

The A-series' real legacy, however, was leading Chris-Craft's entry into the marine engine market. Chris-Craft would continue to offer its boats with other engines, including Chryslers, Kermaths, and Grays, but the launching of the engine division was the beginning of a long history of assembling its own engines.

Model A & B Fours

As the Depression of the early 1930s deepened, Chris-Craft and other boatbuilders worked to reduce the cost of their entry-level models while they attempted to keep sales alive. Along with the introduction of its first stripped-down Utility boats, Chris-Craft also needed its own reliable low-cost engine without taking on the significant costs of original castings. The solution was the four-cylinder Model B. Introduced in 1934, it took the place of the Chrysler four in powering the smaller Runabouts and Utilities as well as small Cruisers.

The Model B was based on a four-cylinder Hercules block, and was built for marine use by Chris-Craft. With 132.7-ci displacement from a 3-1/4x4-inch bore and stroke, it generated 55 horsepower breathing through an updraft carb. The B used six-volt electrics, weighed 450 pounds, and laid the foundation for generations of Hercules-based Chris-Craft engines. As they would do with all Chris-Craft engines, the Model B could be used several transmission options. The B was Direct Drive, the BS model had "Speed Drive" (1.5:1 ratio), and the BR was fitted with "Reduction Drive" (2:1 ratio).

The Model B would end up as Chris-Craft's longest running model. It soldiered on long after World War II as the economy engine in the lineup, and was juiced up in 1954 and reintroduced in two versions, the Model A (basic) and Model B (offering additional tranny options). Both versions generated 60 horsepower at 3,200 rpm. Chris-Craft promoted the little four in *Motor Boating* as "ideal for kit boats and other light hulls where low initial cost and operating economy are important factors." It was less than 32 inches long overall and weighed only 456 pounds. The later Model B was available with reduction drive as well as direct drive as the Models BR and BR3.

It wasn't flashy or overly powerful, but its reliability and low cost gave it tremendous longevity. The Model B continued on in the late 1960s after the K engines were dropped in 1963, even serving as inboard power on Chris-Craft's Motor Sailer 35-foot sailboat more than 30 years after it was introduced.

K Engine Dynasty

Although the four-cylinder Model B may have been the longest running Chris-Craft engine model, it was the K series that came to define Chris-Craft power. The K was based on a Hercules straight-six L-head industrial engine block that had proved to be both rugged and reliable when used as a truck engine or as a irrigation pump engine that needed to run continuously while providing a reasonable horsepower-to-weight ratio. Chris-Craft initially developed a smaller six-cylinder 75-horsepower Model H engine based on a 205.3-ci Hercules block. The H was offered on some Chris-Craft models before 1937, and the K series would be a more powerful version.

Hercules, based in Canton, Ohio, was close enough to Algonac to make shipping cost-effective. Equally important, Hercules was willing to manufacture blocks to Chris-Craft specifications, including modifications to provide high-pressure lubrication required to run the engine at an angle. Chris-Craft could be a hard-to-please taskmaster to its suppliers. This is as evidenced by ongoing correspondence between Chris-Craft engineer Elmer Jasper and suppliers such as J. H. Williams & Company of Buffalo, New York, regarding the quality of forgings for connecting rods in the 1930s. Hercules' ability to satisfy Chris-Craft's demands likely played an important part in their long-time relationship. Other manufacturers, such as Kermath and Scripps, used Hercules blocks as well.

Jasper is credited with much of the success of Chris-Craft's marinization of the Hercules six-cylinder. Chris-Craft machined intake and exhaust manifolds, the cast-iron oil pan, and cylinder heads, and installed oil and water pumps. Carbs and plugs for each model were engineered to Chris-Craft specs. Finished engines were then dyno-tested—records show differences of as much as 5 horsepower among engines of the same configuration.

The first K engines were introduced in the 1937 lineup. The first 221.4-ci base model K put out 85 horsepower at 3,200 rpm, with bore and stroke of 3 3/8x 4 1/8 inches. The KA offered increased compression with an aluminum head (thus the KA designation) and a bigger carb to generate another 10 ponies more at 3,500 rpm. The original 85-horsepower K lasted two years, and then was upgraded to 95 horsepower at 3,200 rpm by boring it out to 3-7/16 inches with the same 4-1/8-inch stroke, giving it a 229.7-ci displacement. Depending on the transmission, it weighed some 660 pounds. The 95-horsepower K would be a stalwart of the Chris-Craft line for years, powering generations of Chris-Crafts. In 1959 the same basic engine went to 100 horsepower and then was finally discontinued in 1963.

For hot-rod boaters, the KB model featured triple Zenith downdraft carbs, a lighter flywheel and high-performance cam, generating a total of 121 horsepower at 3,800 rpm. In 1940, Chris-Craft offered the KB in the 16-foot Racing Runabout with a claimed 44-mile-per-hour top speed. A year later it introduced the rare 16-foot Racing

Chris-Craft produced Model L engines for a brief period in the 1930s. The Model L would be discontinued in favor of the Model M. The L made a modest 110 horsepower at 3,200 rpm out of its 263.2 ci.

The Model M was the big brother of the K, sporting 320.4-ci displacement and generating 130 horsepower at 3,000 rpm in stock tune. It would continue to be a power option in the Chris-Craft lineup for two decades, ultimately replaced by the 283 V-8 in 1959. This Model M continues to power its 22-foot Utility today.

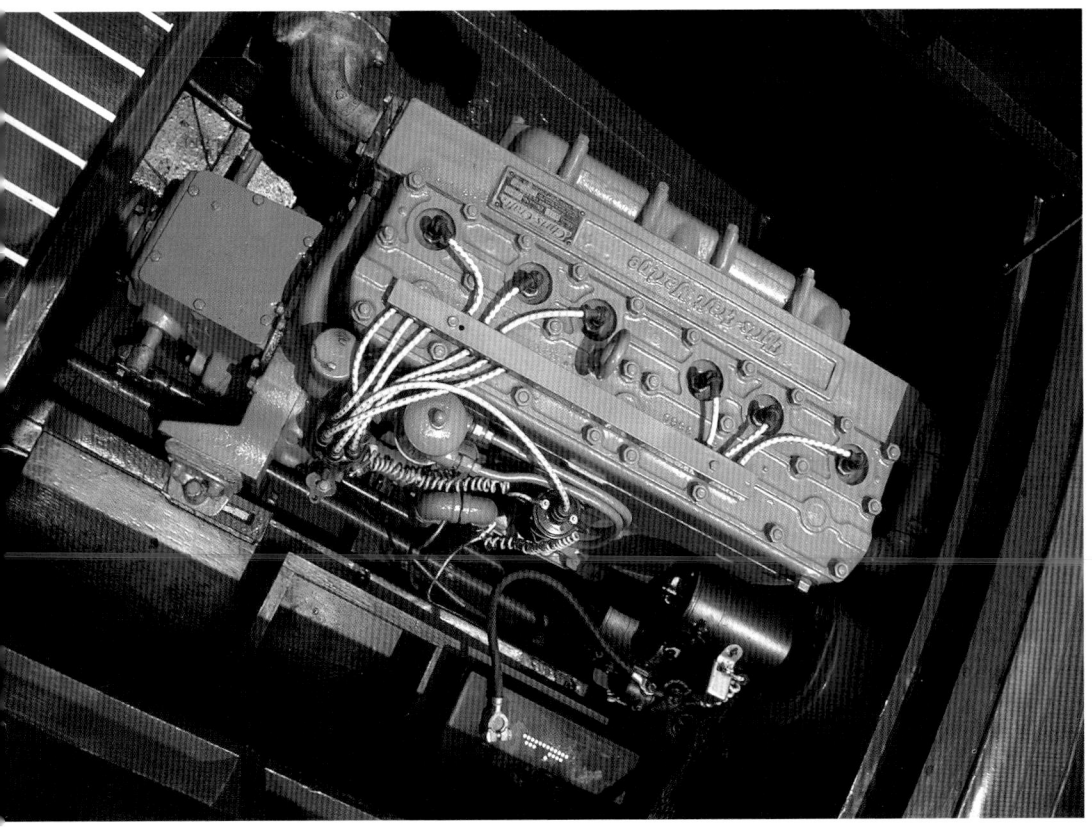

The MBL, which made 158 horsepower at 3,400 rpm, was the hottest engine of the Hercules-based letter series engines. The MBL, a high-performance longstroke version of the M introduced in 1948, was the engine of choice for the classic 19-foot postwar Racing Runabout. *Classic Boating magazine*

by Chris-Craft between 1937 and 1963. Of course, not all of those were installed in Chris-Craft boats—the company sold many engines to other boat-builders and to boat owners as replacements for boats of all marques. The last K, Serial Number 206243, was shipped to Switzerland in 1963.

Model L

For a brief period in 1937–1938, Chris-Craft offered an L-series six-cylinder engine, also based on a Hercules L-head block. The 263.2-ci engine made 110 horsepower at 3,200 rpm with bore and stroke of 3-5/8x4-1/4 inches and weighed 815 pounds in its direct drive costume. By 1938, Chris-Craft engineers apparently had squeezed more horsepower and rpm out of the L, but it would be dropped in favor of the larger displacement M-series engines.

Model M Engines

Like the K-series, the Model M engines were Hercules-based straight sixes, though larger. The M was first produced at the same time as the K, generating 130 horsepower from 320.4 ci at 3,000 rpm with 4x4-1/4-inch bore and stroke in an 880-pound package. With a higher compression head and performance cam, the MB put out 145 horsepower, and pushed happy owners of prewar 19-foot Custom barrelbacks to 41 miles per hour.

As with the K-series, a longstroke version of the M, the ML, was produced after the war, extending the stroke to 4-1/2 inches for 339.2 ci displacement and 145 horsepower at 3,000 rpm. But the engine that captured the hearts of recreational speedboat kings was the MBL, in which the longstroke version of the M was hopped up with separate intake and exhaust manifolds, larger valves and ports, high-lift cam, and lighter flywheel to put out 158 ponies at 3,400 rpm. It weighed 850 pounds when equipped with direct drive. The MBL would push the classic postwar 19-foot Racing Runabout to 44 miles per hour, and it was offered in the 20-foot Custom Runabout when the engine came out in 1948. According to early-1950s brochures, "Equipment furnished with all models [included] rubber mounts, engine buck, gallon of oil, instruction book and lifting ring."

Less common but more powerful was the MCL high-performance engine introduced later, in the 1950s, before the Chevy small-block came along. The MCL breathed through twin updraft carbs on the same longstroke block to make 175 horsepower at 3,400 rpm.

W Series

Once it shook off the effects of the Depression starting in the mid-1930s, Chris-Craft became as much or more a builder of wooden Cruisers as it was a builder of smaller

Hydroplane, also powered by the KB, yielding 50 miles per hour—as long as you didn't try to turn. There was also a KBO, which was an opposite rotation KB, used in twin-engine installations.

Then in 1948, Chris-Craft came out with what would be the most powerful K-series engine, the 131-horsepower KBL. This longstroke version of the KB increased displacement to 236.6 ci by lengthening the stroke 1/8 inch to 4-1/4. With direct drive it weighed only 626 pounds and, as promoted in *Motor Boating,* was "designed especially for uses where quick acceleration and sustained operation at high speeds are required." The KBL would last through 1956. It was replaced by the KFL, which swapped the triple down-draft carbs for dual updraft carbs, with no advertised reduction in horsepower. The KFL lived into 1960, when the Smiths sold Chris-Craft.

The standard KL longstroke version of the K was introduced in 1949. With the standard flywheel and single carb, the KL generated 105 horsepower. In 1951, Chris-Craft introduced a hot-rod version of the longstroke, the KLC, that featured the high-performance cam, lighter flywheel, and higher compression—at 3,800 rpm, the 760-pound KLC put out 120 horsepower. It remained an option through 1956.

According to an article in *The Brass Bell* by Bob Davis, some 200,000 units of the K-series engines were manufactured

Outboard Engines

One of Chris-Craft's great strengths was the ability to recognize opportunities in the recreational boating market, analyze the competition, and then capitalize by launching a product of its own. Following World War II, the company was savvy enough to recognize the oncoming boom in entry-level boating that would be driven in large part by smaller boats powered by improved outboard motors. Many of the young couples who would give birth to the baby boom would have the time for recreation, but not necessarily the money for a Chris-Craft mahogany inboard.

To meet this need and start new boaters off in a Chris-Craft, the company created an outboard motor division, following it up with a Kit Boat Division that offered less expensive plywood boats to go with the motors. Jay W. was reportedly heavily involved in the development of the engine, and Harry Coll would be named manager of the outboard plant in Grand Rapids, Michigan.

As the company did with any new initiatives, it looked at what the competition was producing, then tried to figure out ways to improve upon it. For example, according to one former employee, in developing the outboards it wanted an engine that could be serviced conveniently, in part because it would then lend itself to further development. Its marketing surveys determined that an engine in the 5-horsepower category would be the most popular.

After eight years of development, Chris-Craft had improved the standard magnetos and carburetors on outboards of the day. In 1949 they introduced the 5-1/2-horsepower Challenger two-stroke alternate-firing twin-cylinder outboard with full reverse. With bore and stroke of 2x1-1/2 inches, it displaced 9.42 ci, weighed 46 pounds, carried 1-1/2 gallons of fuel, and offered a gear ratio of 14:25. For Jay W., the entire project must have stirred up memories of fiddling with the Stintz with his father back in 1896.

A year later, Chris-Craft introduced the 10-horsepower Commander engine, and the first Kit Boat brochures featured pictures of happy boaters skimming the waterways with Chris-Craft outboard power. Like its smaller sibling, the Commander was an alternate-firing

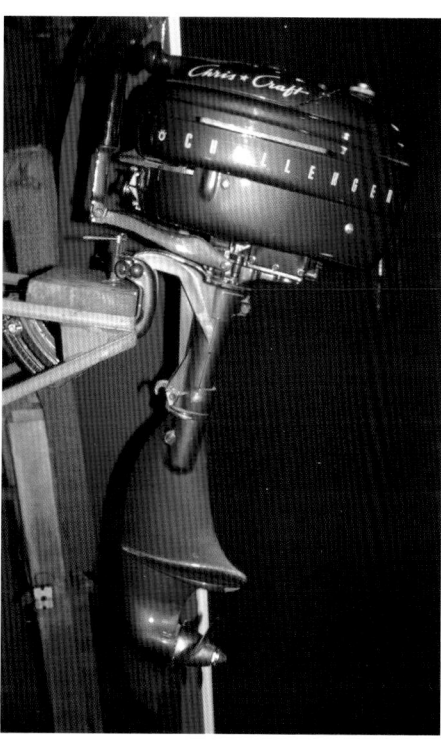

Chris-Craft spent eight years in the 1940s developing the Challenger 5-1/2-horsepower outboard. The 9.42-ci two-stroke offered improved starting and superior idling over many of the competing outboards of its day. When Chris-Craft closed the Grand Rapids outboard engine facility in 1952, the Challengers continued to be manufactured under license in England.

two-cylinder two-stroke with bore and stroke of 2-1/2x2-1/32 inches, displacing 19.94 inches. Fuel capacity was 2 gallons and it weighed 72 pounds. Sales brochures urged consumers to "Try 'em! Troll 'em! Clock 'em!"

The outboard program would be cut short, however, when the doors were locked on the Grand Rapids plant in 1953. As Jeffrey Rodengen chronicles in *The Legend of Chris-Craft*, the official explanation at the time was that the rest of their boat lines demanded all of their attention. And it is certainly true that they were extremely busy developing new products—the Sea Skiff line was in the early stages of development by this time, for example. Another explanation was that success in the outboard business would require a full lineup of motors, something they weren't prepared to commit to.

But backing away from a production challenge, especially after investing more than $1 million, would have been an uncharacteristic move. The Kit Boat Division was going strong, creating a built-in market for outboard engines.

Then there was the charge of patent infringements. The lower unit on the Challenger motor used a bearing that violated a patent held by Mercury, and the reed plate and a few other items were potential patent problems. Carl Kiekhaefer, ultimate competitor that he was, sued Chris-Craft. Rather than fight the suit or change the lower unit, as the story goes, Chris-Craft closed the outboard plant.

Again, a more characteristic response from the Smiths would have been to redesign the offending lower unit. The truth behind the closing of the outboard plant is probably a combination of factors—sales less promising than hoped, along with a program hungry for capital to develop new engines, topped off by fierce competition and a potentially costly lawsuit. Chris-Craft likely decided that the potential pay-off just wasn't worth the time, effort, and money it would take to succeed.

The 5-1/2-horsepower Challenger did not have the same patent problems and would go on to be produced for another 10 years under license in England and elsewhere. But Chris-Craft would leave others to battle over the outboard engine market.

Although the K and the B engines would survive into the 1960s, the end of the letter series engines was in sight with the introduction of Chris-Craft's marinized version of the Chevy small-block. The 283 was particularly adept at powering the smaller Sport and Ski Boats in Chris-Craft's lineup, and continues to be a popular power option today—this engine serves as modern power for a 1948 19-foot Racing Runabout.

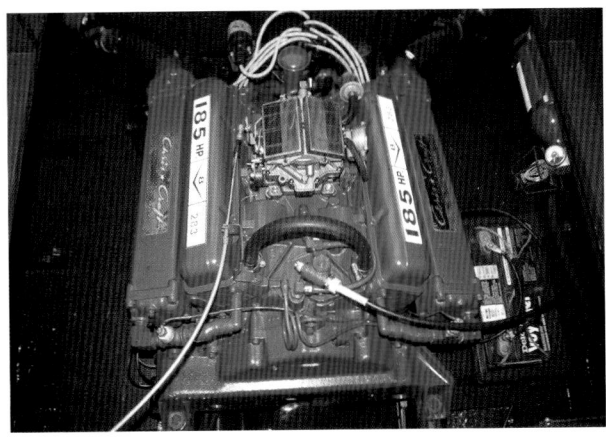

Runabouts and Utilities. Again, the Engine Division would turn to an inline-six block from Hercules for the heavy-duty W series engines. As promoted in *Motor Boating* in 1954, "The real workhorse of the line is the 160-horsepower Model W, which is designed to withstand the rigors of long, continuous service where steady performance and economy of operation are all-important."

The W generated its 160 horsepower at 3,000 rpm from 404.3 ci in a 4-1/4x4-3/4 inch bore-and-stroke configuration, and weighed 1,232 pounds. The WB was introduced new in 1955 at 190 horsepower, then was quickly upgraded, using its twin updraft carbs to boost power output to 200 horsepower at 3,200 rpm with the same displacement as the base W.

Hemis and Cadillac Crusaders

When Chris-Craft came out with the Cobra, its startling new Racing Runabout, in 1955, Chrysler Marine was converting the now famous Chrysler Hemi for marine use. The potential combination proved too tempting—Chris-Craft no longer had an eight-cylinder engine, so the Hemi was just the thing to pack into the 21-foot version of the Cobra to give it 50 miles per hour-plus speed. The Hemi was a 331-ci overhead valve V-8 that generated 200 horsepower at 4,400 rpm in a 1,100-pound package with downdraft carbs and a six-volt electrical system. The first 21-foot Cobras were shipped with the Hemis.

The Cobra was also the recipient of a marinized Cadillac overhead valve V-8 as developed by Detroit Cadillac dealer Cal Connell, who founded Detroit Racing Equipment. DRE's 331-ci conversion generated 285 horsepower at 5,200 rpm, thanks to dual four-barrel Rochester carbs. The Cadillac V-8 could push Century's 21-foot Coronado nearly 60 miles per hour—a speed that generated attention in Algonac. Ultimately Chris-Craft purchased 24 of the hopped up Cadillacs, 17 of which ended up in 21-foot Cobras, giving them 55 miles per hour.

Chris-O-Matic Transmission

As the automotive industry developed, installed, and promoted automatic transmissions, the boating industry would naturally want to follow. Chris-Craft's answer was the Chris-O-Matic tranny, offering electric-hydraulic clutch control. It was offered as an option on all Chris-Craft engines except the four-cylinder Models A and B, and could be retrofitted.

In 1954, *Motor Boating* would announce the new tranny. "Chris-O-Matic, a new marine innovation which actually shifts the gears for the skipper, is available for all but the 60-horsepower series. With this new electric-hydraulic shifting mechanism, the man at the wheel simply flips a selector, much as he would flip a light switch, and instantaneously an electric motor pumps hydraulic fluid into a cylinder to actuate a piston which accomplishes the desired shift. This control, designed for Chris-Craft engines, can be installed on most engines already in operation. It can also be hooked up for dual control installations."

Although it was meant to respond quickly, the Chris-O-Matic developed a reputation for being troublesome. Before long it had acquired the nickname "Crash-O-Matic," supposedly because the pilot's commands weren't always translated into propeller action soon enough, and a boat might continue forward into a dock, for example. The characterization may have been unfair—there were enough new boaters on the water in 1950 that pilot error could have easily played as much role as any faulty transmissions of the day.

Chris-Craft continued to offer the V-8, upgraded to 365 ci in 1956 and 390 ci in 1959 until the introduction of the marinized version of the Chevy small-block. It was three of Connell's Cadillac engines that powered a 53-foot Constellation called *Crusader Rabbit* to an impressive 32 miles per hour. Connell adopted the name from the boat for his company, Cadillac Crusader Marine, leading to the origin of Crusader Marine. When Chevrolet introduced its 409-ci engine in the early 1960s, Crusader Marine ceased marinizing the Cadillac V-8s and switch to the Chevys. Some 800 Cadillacs were marinized from 1952 to 1960, all painted fire engine red.

The New V-8s

Chris-Craft would break from its tradition of inline sixes in 1959 when it introduced a marinized version of the Chevy small-block 283-ci V-8. Company stylists and marketing gurus had long kept their eyes firmly glued to the automotive industry, looking for chances to piggy-back on the trends and major advertising budgets of car manufacturers, and automotive styling was at its peak at Chris-Craft in the late 1950s. Marinizing the small-block Chevy for prospective boat owners was not only a practical move—it was a good engine that would be manufactured in huge quantities, driving engine costs down—it would generate showroom interest as well.

The 185-horsepower 283, which has become a hugely popular engine to modify, was used with great success in Chris-Craft's smaller Sport Boats of the 1960s, making the 17-foot Ski Boat, for example, a 40-mile-per-hour speedster. It was so well matched to the 17-footer that in 1968 it would be incorporated into the model name of the boat: the SS 283 Ski Boat. The small-block powered a Buehler Jet Drive in the short-lived 16-foot Chris-Craft Ski Jet. It was also one of two choices, along with the venerable K, in the Capri Runabouts that were the last of their line in the early 1960s. Twin 283s were common throughout the Cruiser lineup as well.

Chris-Craft had moved its world headquarters from Algonac—home of the Engine Division—to Pompano Beach in 1957. In 1960, the Smiths would sell the company to National Automotive Fibers Inc., and the connection to Algonac would be even more tenuous under the new owners. NAFI discontinued the K engine in 1963, as big-bore power was all the rage during the musclecar era. By 1969, Chris-Craft was taken over by Herbert Siegel, and the Engine Division was moved from Algonac to Gallipolis, Ohio.

In the 1960s, the old inline sixes gave way to the all-American V-8, as bigger and bigger engines were packed into the Utility-style Sport Boats of the decade. As the Chevy small-block was built up and made more powerful on the automotive side, Chris-Craft matched it with marinized

versions. Of particular note was the 327F, known commonly as the Corvette engine, which was used in 17- and 18-foot Super Sports and then the 17- and 20-foot Grand Prix, in which it put out 210 horsepower at 4,000 rpm for 40-plus miles per hour.

Chris-Craft also marinized Ford engines, including the MEL (Mercury/Edsel/Lincoln 430 and 431 V-8, which was used starting in 1959 to replace the larger W-series inline sixes. Commonly referred to as the Lincoln engine, the 431 generated 275 horsepower in boats like the early-1960s 24-foot Sportsman, 21-foot Continental, and 20-foot Holiday. It gave the 20-foot Super Sport a top speed of 47 miles per hour, and served as a workhorse in Cruisers. Then in 1966, Chris-Craft brought out its marine version of the popular Ford 427, sporting four-barrel downdraft carbs and muscling out 300 horsepower in the 20- and 21-foot Super Sports and later in the 20-foot Grand Prix.

In a way, as the wooden boat era came to an end, the engines that powered Chris-Craft returned to their roots. Forty years of engine development had helped shed about 500 pounds and some noise, and add a few thousand revolutions per minute and considerable reliability. But boaters till clamored for that big-bore V-8 power.

V-8s dominated the 1960s on the water as well as the street. The 327F was a marinized version of the Chevy made famous by the Corvette starting in 1963, generating 210 horsepower in Chris-Craft trim.

APPENDIX 1:
Chris-Craft Collection at The Mariners' Museum

The Mariner's Museum in Newport News, Virginia, houses the vast Chris-Craft Collection, the paper records of the Chris-Craft company from 1922 to 1980. The collection includes not only some 15,000 photographs and most of the resources referenced in this book, but most of the nearly 100,000 hull cards. A trained staff continues the extraordinary task of cataloging and preserving the vast Chris-Craft archive, and serves as an invaluable resource for writers and historians who visit the museum.

Throughout its history, Chris-Craft assigned a specific hull number to each boat that was built, and recorded that number along with relevant specifications on the hull card for that boat. Today, thank to The Mariners' Museum, owners of Chris-Craft boats can get background information about their boats. From the hull number, the research staff at the museum can prepare a research package that includes the boat equipment record (hull card), copies of sales literature, the original price sheet, black-and-white photo, engine information, and lists of the technical drawings and wiring diagrams that are available.

Locating Your Hull Number

On Chris-Craft, Sea Skiff, and Cavalier Division boats, the first place to look would be on a metal plate attached to the underside of the engine hatch cover or engine box on single-engine models, and on the underside of the starboard engine hatch cover or engine box on twin-engine models.

You may also find it stamped into the aft surface of the forward header of the engine hatch on single-engine models, and stamped into the aft surface of the forward header of the port engine hatch on twin-engine models.

It could also be stamped into the top edge of the engine stringer starboard next to the engine coupling on single-engine models, and stamped into the top edge of the inboard stringer, port engine, next to the engine coupling on twin-engine models.

They are also sometimes found on top of the wood towing bitt, on the aft face of the bow block, on the extreme forward inboard surface of the port toe rail, or on the aft face of the stem midway between chine and sheer.

On sport boats and runabouts, they may be stamped into the forward surface of the aft deck beam if the seat back is removable. On fiberglass cruisers and sailboats, the hull number can be found glassed over on the interior surface of the port hull side, forward of the foremost bulkhead. Outboard sailboat models will have the number stamped into the engine pad.

For more information about The Mariners' Museum or the Chris-Craft Collection, contact them directly at 100 Museum Drive, Newport News, VA 23606-3759; 757-591-7785.

APPENDIX 2:
Resources and Select Bibliography

Organizations

The Antique Boat Museum
750 Mary Street
Clayton, NY 13624
315-686-4104

Antique & Classic Boat Society
422 James Street
Clayton, NY 13624
315-686-2628
Publishers of quarterly newsletter, The ACBS Rudder.

Chris-Craft Antique Boat Club
217 South Adams Street
Tallahassee, FL 32301-1708
850-224-2628
www.chris-craft.org
Publishers of quarterly newsletter, The Brass Bell.

Gar Wood Antique & Classic Boat Society
315-686-4104

The Mariners' Museum
Chris-Craft Collection
100 Museum Drive
Newport News, VA 23606-3759
757-591-7785

The New Hampshire Antique & Classic Boat Museum
397 Center Street, PO Box 1195
Wolfeboro Falls, NH 03896
603-569-4554
Publishers of newsletter, Boathouse News.

Books

Ballantyne, Philip. Robert Bruce Duncan, Photographer. *Classic American Runabouts: Wood Boats 1915-1965.* Osceola, WI: MBI Publishing Company, 2001.

Duncan, Robert Bruce. *Cutwater: Speedboats and Launches from the Golden Age of Boating.* Top Ten Publishing Corporation, 1993.

Grayson, Stan. *Engines Afloat: From Early Days to D-Day.* Devereaux Books.

Gribbins, Joseph. *Chris-Craft: A History 1922-1942.* Devereaux Books, 2001.

Guetat, Gerald. *Classic Speedboats 1916-1939.* Osceola, WI: MBI Publishing Company, 1997.

Mollica, Anthony. *Gar Wood Boats: Classics of a Golden Era.* Osceola, WI: MBI Publishing Company, 1999.

Rodengen, Jeffrey. *The Legend of Chris-Craft,* 3rd edition. Write Stuff Syndicate, Inc., 1993.

Savage, Jack. *Chris-Craft.* Osceola, WI: MBI Publishing Company, 2000.

Spelz, Robert. *Real Runabouts* Vols. I–VII. Published 1977–1996

Spurr, Daniel. *Heart of Glass: Fiberglass Boats and the Men Who Made Them.* International Marine, 2000.

Wangard, Norm and Jim Wangard. *Classic Powercraft,* Vols. 1-2. Classic Powercraft, Inc., 1986–87.

Magazines

Classic Boating
280 Lac La Belle Drive
Oconomowoc, WI 53066-1648
414-567-4800

WoodenBoat
Naskeag Rd., PO Box 78
Brooklin, ME 04616-0078
207-359-4651

APPENDIX 3:
Production Numbers

Chris-Craft kept detailed records of the boats it manufactured, and so it is possible to determine with reasonable accuracy how many of each model was made. However, total production by model during the Depression years of the 1930s remains somewhat murky. Listed here are production figures for post-war Runabouts, Utilities, and Cavaliers. Note that the years listed include build dates—as with the automotive industry, Chris-Craft would begin building new models in the latter half of the year prior to their introduction.

Runabouts

Length/ Model	Model Name	Years	Production Volume
16-R	Special RA Rocket*	1946–1948	1,040
17-SR	Special Runabout*	1949–1952	726
17-R	Deluxe Runabout	1946–1950	1,880
17-D	Rocket Runabout	1952–1954	243
17-D	Runabout	1955–1956	94
17-D	Runabout	1956–1958	236

Custom Runabout

20-R	Custom Runabout	1946–1949	366

Racing Runabout

19-R	Racing Runabout	1947–1954	503

Riviera

16-RC	Riviera	1949–1951	174
18-R	Riviera Custom	1949–1954	1,210
20-R	Riviera Custom	1949–1954	288
Series Total			**1,672**

Cobra

18-BR	Cobra	1954–1955	51
21-BR	Cobra	1954–1955	55
Series Total			**106**

Lake 'n Sea (fiberglass outboard)

LS-15	Lake 'n Sea	1957	266

Silver Arrow

19-SA	Silver Arrow	1957–1959	92

Capri

Length/Model	Model Name	Years	Production Volume
18-CP	Capri	1959	65
19-CP	Capri	1954–1956	490
19-CP	Capri	1957–1958	296
19-CRA	Capri	1960	112
19-CRB	Capri	1961	60
21-CP	Capri	1954–1956	170
21-CP	Capri	1957–1959	44
Series Total			**1,237**

*Utility-style hulls sold as small Runabouts

Utilities

"Utility" is a generally accepted term for the classification of boats that are generally 15 feet to 29 feet in length, with an interior that is open rather than decked over and a box-like enclosure over the engine. The Utility usually has a forward deck and a small aft deck with the middle two-thirds of the craft open.

Length/ Model	Model Name	Years	Production Volume
Sportsman/Utility			
16-U	Utility	1948–1949	186
17-U	Utility	1949–1952	260
17-CC	Special Sportsman	1952–1955	1,031
17-CC	Sportsman	1955–1956	514
17-CC	Sportsman	1956–1959	1,018
17-CUA	Sportsman	1960–1961	285
18-U	Sportsman/Deluxe Utility	1946–1954	1,186
20-SS	Special Sportsman	1953–1954	194
20-U	Sportsman	1955–1956	68
20-U	Sportsman	1956–1959	214
22-U	Sportsman	1946–1954	2,082
22-S	Sedan	1947–1954	436
24-U	Sportsman	1959–1960	149
24-CUA	Sportsman	1961	38
25-S	Sportsman	1946–1950	208
Series Total			**7,869**
Holiday			
18-H	Holiday	1954–1956	208
18-HY	Holiday	1957–1958	116
19-H	Holiday	1951–1953	384
20-H	Holiday	1953–1954	101
20-HY	Holiday	1954–1957	143
22-H	Holiday	1954–1955	26
23-H	Holiday	1950–1952	88

23-HY	Holiday	1955–1956	28
24-H	Holiday	1953–1954	90
Series Total			**1,184**
18-CUA	Holiday	1962	170
18-CUB	Holiday	1963	110
18-CUC	Holiday	1964	35
20-CUA	Holiday	1962	170
20-CUAZ	Holiday (Italy)	1962	47
20-CUB	Holiday	1963	80
20-CUD	Holiday	1964	10
23-CUA	Holiday	1962	40
Series Total			**662**
20-CUC	Caravelle	1963	80

Continental

18-CL	Continental	1954–1956	280
18-CL	Continental	1957–1958	204
18-CL	Continental	1958–1960	498
20-CL	Continental	1954–1957	68
21-CL	Continental	1957–1959	190
22-CL	Continental	1954–1955	102
23-CL	Continental	1955–1956	97
23-CL	Continental	1957–1958	73
25-CL	Continental	1955	30
26-CL	Continental	1955–1956	48
26-CL	Continental	1956–1959	32
Series Total			**1,622**
19-CUA	Continental	1961	180
21-CUA	Continental	1960–1961	96
21-CUB	Continental	1964	10
Series Total			**286**

Ski Boat

16-CUA	Ski Boat	1962	290
16-CUAJ	Ski Jet	1962–1963	47
K-17	Ski Boat	1958–1960	825
17-CUB	Ski Boat	1961	280
17-CUC	Ski Boat	1963	20
17-CUD	Custom Ski Boat	1963	160
17-CUE	Custom Ski Boat	1964	90
17-CUG	Custom Ski Boat	1965–1967	150
17-CUI	Ski Boat	1968	10
Series Total			**1,872**

Super Sports

17-CUF	Super Sport	1964	110
17-CUH	Super Sport	1965	80
17-CUH	Super Sport	1966	50
17-CUH	Super Sport	1967	40
18-CUD	Super Sport	1964	65
18-CUF	Super Sport	1965	70
18-CUF	Super Sport	1966	40
18-CUF	Super Sport	1967	30
20-CUE	Super Sport	1964	50
20-CUF	Super Sport	1965	40
20-CUF	Super Sport	1966	35
20-CUF	Super Sport	1967	15
21-CUC	Super Sport	1964	40
21-CUD	Super Sport	1965	40
21-CUD	Super Sport	1966	25
21-CUD	Super Sport	1967	20
Series Total			**750**

Grand Prix

17-CUJ	Grand Prix	1968	50
20-CUG	Grand Prix	1968	35
Series Total			**85**

Cavaliers

While Kit Boats did not carry hull numbers, pre-assembled boats from the Plywood Division, later named the Cavalier Division, did carry hull numbers, and those figures are listed below.

Length/ Model	Model Name	Years	Production Volume
Utility/Runabout			
15-V	Cavalier Utility	1955–1959	1,096
15-V	Cavalier Runabout	1956–1958	128
17-V	Cavalier Utility	1954–1959	936
17-V	Cavalier Runabout	1956–1958	104
18-V	Cavalier Utility	1959	20
20-V	Cavalier Utility	1956–1957	40
18-VUA	Custom Utility	1959–1960	389
18-VUB	Custom Utility	1961	140
18-VUC	Utility	1962	160
18-VUD	Custom	1965	60
18-VUD	Custom Ski Boat	1966	40
Series Total			**3,113**
Outboards			
16-KX	Outboard Express	1954–1956	300

16-V	Cavalier Semi-Enclosed	1957–1959	600
16-VT	Cav. O/B Sports Utility	1957–1958	48
Series Total			**948**

Ski Boat

16-VUA	Custom Ski Boat	1962	100
16-VUB	Custom Ski Boat	1963	155
16-VUC	Custom Ski Boat	1964	125
16-VUD	Ski Boat	1965	105
16-VUD	Ski Boat	1966	80
17-VUA	Ski Boat	1967	70
17-VUA	Ski Boat	1968	35
Series Total			**670**

Express Cruiser

19-V	Cavalier Express	1956–1959	224
19-VS	Cavalier Semi-Enclosed	1957–1959	92
Series Total			**316**

Cavalier Sportsman

21-VUA	Cavalier Sportsman	1961	60
21-VUB	Cavalier Sportsman	1962	65
23-VUA	Sportsman	1960	111
Series Total			**236**

Cruisers

21-KC	Cavalier Cabin Cruiser	1955–1956	296
21-VXA	Cavalier Express 2/SL	1961	65
21-VXB	Express Cruiser	1962	80
22-PC	Express 4/SL	1955–1958	406
22-V	Express 2/SL	1956–1958	303
23-V	Express Cruiser	1958–1960	1,260
25-V	Cavalier Express	1958–1960	1,416
30-V	Cavalier	1959–1960	388
Series Total			**4,214**

Golden Arrow

19-VUA-19	Golden Arrow	1963	100
19-VUAZ-19	Golden Arrow (Italy)	1963	20
19-VUB-19	Golden Arrow	1964	50
Series Total			**170**

Dory and Cutlass

22-VUA	Dory	1964–1966	130
22-VXA/B	Cutlass	1964–1968	355
Series Total			**485**

INDEX